Engaging with Shakespeare

Marianne Novy

Engaging with Shakespeare

Responses of
George Eliot
and Other
Women Novelists

The University of Georgia Press

Athens & London

© 1994 by the University of Georgia Press
Athens, Georgia 30602
All rights reserved
Designed by Louise OFarrell
Set in 11/14 Fournier by Tseng Information Systems, Inc.
Printed and bound by Thomson-Shore, Inc.
The paper in this book meets the guidelines for permanence
and durability of the Committee on Production Guidelines
for Book Longevity of the Council on Library Resources.

Printed in the United States of America

98   97   96   95   94   C   5   4   3   2   1

Library of Congress Cataloging in Publication Data
Novy, Marianne, 1945–
Engaging with Shakespeare : responses of George Eliot
and other women novelists / Marianne Novy.
p.   cm.
Includes bibliographical references and index.
ISBN 0-8203-1596-6 (alk. paper)
1. English fiction—Women authors—History and criticism.
2. Eliot, George, 1819–1880—Knowledge—Literature.
3. Shakespeare, William, 1564–1616—Influence.
4. Feminism and literature—Great Britain.   5. Influence
(Literary, artistic, etc.)   6. Women and literature—Great
Britain.   7. Authorship—Sex differences.   8. Sex role in
literature.   I. Title.
PR830.W6N68   1994
823.009'9287—dc20   93-4158

British Library Cataloging in Publication Data available

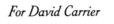

For David Carrier

If one says that X influenced Y it does seem that one is saying that X did something to Y rather than that Y did something to X. But in the consideration of good pictures and painters the second is always the more lively reality. . . . If we think of Y rather than X as the agent, the vocabulary is much richer and more attractively diversified: draw on, resort to, avail oneself of, appropriate from, have recourse to, adapt, misunderstand, refer to, pick up, take on, engage with, react to, quote, differentiate oneself from, assimilate oneself to, assimilate, align oneself with, copy, address, paraphrase, absorb, make a variation on, revive, continue, remodel, ape, emulate, travesty, parody, extract from, distort, attend to, resist, simplify, reconstitute, elaborate on, develop, face up to, master, subvert, perpetuate, reduce, promote, respond to, transform, tackle.

—Michael Baxandall, *Patterns of Intention*

If we need all our knowledge of the old writers in order to follow what the new writers are attempting, it is certainly true that we come from adventuring among new books with a far keener eye for the old, . . . because we can judge more truly what it is that they are doing, and what is good and what bad.

—Virginia Woolf, "Hours in a Library"

Tradition is fine, but you gotta know when to stop being a fool.

—Miranda in Gloria Naylor, *Mama Day*

Contents

Acknowledgments

THIS PROJECT DEVELOPED first of all in dialogue with, and in an imagined dialogue between, the feminist Shakespeare critics I have talked with over the years, mostly at the Modern Language Association and the Shakespeare Association of America meetings, and the feminist criticism and theory study groups that I have been part of at the University of Pittsburgh. My beginning work on it was funded by the American Association of University Women, which awarded me a fellowship for 1985–86. A 1985 conference, "Shakespeare's Personality," for which the organizer, Sidney Homan, even provided babysitting, stimulated some of my initial thought.

Although I knew them only through their books, Carolyn Heilbrun and Nina Auerbach provided early encouragement on this project. I received helpful readings of my first work on it from Deirdre David, Shirley Nelson Garner, Harriet Gilliam, Helene Moglen, Liane Ellison Norman, Jo O'Brien Schaefer, Elizabeth Segel, Alexander Welsh, and especially William J. Sullivan and Richard Tobias. I have also drawn on the resources of the Beinecke Library, the Folger Library, and Dr. Williams' Library in London.

I also thank the Shakespeare Association of America for sponsoring my seminar on women's responses to Shakespeare at its 1988 annual meeting, and the participants in this seminar, especially Carol Thomas Neely and Peter Erickson, for adding to the intellectual context of this project.

Nancy Atkinson, David Carrier, Gwen Gorzelsky, Richard Tobias, Valerie Traub, and Susan Wolfson read and commented generously on specific chapters, and Gwen also searched bibliographies for me. Jonathan Crewe's seminar on rewriting Shakespeare at the 1992 Shakespeare Association Annual Meeting, to which I submitted a version of chapter 8, provoked further thought. Linda Bamber, Jean Howard, Dennis Kennedy, and Catharine Stimpson provided special encouragement and assistance. Jonathan Arac, Carol Kay, David Moldstad, Jo O'Brien Schaefer, and Meredith Skura read the whole manuscript and gave detailed comments that helped enormously.

The book has also developed in dialogue with David Carrier. His interest in ways of writing art history contributed to some of my early formulations, and he has repeatedly found me books relevant to this project and helped in more other ways than I can say. My daughter Elizabeth, whose favorite character in *A Midsummer Night's Dream* is Puck, reads me jokes about Shakespeare in the newspaper comics, among other things, and generally brightens life.

Early versions of portions of this book were published in *Studies in English Literature*, the *Journal of English and Germanic Philology*, and *Women's Re-Visions of Shakespeare*. I am grateful to the editors of these journals and the University of Illinois Press for permission to reprint. G. H. Lewes's marginal comments to *Othello* are quoted with permission from the Art Collection of the Folger Shakespeare Library.

All citations from Shakespeare, except those quoted within quotations from other writers I am discussing, refer to *The Complete Works*, ed. David Bevington, 3d ed. (Glenview, Ill.: Scott Foresman, 1980). Quotations from the letters of George Eliot and her circle come from *The George Eliot Letters*, ed. Gordon S. Haight, 9 vols. (New Haven: Yale University Press, 1954–78), abbreviated *GEL* within the text.

Engaging with Shakespeare

Introduction

THIS BOOK COMBINES feminist criticism of women writers with feminist criticism of Shakespeare by examining how a number of novels by women rewrite his works and his cultural image. I am considering literature by women in its interconnections and also as, in Myra Jehlen's image, "a long border" juxtaposed with literature by men,[1] and focus especially on the nineteenth century because of the important cultural place then of both Shakespeare and women novelists. "The institution of Shakespeare has been created largely by and for men," says Michael Bristol;[2] however, for centuries some women have reached across that border to make space for themselves in that institution, have tried to move that border by appropriating some Shakespearean characters and some aspects of Shakespeare's cultural image for women, or have commented on works from the other side of the border by rewriting them to make plots and characters develop quite differently. This dialogue has been relatively neglected in previous studies of Shakespeare's literary relations, which have focused on male authors, as well as in previous studies of women writers' literary relations:[3] I aim to redress both of these omissions and in the process to show among women novelists, in particular, a tradition of appropriative creativity—reading and rewriting male-authored texts to find their own concerns.

In 1877, Alexander Macmillan asked George Eliot to write the volume on Shakespeare in his "Men of Letters" series, and she declined.[4] Nevertheless, her novels, essays, letters, and journals record an extensive involvement with Shakespeare. In her collected letters, for example, there are far more quotations from Shakespeare's writings than from any other literary source except the Bible and also far more than appear in the works of other women novelists of her time. For this reason she is the key figure in my book, but I also discuss earlier readings of

Shakespeare by women, including Jane Austen and Charlotte Brontë, as well as readings by twentieth-century women who continue, and, in some cases, break with, the traditions of appropriative creativity I examine.

In terms of cultural politics, appropriation can have two different emphases—it may claim that another's writings speak to one's own concerns or it may refer to another's writings in order to transform them, to emphasize the difference of one's position. From Baxandall's list in the epigraph, the first emphasis—which may well go along with claims that the earlier writer takes positions considered progressive or modern—is associated with such phrases as "align oneself with" and the second with such phrases as "differentiate oneself from." In practice, however, these emphases are often combined. A woman novelist of the nineteenth or twentieth century who uses a Shakespearean reference always transforms it to some extent, since the context is so different. On the other hand, the statement that a novel is not going to end like a Shakespearean comedy still suggests that the contrast between the two is relevant and that Shakespearean comedies are known to some of the expected readers. As my discussion will show, recent novelists have been more apt to stress their differences when they recall Shakespeare, but many aspects of nineteenth-century novelists' rewritings, such as the identification of middle-class women with aristocratic male tragic heroes, can also be seen as somewhat oppositional. The word "engaging" in my title should suggest something of both these different emphases, since it can hint at contestation as well as involvement.

Some forms of appropriation in these novels are obvious and small-scale. When Austen includes Shakespearean quotations in what Catherine learns in *Northanger Abbey,* Brontë's Caroline quotes *Coriolanus,* and Eliot's last three novels draw epigraphs from Shakespeare, they are very literally turning Shakespeare's lines into what Bakhtin calls "double-voiced discourse."[5] Narrators sometimes directly compare a character with a Shakespearean figure; comparisons also arise from less obvious or less direct quotations: when Felix Holt attacks Esther with words very like Hamlet's, when Brontë's St. John calls love "delicious poison," echoing Cleopatra, when Gwendolen observes that she hasn't seen any carvings on the trees (like Orlando's) soon after she has been complimented as "having the part of Rosalind." All of these smaller-scale kinds of appropriations of Shakespeare can be combined with suggestions of rewritings that structure more of the novel: for example, the repeated references to the contrast between Gwendolen's life and that for which her reading has prepared her can be related to contrasts between the plots and worlds of *As You Like It* and *Daniel Deronda*. Furthermore, Eliot and other novelists sometimes appropriate Shakespeare's cultural image. This book considers all these kinds of intertextuality.[6]

In the nineteenth century, the practice of many novelists and other prose writers shows that their audience was expected to know Shakespeare well.[7] Shakespeare was part of the cultural system of references, and the "conversations with Shakespeare" in Eliot's novels were far from private jokes. Eliot need not have planned every Shakespearean allusion consciously, any more than she needed to have planned every metaphor consciously, but like her metaphors, her allusions often form patterns that suggest added meanings when we see, for example, the ways in which Gwendolen, in *Daniel Deronda,* resembles the nineteenth-century image of Rosalind and the ways in which she does not. Bakhtin has argued that the novel, in particular, is composed of heteroglossia, or many-voiced discourse; in these novels the heteroglossia often includes, among other elements, the languages of several different Shakespearean genres that contrast with each other.[8] In *Middlemarch,* for example, the language and attitudes of comedy are repeatedly juxtaposed with sonnet language that valorizes idealized love and self-sacrifice.

As a feminist critic of Shakespeare in search of a prehistory, I am especially interested in how writers either use Shakespeare to authorize women or talk back to him about women. This book pays particular attention to issues related to gender or to ideologies of gender: how women writers use Shakespeare's plots of marriage and/or romantic love, his female characters, and potentially gender-crossing aspects of his male characters and his cultural image. It traces a history of women trying to create a Shakespeare of their own, by emphasizing his women and, for a time, his association with sympathy, strongly considered a feminine trait in the nineteenth century. My argument does not depend upon the *truth* of the view that Shakespeare was a good writer because he had sympathy, or that sympathy is feminine, but rather on the well-documented cultural presence of the *belief* in these linkages, within a certain historical period. I am exploring ways in which women could claim a rather paradoxical authority by maneuvering cultural terms largely restrictive to them.[9] I also consider some interactions of Eliot's "aesthetic of sympathy" with issues of class and race. Eliot's nonfictional and fictional writings suggest an interest in extending sympathy to groups less represented in Shakespeare's plays than women, and there are some analogies and some contrasts in her treatments of these different kinds of outsiders.

I do not claim that Shakespeare's work is universal, yet he is one of the best examples of a male writer whose works can at times feel liberating to women readers and not simply constricting.[10] The moments of felt liberation, such as the assertive speeches of his comic women, may be delusive and dangerous and may need to be analyzed as such, but they should not be ignored. My hope in this book is not only to give women novelists a larger place in Shakespearean cultural studies but also to contribute to a feminist criticism that does not perceive men's writing as monolithic, that explores women writers' ambivalence toward a male writer without assuming that the positive side of that ambivalence is just a sign of false consciousness. I am trying to combine two different modes of feminist criticism—the kind that is interested in texts by women as a group, contrasting them with texts by men, and the kind that is interested in breaking down dichotomies between texts by women and texts by men.[11] Both kinds are relevant to the double strategy—alliances among women and integration with men—of many writers I discuss as of other women who have sought to change their culture.

The literary relations I shall trace do not negate women's uses of female writers, nor their often more rebellious uses of male writers other than Shakespeare, nor (for that matter) the importance of socioeconomic context and of biographical events other than their reading to women's writing.[12] But those stories have already been told; this one has not.

Chapter One

Women Novelists' Engagements with Shakespeare: Prehistory, Early Tradition, and Critical Contexts

IN THE CHAPTER ENTITLED "Milton's Bogey: Patriarchal Poetry and Women Readers" of *The Madwoman in the Attic,* Sandra Gilbert and Susan Gubar use the woman writer's relation to Milton as a paradigm for her relation to a male-dominated literary tradition.[1] Women reading *Paradise Lost* find themselves present only as Eve or Sin, they argue, and elsewhere they claim that women reading other canonical texts by men find similar stereotyped images of women as angel or monster.[2] Thus, according to their picture of women writers' psychology, the most important female characters in Shakespeare are, on the one hand, Ophelia and Cordelia and, on the other, Lady Macbeth, Goneril, and Regan: these images diminish women and increase their anxiety about assertiveness in general and about writing in particular.[3] No other Shakespearean woman—none from any comedy or romance—is named in the book.

But these hypotheses are unsupported by any quotations from women writers about how they read Shakespeare or by any passages from their novels in which his female characters are named. Indeed, the texts of the women writers whom Gilbert and Gubar cite often provide evidence that works against their argument. For example, Mary Wollstonecraft, who suggests that Milton "meant to deprive us [women] of souls" by his description of Eve, chose seventeen passages from Shakespeare for her anthology *The Female Reader,* and Virginia Woolf's picture of Milton as "the first of the masculinists" contrasts with her image of Shakespeare as androgynous.[4] In the same novel where Charlotte Brontë depicts Shirley attacking Milton for his picture of Eve, she presents Caroline using a Shakespeare reading to teach Robert sympathy. At these points, women treat Shakespeare and Milton as polar opposites. Although both sets of literary relations are more complex than this formulation admits, a woman's attitude to one writer will not necessarily echo her attitude to the other. A study of women writers' responses to Shakespeare will tell a very different story than does *Madwoman*'s chapter "Milton's Bogey."[5] In particular, a study of women novelists' responses will follow writers who saw themselves, especially in the nineteenth century, as writing in a genre similar to his in its wide popular appeal and concern with characters and who sometimes present even their revisions of him as taking his own values further. But it will also mark the emergence of protest, becoming most explicit with 1960s feminism, against Shakespearean plots for women.

Of all nineteenth-century women novelists' responses to Shakespeare, George Eliot's are the most fully documented. Her most extended treatment of him, in a book review just before she began to write fiction, is a discussion of the assertiveness of his women when in love.[6] In her novels she may reapply his lines, change his plots, and make fun of his characters, but her tone is not rebellious protest against a forerunner who denies her autonomy, as Gilbert and Gubar's hypothesis would suggest. Rather, her relation to Shakespeare suggests a kind of identification acknowledging difference, a model of appropriative creativity rather than the creativity of revolt.[7] This book examines in detail that relation in her novels' intertextuality, places them in a tradition of women's responses to Shakespeare, and explores how those responses change before and after her.

The increased sophistication of feminist criticism today makes it possible to show appropriation as an alternative possibility among women writers, without confusing it with what Judith Fetterley calls "immasculation," or the acceptance of masculine values, and without maintaining the woman writer's subordination as might an earlier "influence study."[8] Appropriation is different from either rebellion or submission. It involves choosing—within a tradition and within a writer's work— what can be made one's own and how. I would align my approach here with the perspective on women's relation to male literary tradition developed by Ann Rosalind Jones and her use of the concept of nego- tiation, which "rather than coerced repetition or romantic rejection of literary models opens up a whole spectrum of women's responses to the logics of power."[9] Jones uses "appropriation" as the most oppo- sitional type of negotiation; in her terms, the negotiations of all the women writers I discuss could be considered "appropriation" because of the large generic and temporal gap between their writing and Shake- speare's.

Gender and the Early History of Responses to Shakespeare

Why have so many women written about Shakespeare and his female characters? An older criticism would say that this proves Shakespeare's universality. Here, however, I historicize and observe that there are many different answers to this question, depending on cultural location. One of the main reasons that many women novelists in the English- speaking world use Shakespeare today is to stress the limitations of his plots as well-known cultural myths about women's possibilities. This was not the aim of the first women who discussed him in print. The generalization that women wanted to gain authority by associa- tion with his prestige omits those who wrote about him before his literary canonization and leaves open the question of why he is, as it seems, the particular prestigious writer most claimed by women. One reason, relevant in many different situations, is that most of his plays include at least one female character with a fair amount of assertive dia- logue, however much the plot contains her.[10] Shakespeare is not unique among male playwrights in this respect—consider Webster, Middleton, Shaw—but many of his characters provide more material for women's appropriation than, for example, Miller's Linda Loman, or Ben Jon- son's Celia, or Marlowe's Xenocrate. Furthermore, unlike the female narrators of such male novelists as Defoe or Richardson, Shakespeare's women were enacted by well-known female performers, on stage from the late seventeenth century on and eventually in lecture halls. The sheer number of his female characters, their relative variety, and the greater potential for interpretation provided by the dramatic genre, distinguish him from Milton even with the most positive interpretation of Eve.[11]

A more complicated set of reasons many women have written about Shakespeare is that there have often been affinities between cultural constructions of Shakespeare and cultural constructions of women, much as both have changed over time. Three images of Shakespeare have particular resonance for women's history: the outsider, the artist of wide-ranging identification—later called sympathy—and the actor. Both men and women have constructed Shakespeare in these ways; at various times, both men and women have used feminine and androgynous imagery of Shakespeare, but women have been more apt to use these comparisons to make a space for their own writing, as they became more apt, when they used character study, to attribute agency to his female characters. These three images of Shakespeare are closely connected: for example, actors were, to a large extent, social outsiders in Shakespeare's time, and descriptions of Shakespeare's ability to create characters often echo descriptions of the protean metamorphoses of successful actors.[12] Uses of them will intertwine—and will intertwine also with discussions of his female characters—as I make a compressed chronological study of gender in early appropriations of Shakespeare, including uses of Shakespeare by novelists in their very early experiments in the form.

One of the first extant references to Shakespeare links actors, women, trespassing, and deceit: the rival playwright Robert Greene called him "an upstart Crow, beautified with our feathers" (probably the words of other playwrights who were not actors)—with a "Tygers hart wrapt in a Players hyde."[13] In other words, he was an actor and therefore a social outsider characterized by pretense and changeability—standard charges in Renaissance attacks on women.[14] In fact, Greene's line parodies a description of a female Shakespearean character—Margaret—as a "tiger's heart wrapt in a woman's hide" (*Henry VI, Part 3* 1.4.137).[15]

In the seventeenth century and much of the eighteenth, Shakespeare

still had the cultural image of an outsider to many established institutions in other ways than his history as an actor. He lacked university
education, he wrote in the popular form of the drama rather than the
more prestigious form of the epic, and he broke many of the rules of
dramatic construction favored by literary critics.[16] If he wrote well—
a debatable question—it was because of gifts of Nature, not of Art.
Women writers at this time might well also have felt outside literary
institutions, since universities were all male, and men dominated literary criticism. At least one woman, another actor turned playwright,
explicitly took this Shakespeare as a model who showed that she could
succeed anyway. In her preface to *The Dutch Lover* (1673), Aphra Behn
wrote, "Plays have no great room for that which is men's great advantage over women, that is learning; We all know that the immortal
Shakespeare's plays (who was not guilty of much more of this than
often falls to women's share) have better pleas'd the world than Jonson's
works."[17] Behn's word "immortal" would not have been the choice of
most critics of the time, who preferred Jonson.[18] Other early women
writers' interest in the image of the nonacademic Shakespeare links his
achievements with theirs obliquely. Margaret Cavendish, in her "General Prologue to all my Playes" (1662), wrote "Although less learning,
yet full well he writ; / For all his Playes were writ by Natures light."
A few lines later, she presents her own plays as lacking in "Learning, Reading, Language, Wit," yet calls them "the buildings of my
natural wit."[19]

In her *Sociable Letters* (1664) Cavendish began (for both sexes) the
traditions of writing at length about Shakespeare's skill in characterization, using imagery of metamorphosis to describe it and attributing
authenticity to his female characters:

> So well he hath Express'd in his playes all Sorts of Persons, as one
> would think he had been Transformed into every one of those Per-
> sons he hath Described. . . . in his Tragick Vein, he Presents Passions
> so Naturally, and Misfortunes so Probably, as he Peirces the Souls of
> his Readers with such a True Sense and Feeling therof, that it Forces
> Tears through their Eyes, and almost Perswades them; they are Really
> Actors, or at least Present at those Tragedies. . . . one would think that

he had been Metamorphosed from a Man into a Woman, for who could Describe Cleopatra Better than he hath done, and many other Females of his own Creating, as Nan Page, Mrs. Page, Mrs. Ford, The Doctors Maid, Bettrice, Mrs. Quickly, Doll Tearsheet, and others, too many to relate.[20]

Cavendish shows the influence of Restoration culture in her delight in female characters who are lively, witty, and in several cases sexually active. Her remarks are earlier than Dryden's 1668 praise of his "comprehensive soul," and the whole passage is much more wide-ranging in the variety of characters it enumerates, from fools to kings, than is Dryden's brief study of Falstaff.[21] It also anticipates later Shakespeare criticism in its emphasis on passions and on metamorphosis.

Cavendish and Behn align themselves with Shakespeare most explicitly as playwrights, although both wrote fiction as well. In 1698, however, when Mary Pix refers to Shakespeare in the preface to her play about Henry V's widow, *Queen Catherine; or, The Ruines of Love,* her tone is quite different.

> Shakespeare did oft his countries worthies chuse,
> Nor did they by his pen their lustre lose.
>
> . . . .
>
> But how shall woman after him succeed,
> And what excuse can her presumption plead.
> Who with enervate voice dares wake the mighty dead.[22]

In the eighteenth century the institution of the theater lost much of the limited accessibility to female authors it had had for a few years.[23] But as possibilities in the theater declined, the novel developed; many more women could become published novelists than performed playwrights, and at the same time the practice of reading Shakespeare's plays—reading them, indeed, as protonovels—was developing.[24] In the eighteenth century, many reading editions of Shakespeare's plays were sold, and at the same time several early fictional experiments clearly positioned themselves in dialogue with him. The uses of Shakespeare in these early novels instantiate theories about the centrality of appropriation and parody to the history of the novel.[25]

Most notably, Sarah Fielding's 1754 novel *The Cry* has as a main character a Portia who says, "I could not hear Shakespear's Portia in the *Merchant of Venice,* freely and without reserve giving herself and all her riches to the disposal of *Bassanio,* without ardently wishing for the power of using the same words, and acting in the same manner towards *Ferdinand.*" [26] Her 1749 children's novel *The Governess,* dealing with girls' education, takes as its epigraph lines, slightly altered, from Helena's reproach to Hermia in *Midsummer Night's Dream:*

> Shall we forget the Counsel we have shar'd
> The Sisters Vows, the Hours that we have spent . . .
> As if our Hands, our Sides, Voices, and Minds,
> Had been Incor'rate? So we grew together,
> But yet an Union in Partition.

Her *Lives of Cleopatra and Octavia* (1757) presents a version of these characters to rival Shakespeare's, as they tell their life stories from the underworld—for her Cleopatra is shallow and insincere, while Octavia is an admirable woman of letters. Although she introduces these characters as historical figures, she describes them in an oddly theatrical way, which would have helped to remind her audience of Shakespeare's characters, as "Persons who have really made their Appearance on the Stage of the World." [27] In *The Countess of Delwyn* (1759), she likens several of her female characters to men in Shakespeare, creating her authority as a scholar, as Susan Lanser has observed, but perhaps also suggesting irreverence: "Lady Dellwyn had full as much reason to call Lady Fanny her evil Genius, as ever Mark Anthony had to give that denomination to Caesar." [28] Her last novel, *The History of Ophelia* (1760), recalls Shakespeare in three ways: its title, the Miranda-like situation of its title character, raised in innocence far from society, and the narration of her visit to her first play, *Macbeth,* when her companions tell her that she "might more properly be said to act the Play, than some of the Persons on the Stage." [29]

Frances Burney's *Camilla* (1796) makes more complex use of a play within a novel. The characters attend a performance of *Othello* by strolling players with provincial accents, all dressed incongruously— Emilia's costume is that of the first witch in *Macbeth.* Desdemona snores loudly, and Othello has trouble putting out his candle and sets fire to his wig, but the novel uses the performance to serious purpose: the audience's comments show how many of them still hold the attitudes about women that Othello acts on. "He's the finest fellow upon the face of the earth. . . . the instant he suspects his wife, he cuts her off without ceremony; though she's dearer to him than his eye sight, and beautiful as an angel. How I envy him!"[30] Furthermore, Margaret Doody has convincingly read the whole novel *Camilla* as "a farcical, deeply absurd rendition of *Othello,* performed by bad actors—that is, by unheroic human beings acting in bad faith."[31] Edgar's words about jealousy, she notes, often echo Othello's—for instance, compare Othello's description of himself as "not easily jealous" (5.2.354) with Edgar's "Jealousy is a passion for which my mind is not framed, and which I must not find a torment but an impossibility." Like Othello, he says he could have borne any other evil. But Burney puts many different views in dialogue with the speeches of the jealous man and his mentor and thus presents more explicit criticism of repressive attitudes toward women. Anticipating the way that Charlotte Brontë's Coriolanus figure will ultimately capitulate to a comic plot, Edgar reforms and marries Camilla, who, unlike Desdemona, survives.[32]

Women Writers, Shakespeare, and Sympathy

In the introduction to *The Cry,* Sarah Fielding praised Shakespeare as the "grand master of human emotion" and took him as an ally in her transgression of neoclassical literary rules, as Behn had in her alignment with him as an unlearned outsider. Her brother Henry had praised her first novel, *David Simple* (1744), for "a vast Penetration into human Nature, a deep and profound Discernment of all the Mazes, Windings and Labyrinths, which perplex the Heart of Man," and he claimed that the book's characterization contained "some Touches, which I will venture to say might have done honour to the Pencil of the immortal Shakespear himself."[33] As the words of the Fieldings suggest, in the mid and late eighteenth century both Shakespeare and women writers (and male sentimentalists as well) were frequently read with an emphasis on their treatment of human emotion. The association of women with sympathy, already present in the Renaissance, had grown during the eighteenth century; according to Janet Todd, in the mideighteenth-century age of sentimentalism women gained cultural (though certainly not political) centrality, and women novelists created feminine writing.[34] Yet the novel was open to women partly because it was a less prestigious form. On the other hand, it was in this same period that Shakespeare was gaining his current status as the most prestigious writer in English, and many critics mentioned his portrayal of human feeling in praising him. They were also beginning to make explicit links between his plays and current fiction: for example, "The Plays of our SHAKESPEARE are many of them formed on the plan of novels, and of novels more evidently romantic."[35] Could the sympathy associated with Shakespeare be linked with the sympathy associated with women and thereby give women novelists more recognition?

In discussing Ann Radcliffe's *The Mysteries of Udolpho* (1794), one reviewer of this time connected her with Shakespeare *not* because of sympathy but because of her ability to create "horror . . . and thrilling fears."[36] But apart from this and the words of the Fieldings, quoted above, Janet Todd's generalization about the middle of the eighteenth century seems to be true for that time and for the end of the century as well: "Women writers were now rarely puffed because of their art. They were not compared with Shakespeare . . . but, instead, apologised for appearing in so unfeminine a way on the public scene."[37] Even though women writers and Shakespeare were both credited with knowledge of human emotions, they were rarely linked in this quality.

The concept of sympathy was discussed in much ethical and aesthetic theory of the eighteenth century but was rarely connected by such theoreticians with its role in the society's assumptions about gender. Edmund Burke, in *A Philosophical Enquiry into the Origin of Our Ideas of the Sublime and Beautiful* (1757), calls it "a sort of substitution, by which we are put into the place of another man, and affected in many respects as he is affected."[38] (Compare Cavendish's imagery of metamorphosis.) He emphasizes the importance of arousing sympathy to poetic response: "We yield to sympathy, what we refuse to description. . . . by the contagion of our passions, we catch a fire already kindled in another, which probably might never have been struck out by the object described" (175–76). In *The Theory of Moral Sentiments*

(1759), Adam Smith writes that sympathy may "denote our fellow-feeling with any passion whatever" and explains that when someone is suffering, "by the imagination we place ourselves in his situation, we conceive ourselves enduring all the same torments, we enter as it were into his body, and become in some measure the same person with him, and thence form some idea of his sensations, and even feel something which, though weaker in degree, is not altogether unlike them."[39] David Marshall emphasizes the qualifying phrases "in some measure" and "as it were" in this definition and argues that Smith describes "what it is like to want to believe in the fiction of sympathy, and what it is like to live in a world where sympathy is perhaps impossible."[40] Smith makes the association between sympathy and women most explicit in condescending terms, in the context of a contrast between humanity, which he associates with women, with generosity, which he associates with men. Although it might sound like progress to associate humanity with women, note his use of the words "merely" and "only." He writes, "Humanity is the virtue of a woman. . . . Humanity consists merely in the exquisite fellow-feeling which the spectator entertains with the sentiments of the persons principally concerned, so as to grieve for their sufferings, to resent their injuries, and to rejoice at their good fortune. The most humane actions . . . consist only in doing what this exquisite sympathy would of its own accord prompt us to do" (274).[41]

As these philosophers' writings show, sympathy is a term of many ambiguities, and the ambiguities about its generally human associations in relation to its associations with women (complicated further by Smith's use of the term "humanity") are among the most important for this book. Smith's qualifications, noted by Marshall, could reflect his attempt to distinguish the concept of sympathy he is developing in the first passage from the "exquisite fellow-feeling" he associates with women. More recently, the analyst Heinz Kohut makes similar qualifications in his definition of the closely related concept of empathy as "'vicarious introspection' or . . . one person's (attempt to) experience the inner life of another while simultaneously retaining the stance of an objective observer."[42] Judith Kegan Gardiner, after quoting Kohut, contrasts this definition of empathy to that of "loving, nurturant understanding," but part of the potential appeal of the concept of sympathy for women writers, especially from the late eighteenth century on, was that it could combine both meanings. The term could affirm both their femininity and their humanity—both Smith's gendered version of "humanity" and the ungendered version. The implication was not that only women could be sympathetic, by any definition, but that in discussing the concept of sympathy women could have some cultural authority.

One of the first critics to discuss Shakespeare's plays extensively in terms of sympathy was a woman, Elizabeth Montagu, who wrote to defend him against Voltaire's attack. She praises Shakespeare for the way his plays "open to us the internal states of the persons interested, and never fail to command our sympathy." Her examples emphasize Lear's "wounded . . . paternal affection," the "tenderness of maternal love" of Constance in *King John,* and Macbeth's "consciousness of guilt." She is also interested in showing sentiment "feminine . . . and perfectly agreeable to the nature of the sex" in Lady Macbeth.[43] While, influenced by the age of sensibility, she cites a different kind of Shakespearean woman than Cavendish does, she resembles Cavendish to a surprising degree in the self-transformation imagery (more vivid than Burke's or Smith's) used in her praise of Shakespeare's characterization: "the art of the Dervise in the Arabian tales, who would throw his soul into the body of another man, and be at once possessed of his sentiments, adopt his passions, and rise to all the functions and feelings of his situation" (1769).[44] She speculates: "I imagine that being an actor might a little assist him in this respect; the writer puts down what he imagines, the actor what he feels."[45] The eighteenth-century development of ideas about the importance of sympathy in aesthetics and ethics meant more influence for Montagu's still pioneering views. Her *Essay on the Writings and Genius of Shakespeare* was reprinted half a dozen times by the turn of the century and helped to focus critical attention on his exceptional capacity for identification and his ability to create sympathy for his characters.[46] Like Cavendish and Behn, she defended him against critics on the grounds that as an outsider he was closer to nature and to ordinary people: by implication she was also defending her own writing against "these connoisseurs, whose acquaintance with the characters of men is formed in the library, not in the street, the camp, or village."[47]

Women Writers and Male Romantics on Shakespeare

The romantic view of Shakespeare that dominated in the nineteenth century developed, at least in part, from Montagu's. Using an image of self-transformation much like hers and Cavendish's, Coleridge wrote that Shakespeare "passes into all the forms of human character and passion, the one Proteus of the fire and the flood."[48] Coleridge went on to add to this description "yet forever remaining himself," a qualification absent from analogous texts of Montagu and William Richardson but like the qualifications in Smith and Kohut.[49] Hazlitt wrote: "He was the least of an egoist that it was possible to be. He was nothing in himself; but he was all that others were, or that they could become. . . . He had only to think of any thing in order to become that thing, with all the circumstances belonging to it. . . . his talent consisted in sympathy with human nature, in all its shapes, degrees, depressions, and elevations."[50] Keats opposed Shakespeare as the "camelion poet" whose poetical character has "no self—it is every thing and nothing"—to the "wordsworthian or egotistical sublime." While in this passage he frequently refers to the poetical character as "it," suggesting a neuter gender, imagery of female procreation appears in the sentence that most specifically identifies the poet as Shakespeare: "It has as much delight in conceiving an Iago as an Imogen."[51]

These passages focus some other controversies about the aesthetic of sympathy that, like its ambiguous gender, will become particularly relevant to nineteenth-century women novelists' uses of Shakespeare. Is the sympathy aroused by good literature fellow feeling with experiences already similar to the reader's own, or does it extend sympathies? Is it moral, amoral, or moral in an extended sense? Is it political or apolitical? These questions could all be posed with regard to the rhetoric of sympathy in our own multicultural world; they are argued or implicit in nineteenth-century discourse. Isobel Armstrong has shown how Victorian critics split in answering the first question and associates the more adventurous position with Keats's chameleon poet.[52] But what would happen if a woman writer seemed to have "as much delight in conceiving an Iago as an Imogen?" Hazlitt argued that while, "in one sense, Shakespeare was no moralist at all: in another, he was the greatest of all moralists" because of his sympathy, which produced a moral vision that was better, because less dogmatic, than more obvious morality, but this was a risky position for a woman writer to take.[53] Hazlitt also argued that sympathy could easily become political—"Jacobin sentiments sprout from the commonest sympathy"—and could very well include anger at injustice.[54] These versions of sympathy were also far from what was expected of women at the time. But as we shall see, Brontë and Eliot took the more risky position that sympathy extends the reader's sympathies and can go beyond conventional morality; Brontë also very explicitly linked sympathy to anger and to politics.

Coleridge and Hazlitt themselves thought of both Shakespeare's female characters and their own female contemporaries in restrictively sentimental terms. They frequently saw both as creatures of emotion devoid of anger, politics, or even thought. Hazlitt said that Shakespeare's women "seem to exist only in their attachment to others. They are pure abstractions of the affections," and show "the true perfection of the female character, the sense of weakness leaning on the strength of its affections for support."[55] Coleridge, similarly, writing that Shakespeare saw "that it, in fact, was the perfection of woman to be characterless," grouped them together and credited them mainly with emotion: "The sweet yet dignified feeling of all that *continuates* society, as sense of ancestry, or sex, etc. A purity inassailable by sophistry, because it does not rest on the analytic processes."[56] They also gave little attention to women writers; Coleridge, in giving advice to would-be authors, assumes they are men who can write in the "restorative atmosphere" of the "social silence, or undisturbing voices of a wife or sister."[57] Dealing with the comedies of Joanna Baillie, Hazlitt writes that she treats the adult characters "as little girls treat their dolls."[58]

Nevertheless, many nineteenth-century women writers negotiated the techniques of character criticism and the idea of sympathy for their own purposes. Such women as Mary Lamb, Anna Jameson, and Mary Cowden Clarke emphasized the diversity, the complexity, and often the strength and intellect of the female characters. Nina Auerbach has shown that by writing character studies and inventing biographies, Jameson, Cowden Clarke, and such actresses as Ellen Terry liberate Shakespeare's women from the confines of their plots.[59] Such readers formed a female interpretive community, where Shakespeare's characters could be used to authorize defenses of women as a group: Anna Jameson, for example, writes, "Shakspeare, who looked upon women with the spirit of humanity, wisdom, and deep love, has done justice to their natural good tendencies and kindly sympathies," and her friend Elizabeth Barrett Browning has her Aurora Leigh say,

> The world's male chivalry has perished out,
> But women are knights-errant to the last;
> And if Cervantes had been Shakespeare too,
> He had made his Don a Donna.[60]

Though these women differ in many ways from twentieth-century feminist critics, their uses of Shakespeare show an even sharper contrast with the uses of Shakespeare as "constitutive of . . . a candidly patriarchal dispensation," discussed by recent male critics such as Michael Bristol.[61] Jameson, for example, introduced her character analyses of women in Shakespeare by writing, "It appears to me that the condition of women in society, as at present conducted, is founded on mistaken principles, and tends to increase fearfully the sum of misery and error in both sexes."[62] In spite of all the contrasts, Jameson anticipates Catherine Belsey's suggestion of utopian moments in Shakespeare's comedic women: they are, says Jameson, "what we persuade ourselves we might be, or would be, under a different and happier state of things, and perhaps some time or other *may* be."[63] George Eliot, as I will note, in her longest extended comment on Shakespeare's women, also saw their behavior as reflecting a different and happier time, and she was bolder than Jameson in associating that happy time with frank passion "partially repressed by the complex influences of modern civilization."[64]

As some women used Shakespearean character criticism for their own purposes, women also began to use literary ideas about the importance of sympathy to justify women's novel writing. Charlotte Brontë and, even more, George Eliot, built on the tradition of seeing Shakespeare's art as one of sympathy. The view that the writer acts through sympathy and extends the reader's sympathy now seems a Victorian commonplace and an obvious way for a cautious woman writer to justify her work: yet this was not an argument frequently made by women writers of the eighteenth and earlier nineteenth centuries. The eighteenth-century followers of sensibility had argued that literature could elevate or refine feelings, but this approach differed from that taken in Brontë's and Eliot's writings, in which sympathy in the novel connects readers with "real life." This argument—and its resonance among the Victorians—may well have required the development of the aesthetic of sympathy by the romantics, the literary criticism of Keats, Hazlitt, and Coleridge dealing with Shakespeare as well as the more recognized influence of Wordsworth.[65]

In the following chapters, then, some of the marked contrast between the uses of Shakespeare by Austen, on the one hand, and by Brontë and Eliot, on the other, result from the changes in Shakespeare criticism during the nineteenth century. The writings of Hazlitt and Jameson are not part of Austen's context, but Brontë probably knew them, and Eliot clearly did. In *Middlemarch,* she referred to Hazlitt as "the most brilliant English critic of the day"[66] (the early 1830s, during which the novel is set) and his milieu in progressive journalism was the immediate antecedent of hers and Lewes's in the *Westminster Review* and the *Leader.* Eliot's letters record at least one long-awaited meeting with Anna Jameson, who worked with Eliot's friend Barbara Bodichon in the Langham Place group of activists for women. Both Hazlitt's *Characters of Shakespeare's Plays* and Jameson's *Characteristics of Women: Moral, Political, and Historical,* or, as later editions were called, *Shakspeare's Heroines,* were extremely popular and were reprinted many times.[67]

The chapters that follow will show that both Brontë and Eliot probably used Hazlitt's ideas about Shakespeare's sympathy and some of the more specific details of his readings. For example, when Eliot wrote, in *The Mill on the Floss,* of "the mingled thread in the web of their life,"[68] and perhaps in her many uses of the web metaphor in *Middlemarch,* she was echoing a line from *All's Well That Ends Well,* "The web of our life is of a mingled yarn" (4.3.70), which Hazlitt quoted frequently in his works.[69] This similarity does not refute Carol Gilligan's claim that the web metaphor suggests a worldview more frequent among women but rather shows, as will many examples in this book, how Eliot appropriated from male authors themes and figures that could be considered feminine.[70] Eliot had much more interest in Shakespeare's women than did Hazlitt, however, and for her allusions to them many passages from Jameson are surprisingly relevant. But her uses of these women are by no means identical to Jameson's; in her criticism she is more interested in their assertiveness; in her novels she considers more probingly their relation to the marriage plots from which Jameson freed them. In her complex revisions of Rosalind, in particular—which take off from Brontë's revision of her in Rosamond Oliver—she anticipates the ambivalent fascination that recent feminist criticism has shown with this complex figure.

Brontë and Eliot are more interested in the men of Shakespeare's tragedies than are most contemporary feminist critics. Eliot, in particular, shared her fascination with Hamlet, common in the nineteenth century, with Jameson, who interrupted her chapter on Ophelia, first to speculate on how Shakespeare's other female characters would have behaved to Hamlet, and then to quote more than two pages of another writer's essay on him and to take issue with it. But Eliot is much more capable than Jameson of taking a critical view of Hamlet, as we shall see in discussing *The Mill on the Floss;* she is also more interested, in another way anticipating recent feminist criticism, in examining and rewriting his attitude toward women. Felix Holt, her hero most explicitly linked to Hamlet, begins by mocking women in a very similar tone, and learns to have a very different attitude toward the woman he originally mocked. *Daniel Deronda,* a more idealized rewriting of *Hamlet,* begins, in contrast, with a special sympathy for women.

Jonathan Bate has argued that Hazlitt and some of his contemporaries could turn "Shakespeare against the power of the state and [repossess] him in the name of liberty."[71] One possibility, for Eliot and some other women, was to turn Shakespeare against male power and claim him for women.[72] This is not the only possibility; sometimes women have identified Shakespeare with male power and deferred (most of those in this position did not write their views, since writing at all was too daring for them), and, especially in recent years, sometimes women have identified Shakespeare with male power and have rebelled; sometimes they have engaged in more ambivalent moves such as claiming some aspects of his presentation of gender but interrogating his treatment of class or race, applying the language of his male tragic heroes to women or playing the languages of different Shakespearean genres against one another.

As feminist consciousness develops, aspects of Shakespeare's plays that women could once ignore reveal their patriarchal assumptions. Yet acknowledgment of Shakespeare's limitations does not preclude an interest in studying ways in which he was appropriated for views that were relatively progressive in their own time. The festive rituals and literary images Natalie Zemon Davis discusses in "Women on Top" did not provide gender equality, but they may have kept "open an alternate way of conceiving family structure" in the generally male-dominated world of fifteenth- to eighteenth-century Europe, as she argues.[73] Some of Shakespeare's plays, including *As You Like It,* which Davis discusses, may have been similarly used through the nineteenth century and even into the twentieth, as I show in chapters 7 and 8. Literature is progressive or conservative partly with reference to its audience and the rest of their culture. For the many women of today, including university students, among whose "better" images of gender relations are the like of *Pretty Woman* and *Thelma and Louise,* some of Shakespeare can still be progressive. By the same token, we shall see, George Eliot found his women refreshing in contrast to "some of Walter Scott's painfully discreet young ladies."[74]

Chapter Two

Jane Austen
and Charlotte Brontë

In Austen's *Mansfield Park,* to Henry Crawford's remark that Shakespeare "is part of an Englishman's constitution," Edmund says, "His celebrated passages are quoted by every body; they are in half the books we open, and we all talk Shakespeare, use his similies [*sic*], and describe with his descriptions."[1] This testimony fits with much other evidence about the novel-reading public in the early nineteenth century, and such widespread reference to Shakespeare continued during the Victorian period. In a connection begun in the late eighteenth century, as we have seen, novelists were often regarded as successors to a Shakespeare who was considered a kind of protonovelist. In his influential essay "On Art in Fiction" (1838), for example, Edward Bulwer Lytton makes many arguments about novelistic technique by analogy to Shakespeare.[2] George Moir, in "Modern Romance and Novel" (1842), writes, "The novel aspired . . . to perform for a reading and refined age, what the drama had done for a ruder and more excitable period," and says that Shakespeare and Scott share "the same general and almost universal sympathies, leading to impartial and kindly views of all men and all opinions, the most remote from their own."[3] And as early as 1821, Archbishop Whateley calls Austen's regard to characters "hardly exceeded even by Shakspeare himself. Like him, she shows as admirable a discrimination in the characters of fools as of people of sense."[4]

Jane Austen and Charlotte Brontë engage with Shakespeare's characters, words, and cultural presence in their novels, in two largely contrasting ways, which George Eliot will later combine. Austen's rewriting is mostly in a comic mode, in two ways: she uses more verbal allusions to love plots in the comedies, and her allusions to Shakespeare's cultural presence are more lightly ironic. Brontë's rewritings more often seem self-conscious attempts to claim what is culturally valued in Shakespeare: she more explicitly aligns his image as a writer of sympathy with her own and more often uses allusions to his tragic or preternatural characters to add to the dignity or mysterious aura of hers. In novels by each one, an attractive, dangerous male character is associated with Shakespeare, in very different ways. Henry Crawford of *Mansfield Park* can read all the characters of *Henry VIII* and feels that he could play all other Shakespeare characters. On the other hand, Robert Moore, in *Shirley,* is much like the stubborn single-minded Coriolanus, and Rochester recalls several other tragic heroes. These contrasting figures of danger are in a sense pejoratively drawn exaggerations of characteristic poses of the two women writers and their narrators—Austen the parodic, ironic observer who can mimic many different kinds of language, and Brontë the serious, self-conscious, individualistic rebel. But both novelists invoke Shakespeare—as we will later see Eliot doing—in a complex, heteroglossic way. Austen recalls both romantic and antiromantic elements of the comedies, and Brontë opposes the Shakespearean individualistic hero and the Shakespearean ideal of sympathy to each other. Still, widely read and influential as Brontë's novels were, critics did not compare her to Shakespeare, while Whateley's comparison between Austen and Shakespeare was developed by many others.[5] Most notably, G. H. Lewes developed the idea of a Shakespeare–Jane Austen tradition, into which he tried to insert George Eliot both by reading the two authors with her during her fictional apprenticeship and also by writing criticism that linked the three. In the process Lewes also used the Shakespearean associations of sympathy to praise women writers more than earlier critics had done.

Mary Poovey, Nancy Armstrong, Margaret Homans, and many other critics have discussed the ways in which nineteenth-century British women writers used the cultural association between women and sympathy.[6] But it is worth noting that, even as the image of the sympathetic writer developed more cultural importance, not all critics wanted it to empower women. E. S. Dallas, in his review of "Currer Bell," specifically mentioned sympathy as inadequate to compensate women novelists for inexperience of life, and J. M. Ludlow used the association of women and emotions to authorize only novels by married women with children.[7] Like the concept of the genius as androgynous, discussed by Christine Battersby, the concept of sympathy as related to both women and art did not in itself promote art by women.[8] It could more easily be appropriated by the woman writer, however, than could the definition of the pen as a metaphorical penis discussed by Gilbert and Gubar.[9] And an exceptional male critic, such as Lewes, could use it to welcome women writers, even if in terms that most late twentieth-century feminists would consider too limiting: "Woman, by her greater affectionateness, her greater range and depth of emotional experience, is well fitted to give expression to the emotional facts of life, and demands a place in literature corresponding with that she occupies in society. . . . We are in no need of more male writers; we are in need of genuine female experience. . . . the very nature of fiction calls for that predominance of Sentiment which we have already attributed to the feminine mind."[10] Even earlier, he wrote of Jane Austen that "her marvellous dramatic power, seems more than any thing in Scott akin to the greatest quality in Shakspeare." According to Lewes, though Scott was compared to Shakespeare by Moir and others, and made many more obvious borrowings of Shakespearean names and plots, unlike Austen, he "had not that singular faculty of penetrating into the most secret recesses of the heart, and of shewing us a character in its inward and outward workings. . . . he had not, above all, those two Shakspearian qualities—tenderness and passion."[11] In his association of Shakespeare with a quality as "womanly," in Victorian terms, as tenderness, as well as his contrast of Shakespeare and Austen, on the one side, with Scott on the other, Lewes is paving the way for the trend in women's appropriation of Shakespeare that involves, most notably in Virginia Woolf, contrasting an androgynous Shakespeare with other, too masculine, male writers.[12] He also anticipated Woolf in using for the first time an image of kinship that she would apply quite differently: he wrote that Shakespeare's "central power of dramatic creation, the power of constructing and animating character, . . . may truly be said to find a younger sister in Miss Austen."[13] Most explicitly, in his 1859 essay "The Novels of Jane Austen," he linked her dramatic power with sympathy, with Shakespeare, and with George Eliot, who had by this time become a novelist with his encouragement. He wrote, "Miss Austen is like Shakespeare. . . . She belongs with the great dramatists," discussed the "effect which her sympathy with ordinary life produces," interjected praise of George Eliot as "equal in truthfulness, dramatic ventriloquy, and humor" to Austen, and "superior in culture, reach of mind, and depth of emotional sensibility," and returned to the claim that Austen, in her "dramatic presentation . . . has never perhaps been surpassed, not even by Shakespeare himself."[14]

Jane Austen

In *Northanger Abbey,* one of her earliest works, Austen's ironies about Shakespeare's cultural presence are part of her ironical treatment of romance. Here Catherine, "in training for a heroine," read

all such works as heroines must read to supply their memories with those quotations which are so serviceable and so soothing in the vicis- situdes of their eventful lives. . . . And from Shakspeare she gained a great store of information—amongst the rest, that

"Trifles, light as air,
"Are, to the jealous, confirmation strong,
"As proofs of Holy Writ."

That

"The poor beetle, which we tread upon,
"In corporal sufferance feels a pang as great
"As when a giant dies."

and that a young woman in love always looks

"Like Patience on a monument—
"Smiling at Grief."[15]

In a Bakhtinian "reaccentuation," the narrator smiles at the com- mon eighteenth- and nineteenth-century habit of considering Shakespeare quotations as information and frames the romantic reading of the *Twelfth Night* passage ironically by using it to set up a picture of Catherine's continued energy when she falls in love. (In *Daniel Deronda,* George Eliot will later draw more ominous ironies from the widespread knowledge of Shakespeare, as people jokingly compare Gwendolen to Rosalind before her disastrous marriage.) The *Twelfth Night* reading that Austen parodies is like the reading of Shakespeare's women quoted from Hazlitt and Coleridge, quoted in the previous chapter; even Anna Jameson wrote of Viola's "deep, silent, patient love."[16] Yet according to much twentieth-century criticism, *Twelfth Night* too is ambivalent about romanticism in this scene. C. L. Barber, for example, sees Viola herself as far from silent and immobile.[17] While Austen is making fun of cultural uses of Shakespearean quotations, she is also employing a technique rather like his own: both of them include and parody ideas of love associated with literary convention. Shakespeare does so most obviously in the comedies, and this may be one reason allusions to the comedies are particularly important in her novels. As Richard Simpson noted in 1870, "she began, as Shakespeare began, with being an ironical censurer of her contemporaries";[18] what Austen is censuring ironically includes her contemporaries' romantic readings of Shakespeare. She often mocks the culturally dominant association of women and feeling found, for example, in the Shakespeare criticism of Hazlitt and Coleridge, yet she also includes echoes of romantic Shakespearean lines that might appeal to a sentimental reader and might, arguably, add to the genre-based reassurance that her novels, like most Shakespearean comedies, will end in marriages. The multiple meanings of works by both authors make them appropriable by both traditionalist upholders of marriage, if they can accept some female self-assertion, and by assertive women, if they can accept some traditional language about marriage. Thus today feminist critics of Austen argue about the final marriages just as do feminist critics of Shakespeare's comedies.[19]

Emma's quotation from *Midsummer Night's Dream* is a good example of how characters' allusions to Shakespeare become multiple-voiced discourse in Austen. Emma's point, in recalling lines from the unhappy lover Lysander, is to argue that her world is very different from that of *Midsummer Night's Dream* and that the romance she is matchmaking will go well: "There does seem to be a something in the air of Hartfield which gives love exactly the right direction; and sends it into the very channel where it ought to flow.

    The course of true love never did run smooth—

A Hartfield edition of Shakespeare would have a long note on that passage."[20] Emma, correcting the voice of the unhappy Shakespearean lover, has the confidence of the Shakespearean comic woman like Rosalind, Olivia, or Viola, all of whom mock similar romantic complaints. In the short range, she is wrong about Harriet's chances with Mr. Elton; but do her two mistakes cancel each other out? That romance does not run smooth, but on the other hand it does not qualify as true love. Before the end of the novel, however, her aspirations have received "the right direction" to complete the comic plot with her own marriage to Knightley. Their romance does not run smoothly during the novel, indeed, but ultimately it does turn into what, by her society's dominant standards, is "the very channel where it ought to flow." So the novel endorses her words, in one sense, and mocks them in another, just as it endorses the Shakespeare line against her, in one sense, and mocks it in another sense, as Shakespeare's comic plotting also mocks it (for Lysander and Hermia too marry at the end, in spite of their complaint).

    Similarly, *Pride and Prejudice* gives Darcy a line that almost echoes Orsino's romantic invitation "If music be the food of love, play on" (*Twelfth Night* 1.1.1), and mocks it with Elizabeth's comment. When Darcy says, "I have been used to consider poetry as the *food* of love," Elizabeth answers, "Of a fine, stout, healthy love it may. . . . But if it be only a slight, thin sort of vibration, I am convinced that one good sonnet will starve it entirely away."[21] This joke, which anticipates the mockery of Will Ladislaw's Petrarchan adoration of Dorothea in *Middlemarch,* is very much the sort of down-to-earth joke about the need for material food, as opposed to spiritual, that often occurs in Shakespeare's comedies: for example Touchstone responds to one of Orlando's poems by saying, "I'll rhyme you so eight years together, dinners and suppers and sleeping-hours excepted" (*As You Like It* 3.2.96–97). Like Touchstone and Rosalind, Elizabeth is mocking the image of the unhappy melancholy lover, but arguably the lines suggest that the novel will find another "fine, stout, healthy" kind of love to portray.

The multiple kinds of irony in Austen's uses of romantic language from Shakespeare are complicated by the fact that usually in Shakespearean comedy the leading woman knows whom she loves (and whom the plot will marry her to) from close to the beginning, while in the Austen novel she very often does not. Think of Rosalind's first meeting with Orlando, of Viola's early expressed desire to be Orsino's wife, and of the persistence with which Helena pursues Demetrius and Hermia Lysander. To some degree, this contrast exemplifies the fact that the nineteenth century represents women in a more repressed and sentimentalized way than the Renaissance. Yet many of Austen's women, if unaware of whom they love, are very articulate from their beginning moments in the presence of the men they eventually marry, and debate with them many ideas, including views on the relation of the sexes.

For this reason, the Shakespearean comedy with most affinity to Austen's novels is *Much Ado about Nothing,* in which Beatrice and Benedick spend much of the play insulting each other. Many critics have seen similarities between this play and, especially, *Pride and Prejudice.* As early as 1813, an anonymous reviewer writes that Elizabeth "thinking him [Darcy] the proudest of his species, takes great delight in playing *the Beatrice* upon him."[22] And as recently as 1959, Sylvia Townsend Warner mentions Beatrice as one of Shakespeare's women who "could almost be taken for women writers' heroines, they are so free and uninhibited, and ready to jump over stiles and appear in the drawing-room with muddy stockings, like Lizzie Bennet."[23] Not only the wit-combats but also the critical view of their society's marriage practices that Beatrice and Elizabeth share link these works; to dramatize this critical view, both contrast their central couples with others in which the women are more passive and conventional (Jane, Hero) or more endangered by men's behavior (Lydia, Hero). Beatrice and Benedick have more indications of psychological development than any other couple in Shakespearean comedy; however, the dramatic mode, and the scenes other characters stage for Beatrice and Benedick to overhear, leave more gaps and ambiguities for an audience's interpretation than does *Pride and Prejudice,* where Elizabeth's inner life is represented in considerable detail.[24] *Pride and Prejudice* rewrites Beatrice as a post-Wollstonecraft woman, demanding to be treated as a rational creature rather than as an elegant female.[25] The hints of economic motivation for marriage in *Much Ado about Nothing*—"she [Hero]'s his only heir"—become explicit discussions in *Pride and Prejudice,* facilitated and made more parodic by the presence of the mother, whose counterpart is absent in the play. Austen presents a more highly developed system of constraints on women, even though no woman has to literally fake death in order to get married; on the other hand she presents more direct criticism of the marital imperative imposed on Lydia and Wickham—"prevailing on one of the most worthless young men in Great Britain to be her husband" (322)—than *Much Ado* presents of Hero's marriage. Both works are antiromantic romances, in which the central characters' anticonventionality produces a large part of their illusion of psychological realism, while at the same time conventions of comic plotting encourage the reader or audience to speculate on a submerged and finally triumphant love plot.

Austen's last novel puts a different kind of ironic framing around its echo of a Shakespearean comedy and makes claims not only for women's love but also for women's pen. *Persuasion,* in contrast to *Emma* and *Pride and Prejudice,* focuses on a woman who knows whom she loves from the beginning, but unlike the typical Shakespearean comic heroine, Anne Elliott thinks her love is hopeless. The dialogue that virtually clinches, instead, a happy ending, echoes *Twelfth Night* so clearly that at least four critics, from Richard Simpson in 1870 to Jocelyn Harris in 1983, have written about the resemblance. Simpson, a Shakespeare scholar, even calls Anne "Shakespeare's Viola translated into an English girl of the nineteenth century."[26] While Captain Wentworth listens, Anne and Captain Harville discuss the respective constancy in love of men and women. In Shakespeare's scene, Orsino advises the disguised Viola that men are inconstant in love and then, the subject having changed somewhat, says that no woman's love can be as constant as his. Viola responds by telling the story of her imaginary sister, who, in the line Catherine remembers in *Northanger Abbey,* sat "like Patience on a monument, / Smiling at grief." The scene dramatizes Viola's persistence and Orsino's changeability and self-deception. In *Persuasion,* on the other hand, Captain Harville consistently argues that men are more constant, and Anne that women are; the scene suggests to Wentworth the likelihood that Anne still loves him. Orsino and Viola debate a literary/cultural tradition that associated women with changeability, dominant in the Renaissance, though the plot of *Twelfth Night* and of most Shakespearean plays challenges it; by Austen's time, women's associations with constancy were more dominant but not unquestioned, and Anne and Harville debate the relevance of what could be called, using Raymond Williams's terms, the residual misogyny still being generated in literature.[27] Harville says, "I do not think I ever opened a book in my life which had not something to say upon woman's inconstancy. Songs and proverbs, all talk of woman's fickleness. But perhaps you will say they were all written by men."[28] Anne responds, "If you please, no references to examples in books. Men have had every advantage of us in telling their own story. Education has been theirs in so much higher a degree; the pen has been in their hands."

When Harville says that all literature emphasizes woman's inconstancy, he forgets precisely the scene from *Twelfth Night* being rewritten here—which, as the allusion in *Northanger Abbey* suggests, was well known to Austen's audience, and was written by a man still regarded as relatively lacking in formal education. To a reader conscious of this intertextuality, Shakespeare's Viola and Austen's Anne are briefly linked as women persistent in love—against androcentric literature's pictures of women—and Anne then goes further than Viola by making the point about literary androcentrism, and other historical points, explicitly in her own voice. Here the novel emphasizes its female authorship and offers it as a promise of bringing to literature the untold stories of women's experience. While many of Austen's allusions to Shakespeare's comedies associate her female characters with mockery of romanticism, Anne takes a romantic stance, emphasizing women's emotionality, at the same time that she protests the male dominance of literary tradition. Arguably this is the point where Austen's style of alluding to Shakespeare is the closest to Charlotte Brontë's.

The treatment of the one character in her novels who actually reads a scene from Shakespeare, however, exemplifies Austen's contrast to Brontë. In *Mansfield Park* Henry Crawford, contemplating private theatricals, says, "I really believe . . . I could be fool enough at this moment to undertake any character that ever was written, from Shylock or Richard III down to the singing hero of a farce in his scarlet coat and cocked hat. I feel as if I could be anything or every thing" (94). This passage has an odd resemblance to Keats's description of Shakespeare discussed in chapter 1—"every thing and no thing," written very close in time—and as in Keats, rather than in Hazlitt or Brontë, suggests an amoral sympathy rather than one leading to a higher morality. While many of Shakespeare's characters are actors, Richard III is one whose acting involves the most villainy, and furthermore, he makes a speech comparable to Henry's about all the different roles he can play, as he will

> frame [his] face to all occasions,
> . . . .
> . . . add colors to the chameleon,
> Change shapes with Proteus for advantages,
> And set the murderous Machevil to school.
> (*Henry VI, Part 3,* 3.2.185, 191–93)

When he reads from *Henry VIII,* he acts all different emotions, as he predicts: "whether it were dignity or pride, or tenderness or remorse, or whatever were to be expressed, he could do it with equal beauty" (255). In the more Victorian Brontë a Shakespeare reading will be at least temporarily a moral lesson to Robert Moore in its expansion of his perspective to sympathy with others, but here Henry is more like the amoral poet who conceives Iago and Imogen with equal delight, and his changeability in this scene (like his interest in the polygamous Henry VIII himself) is a predictor of the later fickleness with which he will break his promise to Fanny and instead seduce Maria Rushworth. As Edmund says, Henry's *"feelings* . . . [are] too much his guides." While in Brontë feelings will generally be a guide to good, here they can be dangerous. Thus Austen's invocation of the image of the changeable actor, so close to the image of the many-sided Shakespeare, is of a piece with her interest in both romantic and antiromantic aspects of his comedies, and perhaps Henry's elusiveness is a dark parody of her own. "It was truly dramatic," the narrator says of Henry's performance in *Henry VIII,* and as we have seen, "dramatic" is one of the words most often used in praise of Austen.

Charlotte Brontë

Brontë's uses of Shakespeare contrast with Austen's most importantly in two ways: Brontë generally evokes tragedies rather than comedies, and she more explicitly appropriates Shakespearean sympathy as a concept that can make moral and political demands. Both of the contrasts suggest Brontë's more open literary ambition and her greater participation in a more highly developed romantic-Victorian line of Shakespeare reading. Austen is very skillful in her novelistic uses of Shakespeare's comedies, but Brontë engages in a more daring endeavor of using allusions to claim tragic dignity for characters below the usual class of the tragic hero, even though her narrators, unlike Eliot's, do not call explicit attention to this expansion of boundaries. Brontë is also more daring in linking the sympathetic Shakespeare to the activist concept of women's sympathy used by writers such as Elizabeth Gaskell. It is part of the dialogic quality of *Shirley,* in particular, that these two Shakespearean ideals, the individualistic tragic hero and the communal value of sympathy, are both put in play.

One letter of Brontë's is particularly suggestive of her interest in intertextuality. To her publisher, George Smith, she writes, playfully, "You should be very thankful that books cannot talk to each other as well as to their reader. . . . Still I like the notion of a mystic whispering amongst the lettered leaves, and perhaps at night, when London is asleep and Cornhill desert, when all your clerks and men are away, and the warehouse is shut up, such a whispering may be heard—by those who have ears to hear."[29]

Given this consciousness of books' dialogues with each other, it is not surprising that Brontë provided Gilbert and Gubar such good evidence of rebellion against Milton. Not only does Shirley attack Milton for his presentation of Eve, but also Rochester echoes Milton's description of Satan in denying he is a villain.[30] On the other hand, Shakespeare is an explicit presence in *Shirley* for at least as long as Milton is, and several of his plays are intertexts for *Jane Eyre* as well.

Brontë's interest in Shakespeare and her preference for the tragedies are already clear in her prose of the 1830s. According to Christine Alexander, "Quotation from Shakespeare is as much a part of the texture of her early prose as is Biblical allusion. She appears to have been especially fond of *Othello, Macbeth,* and *A Midsummer Night's Dream.*"[31] Although she advised Ellen Nussey to "omit the comedies of Shakespeare," perhaps accommodating herself to Ellen's conservative and sheltered taste, she found tragedies and histories morally admirable— in the same letter she went on to write, "That must indeed be a depraved mind which can gather evil from Henry the 8th, from Richard 3rd, from Macbeth and Hamlet and Julius Caesar."[32]

The later Brontë is still concerned with Shakespeare's morality but in a more complicated way. Her novel *Shirley* shows most explicitly how a Victorian woman writer could link the cultural ideal of Shakespearean sympathy to the cultural ideal of womanly sympathy. In *Mansfield Park,* Shakespeare's protean power of characterization, as reenacted by Henry Crawford, could be dangerous; in *Shirley,* Caroline thinks it may be ethically improving. Victorians who argued in favor of expanding women's participation in society often did so on the grounds that women's compassion would help heal social wounds; accordingly, when concerned about violence impending from class conflict, Caroline appropriates the sympathetic Shakespeare to educate her cousin Robert Moore, a mill owner, about how he should deal with working people.[33] She believes that the emotional impact of reading *Coriolanus* will improve him morally: "It is to stir you; to give you new sensations. It is to make you feel your life strongly, not only your virtues, but your vicious, perverse points."[34] The narrator—the only third-person, omniscient one in Brontë and a testimony of her attempt to expand her own viewpoint in this book—confirms Caroline's emphasis on Shakespeare's wide-ranging sympathy and describes its influences on Robert: "Stepping out of the narrow line of private prejudices, [he] began to revel in the large picture of human nature, to feel the reality stamped upon the characters who were speaking from that page before him" (116). But

Caroline wants the reading to have a more lasting effect on Robert: she explains the play's meaning to him as "you must not be proud to your workpeople; you must not neglect chances of soothing them, and you must not be of an inflexible nature, uttering a request as austerely as if it were a command" (117).

Caroline first introduces her proposal of Shakespeare reading to Robert on behalf of England rather than on behalf of sympathy, saying, "Tonight you shall be entirely English; you shall read an English book. . . . Let glorious William come near and touch it [your heart]; you will see how he will draw the English power and melody out of its chords" (114). Claiming a Shakespeare both "out of the narrow line of private prejudice" and promoting "English power," *Shirley* is in a tradition exemplified earlier by Elizabeth Montagu, whose sympathetic Shakespeare, discussed in chapter 1, was developed in part as a patriotic answer to Voltaire's attack.[35] English nationalism is a frequent motif in Brontë's novels, but here it is also a strategy to suggest that sympathy between classes is the true English attitude and that Robert's lack of fellow feeling with his workers results from his half-Belgian ancestry and his many years away from England.[36]

Setting the political use that Caroline wants to make of Shakespeare in the context of both nineteenth-century women's writing and nineteenth-century Shakespeare criticism—and the controversy about the political status of sympathy, discussed in the previous chapter—helps to synthesize and revise the opposing views of two influential recent critics, Nancy Armstrong and Annabel Patterson.[37] As Armstrong says, sympathetic identification is important to Caroline in her reading of *Coriolanus,* and the Victorian association of women with sympathy is relevant; in the novel as a whole, sympathy is often associated with a woman's subculture, and both Caroline and Shirley frequently comment on male characters' lack of sympathy.[38] On the other hand, as Patterson says, Caroline "insists on the political and class dimensions of the tragedy," although it is true, as Armstrong writes, that she sees those dimensions in relation to Coriolanus's (and Robert's) psychology and does not use the play to motivate Robert's workers to struggle against him. Caroline's politics could be compared to Hazlitt's when he wrote, "Jacobin sentiments sprout from the commonest sympathy."[39] Later in the novel, she is indeed called "a little Jacobin."

Hazlitt had written an essay on *Coriolanus* that, while admitting that the play contains "arguments for and against aristocracy or democracy," found a message in the play quite different from the one Caroline finds. He wrote, "the whole dramatic moral of *Coriolanus* is that those who have little shall have less, and that those who have much shall take all that others have left."[40] This interpretation, the opposite of Hazlitt's own political position, seems to be what Robert draws from the play. "He delivered the haughty speech of Caius Marcius to the starving citizens with emotion; he did not say he thought his irrational pride right, but he seemed to feel it so" (116). Caroline's response to his attitude exemplifies the crucial ambiguity of the word "sympathy": "You sympathize with that proud patrician who does not sympathize with his famished fellow-men." Robert's sympathy is amoral and, like Henry Crawford's, can be connected with the Keatsian vision of Shakespeare's "poetical character" with "as much delight in conceiving an Iago as an Imogen."[41] Earlier in the reading he was able to sympathize with a wide range of characters ("outside of private prejudice"), but upon its conclusion he only retains sympathy with experiences already similar to his own, while Caroline, like many Victorian women, takes the view that sympathy is moral, should expand the reader's experiences, and should lead to action. Robert's principal response to the play seems to be identification with the character who shares his own flaws and his own feeling of being threatened by people he despises. Caroline's critical view of Coriolanus, which anticipates elements of the analysis that many feminist critics today would make of him, baffles Robert. Armstrong's emphasis on the power of Caroline's reading needs to be qualified by recognition of Robert's resistance to it: "That is the moral you tack to the play. What puts such notions into your head?" As their contrasting approaches to Shakespeare are juxtaposed, irony cuts against the confidence both of them have that the meaning of the play is obvious.

Later in the novel, unlike any character in *Coriolanus,* Caroline makes explicit connections between gender and class "Old maids, like the

houseless and unemployed poor," she thinks ironically, "should not ask
for a place and an occupation in the world" (377). Issues of gender
inequality as well as class inequality are at stake in this scene as well.
Reading the play, thinking Shakespeare will authorize her own viewpoint, seems to energize Caroline; in the comic scenes, where she must
speak, among other roles, the parts of rebellious workmen, she shows
"a spirit no one could have expected of her, with a pithy expression with
which she seemed gifted on the spot, and for that brief moment only"
(116). Yet the narrator emphasizes the ephemerality of her liveliness,
and in language that echoes Anna Jameson's comparison of analyzing
Cleopatra, Miranda, and Ophelia to catching a meteor, dewdrop, or
snowflake, she says that Caroline's conversation was "untaught, un-
studied, intuitive, fitful; when once gone, no more to be reproduced as
it had been, than the glancing ray of the meteor, than the tints of the
dew-gem, than the colour of form of the sun-set cloud, than the fleeting
and glittering ripple varying the flow of a rivulet."[42]

Caroline is no Cleopatra, but Robert resembles a prose Antony in
a Roman mood when he says to himself, at the end of the evening,
"This won't do! There's weakness—there's downright ruin in all this.
However, . . . the frenzy is quite temporary. I know it very well: I
have had it before" (120). The novel undercuts Caroline's optimism
about the effect of Shakespeare reading while identifying it with her
personal as well as social hopes: just as Robert can be moved by the
play but not make the ethical application to treat his workpeople differently, he can be strongly attracted to Caroline and then withdraw
from her. Perhaps *Coriolanus* even accomplishes the opposite of Caroline's intent by giving Robert a snobbish, proud hero with whom to
identify, one whose behavior, as Margaret Arnold has shown, he follows in many later details.[43] At the end of the novel, Robert does adopt
much of Caroline's message, after he is humbled by Shirley's rejection
of his mercenary proposal of marriage and by his convalescence and
educated by his investigation of poverty in Birmingham and London.
But much of this change seems, in Deirdre David's phrase, a "fiction
of resolution," determined by the novel's ideological commitment to
show that individual conversion can bring about social harmony.[44]

The novel is divided in its interest in both individualism and sympathy; it appropriates Shakespeare on both sides of the conflict—the tragic hero on one, the social ideal on the other—and then converts the tragic hero to provide a Shakespearean comic ending. The comic ending is possible partly because *Shirley*'s women, particularly the title character, have some power to help bring about a more compassionate society. Shirley and Caroline are leaders in trying to alleviate class conflict by promoting help for the poor; their value system offers an alternative for the novel's world.[45] In contrast, in *Coriolanus* Volumnia's pride and militarism are the source of her son's; her greater political interest and wish not to have her city burned provide little sense of profoundly different values, and the silent, tearful Virgilia has little possibility for influencing change. The location of moral strength in Shirley and Caroline shows some of the greater possibilities for women that Victorian women novelists and reformers could develop.

Yet, even though no woman in *Shirley* has the destructive power of Volumnia, the novel seems ambivalent about female power. Forceful women are caricatured in Hortense, Robert's sister, and Nurse Horsfall, who nurses him after he is shot. Shirley ritually tames herself for Louis in much more prolonged and melodramatic dialogue than occurs when characters in Austen or Shakespeare decide to marry. Caroline's complaints about the condition of women are mostly made to herself or directly to the reader; she submits to her uncle's demands, including his demand that she not see Robert, much too meekly. It may be symptomatic that Robert is most moved by her not when she is reading or discussing Shakespeare but when she is reciting a poem in the voice of a female victim—"La Jeune Captive," by Chenier. In the background of their relationship are the images of male power and female weakness, and the erotization of these roles contradicts the ideal of gender equality for which Caroline and Shirley often speak.[46] In a composition written for her masterful Belgian teacher, M. Héger, in 1843, Brontë had praised Wellington, one of her childhood heroes, as "le moderne Coriolan," caring only for the approval of his own conscience.[47] Her interest in powerful masculine figures, persistent since the early fantasy world of Angria, is still present when Robert Moore becomes the "modern Coriolanus."[48] The contradictions in *Shirley* are more problematic than those resolved in Austen and in Shakespearean comedies because of the greater use of an individualistic male hero and more explicit concern with class oppression. Hazlitt had written of *Coriolanus,* "Any one who studies it may save himself the trouble of reading Burke's Reflections, or Paine's Rights of Man, or the Debates in both Houses of Parliament since the French Revolution or our own."[49] Brontë draws the dialogue of attitudes in her novel as a direct continuation of the dialogue in the play, while adding conflicting attitudes about gender as well. It is no wonder the solution seems inadequate.

Jane Eyre contains no explicit discussion of the woman writer's relation to tradition, but its frequent allusions to Shakespearean tragedy suggest claims for the stature of its characters. While in Austen allusions to romantic Shakespearean lines, from comedies, are often followed with an antiromantic comment, in *Jane Eyre* the Shakespearean allusions, usually to tragedies, sometimes have a hyperbolic and perhaps self-mocking tone but are not explicitly critiqued. As in *Shirley,* the male hero is linked with tragic men, but here the allusions suggest that the central woman also endures tragic suffering. The sympathy of their final union has echoes of the temporary union of Cordelia and Lear, with the blinding and maiming of Rochester resulting in a change in the balance of power analogous to the change Lear undergoes on the heath.

Near the beginning of the novel, Rochester is linked less with Lear than with younger Shakespearean tragic heroes who communicate with preternatural forces. Speaking to Jane enigmatically of his plan for her, he likens his "notion" to the ghost who appeared to Hamlet: "It is no devil, I assure you; or if it be, it has put on the robes of an angel of light. . . . By which instinct do you pretend to distinguish between a fallen seraph of the abyss, and a messenger from the eternal throne?"[50] More explicit echoes ominously associate Rochester with Macbeth. In the next chapter, he says, "During the moment I was silent, Miss Eyre, I was arranging a point with my destiny. She stood there, by that beech-trunk—a hag like one of those who appeared to Macbeth on the heath of Forres. 'You like Thornfield?' she said, lifting her finger; and then she wrote in the air a memento, which ran in lurid hieroglyphics all along the house-front, between the upper and lower row of windows, 'Like it if you can! Like it if you dare!'

" 'I will like it,' said I. . . . I will break obstacles to happiness" (143). Rochester thus identifies his own determination to have Jane for his own, in spite of his living, mad wife, with Macbeth's determination to have the throne of Scotland. Like Macbeth after he sees the witches, Rochester often seems preoccupied; on their abortive wedding day, Jane says, "I know not whether the day was fair or foul. . . . I wanted to see the invisible thing on which, as we went along, he appeared to fasten a glance fierce and fell" (290). Compare the witches' "Fair is foul, and foul is fair" (*Macbeth* 1.1.11) and Macbeth's "So foul and fair a day I have not seen" (1.3.38). Rochester is thus a Macbeth who confides—up to a point—in the innocent Jane, and Margaret Smith has pointed out how the description of Bertha when she enters Jane's room "dressed in a long white garment and bearing a candle," associates her with Lady Macbeth.[51]

Rochester links Jane herself with less ominous, more subordinated versions of the Shakespearean supernatural. He often calls her "fairy" and once describes her as "delicate and aërial" (261); this may recall the relationship between Prospero and his "delicate Ariel" (*Tempest* 4.1.18), usually played by a woman in the nineteenth century; it is one of the few Shakespeare echoes undercut in this novel, when Jane says, "puny and insignificant, you mean." "Fairy" is also part of a set of allusions to the century's favorite comedy, *A Midsummer Night's Dream.*[52] Rochester calls Jane "Mustard-Seed" (260), after a fairy in that play, and it is Midsummer Eve when Jane goes to walk in the garden and finds him there. Briefly, it seems that the tragic hero's break with convention is merely analogous to the lovers' escape to the forest outside Athens; Rochester's imagery keeps Jane tiny and domestic at the same time that he associates her with nonhuman mystery. At the same time, Rochester's midsummer night outside with Jane, when they declare their love, is more significant than Emma's midsummer picnic, where she flirts with Frank Churchill and insults Miss Bates. In *Emma,* unconventional behavior associated with nature needs to be disavowed; in *Jane Eyre* it is ultimately rewarded.

But first Jane must endure a more arduous stay in nature in *Jane Eyre*—her journey on the heath, which recalls not a comedy but a tragedy, *King Lear,* and is part of the structurally most important set of allusions. These allusions begin comically: when Rochester removes the gypsy disguise he has assumed partly to learn the thoughts of the contrasting women Blanche and Jane, he exclaims, "Off, ye lendings!" (204).[53] Here he borrows words from Lear in one of his early mad scenes; like this whole episode, they emphasize Rochester's eccentricity. Is Rochester also an old man who wants daughterly affection? Yes and no. Jane has just noticed that his hand is young and not that of the old woman he has been pretending to be. Their age difference, however, is significant; in the scene with the Hamlet allusions, he has described himself as "old enough to be your father." The novel both indulges and denies the parent-child fantasy.[54] The young woman (determined not to flatter) who, after leaving Rochester, returns to find him weakened and humbled and stays with him, might even suggest Cordelia listening to Lear saying, "We two alone will sing like birds i' th' cage" (5.3.9). In a prose version of this, Rochester says, "Oh, you are indeed there, my skylark! All the melody on earth is concentrated in my Jane's tongue to my ear" (444).

But in the novel, unlike the play, we follow the woman's side of the story, while associations link her not only with Cordelia but also with Lear himself; unlike *Shirley* this novel gives a female character as well as a male one the stature of a tragic hero. When Jane leaves Thornfield on discovering Rochester's marriage, she is, like Lear, going to the heath in order to keep her own integrity. Like Lear she must deal with the "torture of thought" (328) as well as physical pain; she wishes to die but struggles on; her questioning of God and man is far less probing, but Brontë would have seen it as an improvement that her religious faith remains strong. When she reaches the Rivers's house, Diana and Mary are as kind and straightforward in their help as Cordelia, and in using an image like Cordelia's about Lear's sufferings, she expresses her faith in their sympathy. When she says, "If I were a masterless and stray dog, I know that you would not turn me from your hearth tonight" (342), she echoes Cordelia's speech, "Mine enemy's dog, though he had bit me, should have stood that night / Against my fire" (4.7.37–38). The novel in many ways suggests that Jane and Rochester belong together because they are two outsiders with a mysterious kinship (at a crucial point [177] she uses the phrase "I feel akin to him"); part of this effect are the hints that somehow they are both Lears, as well as Lear and Cordelia.

Most of the important Shakespearean allusions in *Jane Eyre,* as in *Shirley,* are to tragedies, but *Jane Eyre* does evoke one woman from Shakespeare's comedies, though not in the description of Jane. And unlike allusions to the tragedies in this novel, the allusions to comedy, though initially attractive, ultimately critique the character and her world. In both her first name and her last, Rosamond Oliver recalls characters from *As You Like It.*[55] Jane says that "all advantages, in short, which, combined, realize the ideal of beauty, were fully hers. . . . Nature had surely formed her in a partial mood; and, forgetting her usual stinted step-mother dole of gifts, had endowed this, her darling, with a granddame's bounty. . . . [she is] favored, it seems, in the gifts of fortune as well as in those of nature" (367–68). Jane's praise combines elements from Orlando's poem about Rosalind ("Therefore Heaven Nature charg'd / That one body should be fill'd / With all graces wide enlarg'd / Nature presently distill'd / Helen's cheek, but not her heart" [3.2.139–43]) as well as Rosalind's conversation with Celia about the gifts of Fortune and Nature. There Rosalind says of Fortune, "her benefits are mightily misplac'd, and the bountiful blind woman doth most mistake in her gifts to women" (1.2.33–35). Rosamond is as aggressive with St. John in her first appearance in the novel as Rosalind was in her first meeting with Orlando, and St. John, about as uncomfortably silent as Orlando there, unlike Orlando never changes his attitude later. Jane presents Rosamond as rather shallow in contrast with herself and by implication as belonging in a comic world dismissed as trivial: "she was very charming, in short, even to a cool observer of her own sex like me; but she was not profoundly interesting or thoroughly impressive" (373).

St. John, indeed, sees limitations in her decisive enough to make him suppress his attraction to her and in his language about her rejects comic values. When he speaks of her, he uses imagery reminiscent of *Antony and Cleopatra,* but, like Robert at the beginning of *Shirley,* he has decided to behave like a Roman. He sees love of Rosamond as "delicious poison" (1.5.27–28), and when thinking of indulging that love, he recalls the agent of Cleopatra's suicide as he says, "there is an asp in the garland" (378). Rejected by St. John, Rosamond quickly marries someone else, turning into the stereotype of the inconstant woman that Rosalind, in the character of Ganymede, applied to herself—"for every passion something and for no passion truly anything" (3.2.401–402).

In the world of *Jane Eyre,* where passion is so important, Shakespearean allusions give tragic depth and otherworldly qualities to Jane and Rochester but reinforce the sense that St. John is cold and that Rosamond has warmth that is only superficial. The rewriting of Shakespeare's Rosalind, however, may have provided a germ for the plot in *Middlemarch,* where another dedicated man marries a beautiful and shallow Rosamond. St. John says, "She is not the partner suited to me. . . . to twelve months' rapture would succeed a lifetime of regret. . . . she could sympathize [that word again] in nothing I aspired to." Chapter 5, on *Middlemarch,* will show how Lydgate's marriage develops this alternative plot and plays it against other Shakespearean echoes.

Brontë's Shirley says, "The cleverest, the acutest men are often under an illusion about women; they do not read them in a true light. . . . their good woman is a queer thing, half doll, half angel; their bad woman almost always a fiend. . . . women read men more truly than men read women" (343). Unlike Anne's comments in *Persuasion* about the falsity of male pictures of women, these lines are not accompanied by any hints that Shakespeare is an exception. Probably it is significant that the Shakespearean characters she appropriates to give resonance to hers are almost all male, and the rewriting of Rosalind as Rosamond is rather close to "half doll, half angel." There is much creative energy in Shirley's attack on Milton's Eve: "Milton was great; but was he good? . . . Milton tried to see the first woman; but he saw her not. . . . It was his cook that he saw." Yet there is also creative energy in Caroline's use of *Coriolanus* against Robert and in the rewriting of *Lear* to give Jane some of both Lear's and Cordelia's tragic stature and emotional weight. Brontë exemplifies both rebellious and appropriative rewritings of male predecessors. More of a romantic, she is more interested than Austen in Shakespeare's tragic men, his use of the supernatural, and his associations with sympathy considered, in part, as an ethical value. Her interest in his comic women, less than Austen's, seems most evident in her portrayal of Rosamond, to whom Jane feels alien much as Brontë felt alien to Austen's world, of which she wrote,

"I should hardly like to live with her ladies and gentlemen, in their elegant but confined houses."[56] Brontë appropriates most positively a Shakespearean woman who also leaves a confining social world in the echoes of Cordelia she uses in creating Jane Eyre.

George Eliot read *Jane Eyre* and, probably, *Shirley*, close to the time she began writing fiction, and during her work on her first short stories, she and Lewes read both Austen and Shakespeare.[57] In "Recollections of the Scilly Isles," about spring-summer 1857, she writes, "Our readings were . . . Life of Charlotte Brontë, Twelfth Night, Macbeth, Northanger Abbey, and Persuasion." Lewes's journal for spring 1857 includes, as well, *Emma, Sense and Sensibility, Much Ado About Nothing,* and *As You Like It:* they read aloud to each other.[58] Eliot's novels, like Austen's, sometimes make fun of cultural uses of Shakespeare (see the implied critique of Gwendolen's superficial reading of Shakespeare in *Daniel Deronda*). She is even more interested than Austen in Shakespeare's female characters (partly because of the intervening development of character criticism, especially by Anna Jameson), and like Brontë, she rewrites Rosalind and several tragic heroes. Like Brontë, she can use Shakespeare allusions to add stature, even a sense of preternatural vision, to her characters. She can also, like Brontë, emphasize contrasts between her characters and the Shakespearean figures allusions recall, making her characters alternatively more generous (Felix, Daniel) or more narrow (Rosamond) than their Shakespearean counterparts. She is even more self-conscious and persistent than Brontë in her explo- ration of the ideal of sympathy associated with Shakespeare. While she had been appropriating Shakespeare in her letters even before she read Brontë or Austen, as we shall see in the next chapter, among the many things she might have learned from these literary mothers was that women novelists could rewrite Shakespeare from their own points of view.

Chapter Three

George Eliot: Early Works

GEORGE ELIOT's interest in Shakespeare, and particularly in his female characters, began when she was still Mary Ann Evans.[1] Most of her responses to him, throughout her career, contradict the claim in *The Madwoman in the Attic* that women writers think the male canon portrays women only as "extreme stereotypes (angel, monster)."[2] Indeed, in at least one passage she emphasized the autonomy of his female characters even more than the many other Victorians who also wrote about them. I suggest that she enjoyed Shakespeare partly because she saw him as a creator of powerful women and that she saw herself as writing both in his tradition and from a female viewpoint.

Many of her contemporaries placed George Eliot in some sense within a Shakespearean tradition. In 1873, John Fiske, an American disciple of Herbert Spencer, wrote, "Spencer thinks she is the greatest woman that has lived on the earth—the female Shakespeare, so to speak; and I imagine he is not *far* from right."[3] The earliest explicit use of the comparison is only slightly less hyperbolical: in her journal for March 26, 1859, George Eliot notes exultantly that Charles Reade says that *Adam Bede* is "the finest thing since Shakespeare."[4] This chapter will explore the Shakespearean appropriations and revisions in her letters, essays, and early fiction. It will examine her interest in Shakespeare's women and in his cultural image as an artist of sympathy, discuss the contexts in her biography for these interests, and show how her early fiction alludes to both women and men from Shakespeare's plays in trying to extend literary attention to people usually subordinated by class and gender.

Eliot and Shakespeare's Women

In one of her very earliest letters (March 16, 1839), her attitude to Shakespeare sounds wary: "we have need of as nice a power of distillation as the bee to such nothing but honey from his pages" (1:22); in retrospect this foreshadows her many creative transformations. The wariness in this letter stems mostly from the austere religiosity she still had at nineteen but would soon repudiate. By October 1842, her friend Mary Sibree wrote her brother that Mary Ann said she "could be content were she allowed no other book than Shakspeare; and in educating a child, this would be the first book she would place in its hands." She thought that objecting to Shakespeare's plays was like objecting to walk in a beautiful garden "because toads and weeds are to be found in it."[5] Fourteen years later, she could take her high opinion of Shakespeare more for granted and use it in praising other writers. For example, in an essay on *Antigone,* she praised Sophocles by saying that he is "the single dramatic poet who can be said to stand on a level with Shakspeare. Sophocles is the crown and flower of the classic tragedy as Shakspeare is of the romantic."[6]

Her letters, especially the first volume (written between the ages of sixteen and thirty-two), abound in Shakespearean references, many of which strongly suggest that she identified with his female characters. Ten of the more than twenty in that volume are from *As You Like It,* and throughout her life it is the play she most often recalls in her correspondence.[7] This preference was unusual in her time; one reason for her interest is that the friendship between Rosalind and Celia is often a model for her own friendship with other women. To Maria Lewis, she writes, "I heartily echo your kind wish that we should be 'like Juno's swans' coupled together" (1:51; *As You Like It* 1.3.75). To Martha Jackson, "I have as many queries rising to my lips as, if you were here to have them orally delivered, would make you wish, like Rosalind, that the answers were corked up in you like wine in a bottle" (1:92; based on

As You Like It 3.2.197–200). To Sara Sophia Hennell, "Not a word more
to throw at a dog. So said Rosalind to Celia and so says one to thee,
who loves thee as well as Rosalind did her Coz" (1:203; based on *As You
Like It* 1.3.3). In some of her other letters from this time she playfully
puts on a male identity to express this affection, suggesting another dimension of her interest in the cross-dressed Rosalind and anticipating
her later use of a male pseudonym. "I have not been beyond seas long
enough to make it lawful for you to take a new husband—therefore
I come back to you with all a husband's privileges and command you
to love me whether I shew you any love or not" (1.279). These letters
place her relationships within the tradition of romantic friendship identified by Lillian Faderman.[8] Yet the *As You Like It* allusions make the
note of playfulness more explicit.

Eliot's longest discussion of Shakespeare, dating from the year before she began writing fiction, focuses on his representation of women.
In 1855, writing criticism for the *Leader* while living with its cofounder,
G. H. Lewes, in spite of the English laws prohibiting him from divorc-
ing his unfaithful wife, she uses Shakespeare's women as models to
attack what she calls "The doctrines of modern propriety."[9] Discussing Girardin's *Cours de Littérature Dramatique,* she energetically refutes
the claim that Shakespeare's women, unlike those of ancient dramatists, declare their love only after a lover has declared himself to them.
On the contrary, "Shakspeare's women have no more decided characteristic than the frankness with which they avow their love, not only
to themselves, but to the men they love." In contrast to Hazlitt's view
that these characters show "weakness leaning on the strength of its
affections for support,"[10] note the active power that George Eliot finds.

> If Romeo opens the duct [duet?] of love with a few notes *solo,* Juliet
> soon strikes in and keeps it up in as impassioned a strain as he. Sweet
> Desdemona, "a maiden never bold," encourages Othello, not only by a
> "world of sighs," but by the broadest possible hint that he has won her
> heart. Rosalind, in her first interview with Orlando, tells him he has
> "overthrown more than his enemies;" Portia is eloquent in assurances
> of her love before the casket is opened. . . . Curious it is to contrast

these Shakspearean heroines with some of Walter Scott's painfully discreet young ladies.

She sees the "respectability" of Scott's ladies as a violation of nature: "they are like trees trained in right lines by dint of wall and hammer." Many nineteenth-century writers associate Scott with Shakespeare, but like Lewes, she dissents.[11] At the end of the paragraph she explicitly uses the concurrence of Shakespeare and Greek dramatists in portraying "feminine frankness" as evidence that "it must be simply a natural manifestation which has only been gradually and partially repressed by the complex influences of modern civilization."

Her enthusiastic emphasis on the initiative of Shakespeare's women was unusual. Her view differs markedly from Hazlitt's, and even Anna Jameson, who celebrated them at great length, was more cautious and concerned with propriety in her praise.[12] For many Victorian critics, as Russell Jackson has shown, "Rosalind, Beatrice, and Viola, for all the affection they attracted, could not be accepted without some special pleading. They enjoyed a freedom of speech and mind beyond what was proper in a well-brought-up Victorian girl."[13] In her notebook, Eliot herself commented on this peculiarity of Victorian criticism: "It is remarkable that Shakespear's women almost always *make love,* in opposition to the conventional notion of what is fitting for woman. Yet his pictures of women are belauded."[14]

The few occasions on which Eliot criticizes women's roles in Shakespeare's plots further confirm the protofeminism of her responses. In her journal for March 16, 1855, the same year, she wrote, "After dinner read 'Two Gentlemen of Verona'. . . . That play disgusted me more than ever in the final scene, where Valentine, on Proteus' mere begging pardon, when he has no longer any hope of gaining his ends, says 'All that was mine in Silvia, I give thee!' Silvia standing by."[15]

Each of these Shakespearean allusions had a strong personal resonance for Eliot. She borrowed phrases from the dialogues between Rosalind and Celia at times when female friendships were the most important ones in her life; when her defining relationship became her love of G. H. Lewes, she wrote on Shakespeare's portrayal of unconventional, frankly passionate women. And Lewes was away, trying to determine whether his marriage with Agnes was definitely broken, when she noticed and objected to the assumption of Silvia's passivity.[16]

Rosalind, Portia, and many of Shakespeare's other transgressive women take on masculine disguise and a masculine name, as did the Victorian actresses who played them. Comparing herself as a writer to Rosalind, whose words she had often appropriated, seems at least as plausible a psychology for Eliot as the fear of being like Lady Macbeth that, according to Gilbert and Gubar, nineteenth-century women writers might have had.[17] Before Eliot began writing fiction, she had compared some works by women to "the swaggering gait of a bad actress in man's attire" (*Essays*, 53), but this was because they were "an absurd exaggeration of the masculine style" as her own writing, I will discuss shortly, would not be.

Eliot, Shakespeare, and Sympathy

The passion Eliot noted and valued in Shakespeare's female characters, I argue, is closely linked with the strong emotions she experienced while watching his plays. A letter she wrote in 1859 indicated how central to Eliot's image of Shakespeare is this experience. "In opposition to most people who love to *read* Shakspear I like to see his plays acted better than any others: his great tragedies thrill me, let them be acted how they may. I think it is something like what I used to experience in the old days in listening to uncultured preachers—the emotions lay hold of one too strongly for one to care about the medium. Before all other plays I find myself cold and critical, seeing nothing but actors and 'properties'" (3:228).

It was a Victorian commonplace that Shakespeare's art could arouse sympathy, but criticism of Shakespeare's women, and later of her own, shows that not all Victorian critics could go as far as Eliot in sympathizing with passion. For her, the aim of sympathy could justify the portrayal of frank female desire. She used it this way in defending a story in her *Scenes of Clerical Life* against the criticism that it portrayed a woman's love as too open and undignified: "My artistic bent is directed . . . to the presentation of mixed human beings in such a way as to call forth tolerant judgment, pity, and sympathy" (2:299). Eliot found the message of sympathy in many other writers, ranging in time from Sophocles to Wordsworth, but, in Victorian England, Shakespeare was both the writer most praised for creating sympathy for his characters and, as the Girardin review shows, one of the few earlier writers she saw as presenting strong female desire: this combination contributed to his importance for her.[18]

Lewes, as a man of the theater, helped sustain Eliot's interest in Shakespearean performance. She and Lewes read the plays to each other many times, and, since he wrote theater reviews, together they saw Shakespeare acted by Helena Martin, Fechter, Rossi, Aldridge, and Salvini, to mention only those discussed in her letters.[19] Lewes emphasized the role of sympathy in the theater as well as the novel: before most of the discussions of Austen and sympathy quoted in the previous chapter, he wrote that the dramatist appeals "to that sympathy which man feels for man."[20] Lewes also phrased one of the earliest implicit comparisons between Eliot and Shakespeare. He wrote to his publisher, Blackwood, describing the anonymous manuscript of "Amos Barton" as "exhibiting in a high degree that faculty which I find to be the rarest of all, viz. the dramatic ventriloquism" (*GEL* 2:274). His image is one Hazlitt used for Shakespeare: "By an art like that of the ventriloquist, he throws his imagination out of himself, and makes every word appear to proceed from the mouth of the person in whose name it is given."[21] After the publication of *Adam Bede,* others made the Eliot/Shakespeare comparison explicit: Theodore Martin wrote Blackwood, "The views of life and character are so large, so Shakspearian in their breadth of sympathy . . . that one almost forgets it is a book" (*GEL* 3:42). It was shortly after this that Lewes wrote the review essay constructing the Shakespeare/Austen/Eliot tradition—"The Novels of Jane Austen"— mentioned in the previous chapter (*GEL* 3:46). As Eliot's writing continued, more and more Victorians compared her to Shakespeare in terms of the wide-ranging sympathy seen in both of their works.[22]

In Eliot's culture, the image of Shakespeare as sympathetic was the perfect example that it was possible to be great without egotism, to write while seeming to put the self aside, projecting it into a variety of other characters. This view of the great writer as sympathetic was particularly important to Eliot because, influenced by Victorian constructions of womanhood, she was extremely anxious about egotism, though extremely ambitious.[23] She calls herself too egotistical at least sixteen different times in the first volume of her letters—usually with regard to writing too much about herself. As Ruby Redinger shows, she frequently felt uneasy about an interest in herself that she could not suppress; indeed that very uneasiness added to her self-consciousness.[24] She made unusual self-comparisons for a teenage girl—to the philanthropist Wilberforce (1:12); to Erasmus (1:92). Each time she then recoiled and abased herself. Much later, she described herself as having been "too proud and ambitious to write: I did not believe that I could do anything fine, and I did not choose to do anything of that mediocre sort which I despised when it was done by others" (8:384).

One model for interpreting this period, suggested by the religious emphasis of Eliot's background, the "all-or-nothing" themes in her youth, the rebellion against going to church with her father, and her focus on the person of Jesus (in translating Strauss), is the uncertainty about identity discussed by Erik Erikson in *Young Man Luther.*[25] In Erikson's interpretation, Luther resolved his crisis of identity by writing lectures on the Psalms and by reformulating his theology. Similarly, Eliot helped herself resolve her crisis by her work as an essayist and translator, about which she herself used religious imagery. "I began, however, by a sort of writing which had no great glory belonging to it, but which I felt certain I could do faithfully and well [translation of Strauss's *Life of Jesus*]. This resolve to work at what did not gratify my ambitions, and to care only that I worked faithfully, was equivalent to the old phrase—'using the means of grace'" (8:384). Like Erikson's Luther, whose religious imagination met the psychological needs he shared with many others in his culture, she began to see the growth out of egotism into sympathy not simply as a need of her own but as a process of maturing more generally necessary. "When we are young we think our troubles a mighty business—that the world is spread out expressly as a stage for the particular drama of our lives and that we have a right to rant and foam at the mouth if we are crossed. I have done enough of that in my time. But we begin at last to understand that these things are important only to one's own consciousness" (2:156).

She would take this process of maturing as one of the main subjects of her fiction and one of her aims for her readers. Thus she synthesized her ambition and her critical view of egotism.

Gender theory such as Chodorow's, added to Erikson's psycho-historical analysis and Showalter's study of the language of many Victorian women writers, suggests that because of Eliot's upbringing in a nineteenth-century family and acculturation as a nineteenth-century woman, she needed to find a kind of creativity that she could see as relational.[26] Her choice of translating meant, in part, a structured, limited kind of identification with another writer. Soon after she begins her translation, in February 1848, a new note enters the self-description in her letters: "Everyone talks of himself or herself to me, and I beg you will follow everyone's example in this one thing only" (1:251–52). It is becoming part of her developing self-concept to be interested in others. Later, in "Woman in France: Madame de Sablé" (October 1854), she would praise a woman whose "forte was evidently not to write herself, but to stimulate others to write; to show that sympathy and appreciation which are as genial and encouraging as the morning sunbeams. She seconded a man's wit with understanding—one of the best offices which womanly intellect has rendered to the advancement of culture" (74).[27]

But Eliot was not satisfied to be, like her version of Madame de Sablé, "all the more receptive towards the originality of others" because of her own "absence of originality," and one of her own previous uses of the Shakespeare passage she paraphrases in "seconded a man's wit with understanding" helps to make this point. In an earlier letter, referring to her own need for a response, not to "a man's," she had written (echoing Wordsworth as well as Shakespeare), "O how lusciously joyous . . . to feel one's 'heart leap up' after the pressure that Shakspeare so admirably describes, 'When a man's wit is not seconded by the forward child understanding it strikes a man as dead as a large reckoning in a small room'" (*GEL* 1:71; *As You Like It* 3.3.10–12). In "Woman in France" she uses the view that women possess distinctive maternal sensations and emotions as part of an argument for access to writing, as well as to other kinds of achievement: "woman has something specific to contribute. . . . Let the whole field to reality be laid open to woman as well as to man. Then we shall have that marriage of minds which alone can blend all the hues of thought and feeling in one lovely rainbow of promise for the harvest of human happiness" (53, 81). This last sentence, the final one in the essay, echoes the most famous of Shakespeare's sonnets, which begins, "Let me not to the marriage of true minds / Admit impediments." She herself would not allow legal impediments to keep her from seeing her relationship with Lewes as marriage and here urges an analogous defeat of social obstacles to women's achievements, achievements that she once more envisions in relational terms.[28]

Nevertheless, her emphasis on women's specific contributions does not always lead her to a clear support of women's access to writing. In her essay "Silly Novels by Lady Novelists" (October 1856), like the one on "Woman in France," she would imagine "a really cultured woman" in terms of sympathy: "She does not write books to confound philosophers, perhaps because she is able to write books that delight them. . . . She does not give you information, which is the raw material of culture—she gives you sympathy, which is it [sic] subtlest essence" (317). But this definition, which begins with the phrase "a really cultured woman, like a really cultured man," shows tension between the view that sympathy is a human virtue and the view that it is especially necessary for women. Furthermore, it is ambiguous about whether the cultured woman so described really does write the books she is able to—perhaps because Eliot herself was still uncertain.

The traditions of women novelists, evangelicalism, and sensibility provided possibilities for justifying her writing with regard to moral sentiment, but she found all these traditions, on the whole, inadequate models, according to this and other reviews she wrote close to the time she began writing fiction. In separate, lengthy essays, she attacked both an influential evangelical preacher, Dr. Cumming, and a poet of sensibility, Edward Young, explicitly for their lack of sympathy, in spite of the charity that both of them claimed to teach.[29] Her essay "Silly Novels by Lady Novelists" described the "really cultured woman" as part of an attack on the "oracular species" of woman novelist for their lack of sympathy and many other defects and shows that she found severe limitations in many other kinds of women writers. In "Three Novels," when discussing a novel by Fredrika Bremer, she declared, "Women have not to prove that they can be emotional, and rhapsodic, and spiritualistic; every one believes that already" (334). Though she could adapt some of her society's ideology of gender to her own purposes, responded in her fiction to many novels by earlier women, and would later make an allegorical use of some of the teachings of evangelicalism, she had rejected evangelical beliefs and her society's dominant behavioral expectations of women for herself and needed to find models of sympathetic writing in other traditions in addition to those of women and evangelicals.[30]

I do not suggest anything so simple as a moment here when Eliot thought, "I will be a sympathetic writer like Shakespeare," anticipating the identification that would later be made by Lewes, Theodore Martin, and many other Victorians, nor do I deny her interest in many other writers. Nevertheless, during these years of exploration, Shakespeare was clearly important to her. As she finished her translation of Strauss's *Life of Jesus,* she told her friend Cara Bray that she "means to come and read Shakespeare through to us as her first enjoyment."[31] Her letters contain many more appropriations of Shakespeare than I can quote or discuss, but two at this period seem particularly significant. Writing to the Brays from Geneva in 1849 about how important they are to her, she defines herself with one allusion to a Shakespearean text (*Macbeth* 3.4.24) and one to the animal that was one of Keats's images of Shakespeare in a letter published just the previous year.[32] "My nature is so chameleon I shall lose all my identity unless you keep nourishing the old self with letters" (1:302); "When one is cabin'd, cribbed, confined in oneself, it is good to be enlarged in one's friends" (1:324).[33]

During her apprentice period, her works were translating, editing, and anonymous reviewing—all relational modes; she chose to translate, after Strauss, Feuerbach's *Essence of Christianity,* in which sympathy was an important concept.[34] But she had been finding sympathy in literature longer than in philosophy, and she felt that art could do more than other modes of discourse to arouse sympathy in others. For example, in "The Natural History of German Life" (July 1856), she wrote, "Appeals founded on generalizations and statistics require a sympathy ready-made, a moral sentiment already in activity; but a picture of human life such as a great artist can give, surprises even the trivial and the selfish into that attention to what is apart from themselves, which may be called the raw material of moral sentiment" (*Essays,* 270).

This is one of the several essays that, in contrast with those critiquing Cumming and Young, set out a positive statement of goals for her own writing. Although she discussed a number of writers favorably, her echoes of Shakespeare and of Shakespeare criticism in these essays reinforce the sense that his association with sympathy was important to her. Reviewing a new translation of *Wilhelm Meister,* she wrote, "The novelist may place before us every aspect of human life where there is some trait of love, or endurance, or helplessness to call forth our best sympathies" (146), and praised Goethe with an argument close to Hazlitt's argument in defense of *Measure for Measure.* Hazlitt had written, "Shakespear was in one sense the least moral of all writers; for morality (commonly so called) is made up of antipathies; and his talent consisted in sympathy with human nature, in all its shapes, degrees, depressions, and elevations. The object of the pedantic moralist is to find out the bad in everything: his was to shew that 'there is some soul of goodness in thing evil.' In one sense, Shakespear was no moralist at all: in another, he was the greatest of all moralists."[35] Eliot, similarly, made Goethe's sympathy a justification for portraying behavior sometimes considered immoral: "The large tolerance of Goethe, which is markedly exhibited in *Wilhelm Meister,* is precisely that to which we point as the element of moral superiority. . . . the line between the virtuous and the vicious, so far from being a necessary safeguard to morality, is itself an immoral fiction" (*Essays,* 147). She would soon use the same argument in defense of her own writing.

"The Natural History of German Life" most clearly articulates her relational view of art: "The greatest benefit we owe the artist, whether painter, poet, or novelist, is the extension of our sympathies" (270). Many Victorian critics discussed literature in terms of sympathy, but Eliot is taking the minority and more adventurous side against the view, as Isobel Armstrong formulates it, that sympathy in literature simply "corroborates the familiar, basic facts of our moral and emotional experience and confirms us in the ordinary duties and obligations of existence." Armstrong relates the more adventurous view to Keats's idea of the "camelion poet," for whom, as we have seen, Shakespeare is the prototype, but Eliot emphasizes the writer's responsibility more.[36] The essay argues against the inadequacy of a kind of sympathy that simply, in today's terms, reinforces stereotypes: Eliot finds it "pernicious" that in art representing lower-class characters, in particular, "our sympathy . . . should be perverted, and turned towards a false object instead of the true one" (271).

In her view, to represent truthfully the lives of the people, a writer needs both tragic and comic modes. Dickens, she says, although "gifted with the utmost power of rendering the external traits of our town population, . . . scarcely ever passes from the humorous and external to the emotional and tragic, without becoming as transcendent in his unreality as he was a moment before in his artistic truthfulness" (*Essays,* 271). Praising him, however, she grants him "the same startling inspiration in his description of the gestures and phrases of 'Boots,' as in the speeches of Shakspeare's mobs or numbskulls."

This passage combines the image of Shakespeare as sympathetic and a residual conservatism that sees inspiration in the presentation of the people as a mob, a mix frequent in nineteenth- and early twentieth-century Shakespeare criticism.[37] Still, this essay also recalls Samuel Johnson's defense of Shakespeare's "mingled drama," mixing tragic and comic modes, as exhibiting "the real state of sublunary nature, which partakes of good and evil, joy and sorrow."[38] In a letter written a few years before, foreshadowing some critical descriptions of her fiction, Eliot had jokingly claimed a similar characteristic for her epistolary style: "It is the immemorial fashion of lady letter-writers to be glad and sorry in the same sentence, and after all, this feminine style is the truest representation of life" (*GEL* 9:115; August 6, 1854). While "Natural History" uses Shakespeare as the model against which Dickens is judged—since by implication Shakespeare has written true tragedy as Dickens has not—it also suggests, as Johnson does not, the possibility of rewriting Shakespeare's plays to take an even larger social range into account. Discussing Riehl's presentation of German peasants, she says, "If any Romeo among the 'mattocks' were to marry a Juliet among the 'water-snakes,' there would be no lack of Tybalts and Mercutios to carry the conflict from words to blows, though neither side knows a reason for the enmity" (*Essays,* 277). Here is a germ of the uses of

Shakespeare in her fiction. In "Mr. Gilfil's Love Story," *Adam Bede, The Mill on the Floss,* and later works, she seeks to extend the areas of literary sympathy shown by Shakespeare and to maintain both comic and tragic perspectives.

"Mr. Gilfil's Love Story" and *Adam Bede*

We have seen how Charlotte Brontë used allusions to Shakespeare's tragic heroes to add resonance to both male and female characters, while extending the realm of tragedy to include characters of lower class than Shakespeare's. Eliot's early fiction uses a similar strategy, but some differences should be noted. While the Shakespeare allusions in Brontë's novels (and in Austen's novels as well) tend to occur in the characters' quoted speech, rather than in the voice of either the first-person narrator of *Jane Eyre* or the omniscient narrator of *Shirley,* Eliot gives more of her allusions to her narrator. Eliot's narrator, a more fully realized voice promoting sympathy, makes more explicit claims for the characters' literary stature and, especially in *The Mill on the Floss,* for their tragic stature. In addition, Eliot makes more references than Brontë to Shakespeare's tragic women as well as to his men.

I will focus on two aspects of "Mr. Gilfil's Love Story" and *Adam Bede* in relation to Shakespeare: the treatment of passionate women and the characterization of the narrator as both sympathetic and gender-crossing. In "Gilfil," the second story Eliot wrote, she begins her pattern of putting a passionate female character for whom she wants to create sympathy in a tradition of Shakespeare's women, and links her not just with the comic characters among whom she might belong by class but with tragedy. The narrator modulates a comment on Caterina's educational limitations into a claim for her rank as a tragic heroine: "It is very likely that to her dying day Caterina thought the earth stood still, and that the sun and stars moved around it; but so, for the matter of that, did Helen, and Dido, and Desdemona, and Juliet; whence I hope you will not think my Caterina less worthy to be a heroine on that account. The truth is that, with one exception, her only talent lay in loving; and there, it is probable, the most astronomical of women could not have surpassed her."[39]

Caterina is Eliot's first experiment in portraying the frank passion in women that she so enjoyed seeing in Shakespeare, and her publisher was rather taken aback. Blackwood suggested that she improve the story by "making Caterina a little less openly devoted to Wybrow and giving a little more dignity to her characters" and later complained about the dagger with which she goes to meet him after she learns of his falsehood (2:297). As Blackwood and Eliot discuss the story, they reenact the conflict between civilized respectability and passion that Eliot sees exemplified in the contrast between Scott's women and Shakespeare's. Like Madame de Staël, who wrote in *Corinne* that *"Romeo and Juliet,* translated into Italian, seems but resuming its own mother-tongue,"* she depicts an Italian heroine who shocks English decorum but seems somewhat closer to the mores of the stage Italy of Shakespeare's comedies and love tragedies.[40] In defense of Caterina's behavior, she could have cited that of Helena in *All's Well,* also a ward in a family that includes a cold-hearted man she loves; this character is one of her long list in her Girardin review of "women who love without being loved in return, and some of whom even sue for love"—she also mentions "the Helena in *Midsummer Night's Dream,* the shepherdess Sylvia [Phebe?], Viola, and Olivia, who woos so prettily that the action justifies itself."[41]

The argument that Eliot actually makes to Blackwood, however, justifies her details not in terms of Shakespeare's characters but in terms of the literary aim that she shared with the Victorian image of Shakespeare. "My artistic bent is not at all to the presentation of eminently irreproachable characters, but to the presentation of mixed human beings in such a way as to call forth tolerant judgment, pity, and sympathy" (2:299). In the combination of her class origin—she is the daughter of an Italian copyist—and the serious treatment of her passion, Caterina *extends* the sympathy we might give to one of Shakespeare's heroines.

It is not only the narrator who associates her with them; Gilfil makes the connection *almost* explicit when he fears that moving up her marriage will precipitate suicide, as happened with Juliet, and imagines her drowned like Ophelia when he "seems to see part of her dress caught on a branch, and her dear dead face upturned" (165).[42] Instead of staging a dramatic death scene, however, Caterina survives long enough for a subdued wedding to Gilfil, tries to make the best of the calm love she develops for him, and then dies in pregnancy.[43]

But what if Caterina's relation with Wybrow had led to pregnancy?

This question might suggest some of the plot of *Adam Bede*. Eliot's portrait of Hetty can be seen as a continuation of her interest in women's passion, here dissected and demythologized. As Gillian Beer writes, "Hetty's passion is physical and self-directed, not sustained by moral endurance. Her plight is, therefore, . . . *worse* than that of the high-minded heroines with inner resources who were the Victorian liberal version of fallen women."[44] While Hetty's suffering is painfully unromantic, details of *Adam Bede* subtly suggest comparison between Hetty's sufferings and the anguish experienced in Shakespearean tragedy. Like Lear (and in the first respect like Jane Eyre), Hetty wanders in exile on the heath, seeming mad, without shelter; like Lady Macbeth, who could not kill Duncan when she was reminded of "my father as he slept," she cannot kill her unwanted child *directly* and then suffers from the pain of her victim; as Lady Macbeth remembers, "Here's the smell of the blood still" (5.1.49), Hetty keeps hearing her dead child cry until she tells her story to Dinah.[45]

But the Shakespearean character Hetty most resembles, Ophelia, is evoked in an indirect way that emphasizes again how Eliot is extending tragedy to characters of lower-class position and fewer resources. Hetty's wanderings bring her to Stratford-on-Avon, first because she confuses it with Stony Stratford; later she chooses to go back there because she remembers its grassy fields and thinks they might provide a pool in which she could drown herself. The place name has particular impact in the novel because this is one of the few sections where the names are not fictional. It was, of course, near George Eliot/Mary Ann Evans's own birthplace in Warwickshire, but by this time it had been clearly established as a shrine to Shakespeare; he is never mentioned, but the contrast between Hetty's Stratford and the reader's is explicitly evoked: Stony Stratford to Stratford-on-Avon "seems but a slight journey as you look at the map, or remember your own pleasant travels to and from the meadowy banks of the Avon."[46] When Hetty thinks of drowning herself in the pool, neither she nor the narrator mentions Ophelia, who also loved a man of higher rank—"a prince out of thy star" (2.2.141)—and who sang about seduction and betrayal, but the reader may very well remember her—especially the Victorian reader, for whom her madness and drowning produced such familiar visual images.[47] When Hetty wonders "if there would be anything worse after death than what she dreaded in life" (321), some readers might also have thought of Hamlet's familiar soliloquy, which speaks of "the dread of something after death" (3.1.79). The next sentence explicitly tells us, "Religious doctrines had taken no hold on Hetty's mind," and emphasizes that the religious rituals imposed on her have given her no "strength in life, or trust in death." Readers who remember Ophelia and Hamlet might think likewise that part of Hetty's poverty of experience is the lack of any perspective that might be gained from literature.

Allusions to Shakespeare by the narrators of *Scenes of Clerical Life* and *Adam Bede* are part of Eliot's strategy for giving readers the perspectives that characters do not have. Other strategies include direct statement about the importance of sympathy. In the passage Lewes quoted when arguing that George Eliot surpassed Jane Austen, the narrator of "Amos Barton," the first story in *Clerical Life,* says, "Perhaps I am doing a bold thing to bespeak your sympathy on behalf of a man who was so very far from remarkable. . . . you would gain unspeakably if you would learn with me to see some of the poetry and the pathos, the tragedy and the comedy, lying in the experience of a human soul that looks out through dull grey eyes, and that speaks in a voice of quite ordinary tones" (41–42). Similarly, in *Adam Bede,* Eliot's narrator defends novelistic realism on the grounds of aiming to expand the reader's sympathies: "It is these more or less ugly, stupid, inconsistent people, whose movements of goodness you should be able to admire—for whom you should cherish all possible hopes, all possible patience. . . . let us love that other beauty too, which lies in no secret of proportion, but in the secret of deep human sympathy" (151–53).

These narrators, emphatically positioned on the side of sympathy, are both generic contrasts with Shakespeare and one of the major ways Victorians saw her as continuing his tradition. The sympathy she and other Victorians saw in Shakespeare was manifested by his self-projection into the voices of other characters, not by speaking in his own voice. In Eliot's novels, however, sympathy is not only an inferred attribute of the author but also an explicit aim of the narrative voice.

The sympathetic narrator in Eliot's early works is positioned in two other ways: with childhood memories of the relevant geographical areas (close to the area of Shakespeare's childhood, as the *Adam Bede* passage recalls) and with masculine cultural and biological possibilities as well as a male pseudonym.[48] In *Clerical Life,* he distances himself from the "lady readers": "dear ladies, allow me to plead that gin-and-water, like obesity, or baldness, or the gout, does not exclude a vast amount of antecedent romance, any more than the neatly executed 'fronts' which you may some day wear, will exclude your present possession of less expensive braids" (82). In *Adam Bede,* speaking of Hetty's difficulties in pregnancy, he says to the reader, "God preserve you and me from being the beginners of such misery!" The narrator is by implication placed as a sympathetic male, comparable to the male characters in each work described occasionally with maternal comparisons. Describing Gilfil's love for Caterina, the narrator writes, "In the love of a brave and faithful man there is always a strain of maternal tenderness; he gives out again those beams of protecting fondness which were shed on him as he lay on his mother's knee" (174). *Adam Bede* critiques the idea of maternal instinct in the portrayal of Hetty, but the glorified image of the mother returns, applied to Adam when he sees Hetty at the trial: "the mother's yearning, that completest type of the life in another life which is the essence of real human love, feels the presence of the cherished child even in the debased, degraded man; and to Adam, this pale hard-looking culprit was the Hetty who had smiled at him in the garden under the apple-tree boughs" (361).[49] Furthermore, the narrator surrounds Hetty, throughout the novel, with imagery of childhood. This is not just condescension toward her, but an attempt to share with the reader (as here with Adam) the sympathy associated with an idealized maternal attitude, combined with nostalgia for a time before a fall into adulthood.[50] Furthermore, the narrator in these early works often uses qualifying tags, such as "Perhaps I am doing a bold thing" (quoted above) or "if I have read religious history aright," which gives him a tone of contingency often associated with women's language.[51] While the pseudonym protected Eliot from readers' assumptions about women authors, these early works provide more than a few hints of a gender-crossing quality in their narrator, which links this narrator to the gender-crossing image of the poet, particularly Shakespeare, suggested by the imagery of Keats or Coleridge.

In two main ways, then, the uses of Shakespeare in George Eliot's early works are related to issues of gender. Allusions to Shakespearean women provide prototypes for female characters whose behavior escapes the social constraints of propriety, and allusions to the idea of sympathy, associated with a masculine-named narrator and other male characters, sometimes recall his image as androgynous. Later the narrator will give up the masculine details in autobiographical comments; as Eliot's female identity becomes known (after the publication of *The Mill on the Floss*), her pseudonym recalls, rather, the other kind of androgyny of his female characters in masculine disguise. But Eliot's novels continue to engage with the idea of sympathy associated with Shakespeare; they also work various transformations on Hamlet, first linking him too with a transgressive female character (Maggie), and on less ambiguously masculine characters from Shakespeare's tragedies and histories.

The Mill on the Floss

The Mill on the Floss rewrites Shakespeare in a more complex way than any of Eliot's earlier writings: it rethinks both tragedy and history play to deal more with the experiences of those subordinated by class and gender but also to contrast tragic and historic perspectives. Furthermore, it meditates on both the necessity and the inadequacy of sympathy, explicitly associated with the Shakespeare book Philip gives Maggie, in relation to women's passion.

While in *Adam Bede* the literary allusions are underplayed, and the narrator's aesthetic theory presented in chapter 17 aims primarily at justifying its characters as subject matter, in *The Mill on the Floss* the narrator makes more explicitly the claim that its characters are subject matter specifically for *tragedy*, in spite of the class bias in traditional tragic theory and in Shakespeare's choice of heroes. Maggie's father has his hubris and his fall: "The pride and obstinacy of millers, and other insignificant people, whom you pass unnoticingly on the road everyday, have their tragedy too" (172).[52] The insignificant people whose tragic qualities are emphasized here include children, especially Maggie as a child: "There were passions *at war* in Maggie . . . to have made a tragedy, if tragedies were made by passion only" (88). But more emphatically *The Mill on the Floss* goes beyond Shakespeare in putting a woman at the center of the tragedy, without a heroic lover comparable to Cleopatra's Antony or Juliet's Romeo.[53] Even Brontë, in giving Jane Eyre echoes of Lear and Cordelia, gave Rochester also some of the tragic resonance that Eliot denies to Stephen.

In some ways, Maggie's plot seems more like that of a tragic victim than that of a tragic hero. She has more of Ophelia's dutiful side than do Caterina and Hetty; she tries to accommodate to her family's antagonism to Philip, and the horror they would have at her attraction to her cousin's quasi-fiancé, as Ophelia obeys her father's cautions about her relationship with Hamlet. Maggie's relationship with her brother Tom, like Ophelia's with her brother Laertes, is shaped by traditional contrasts between expectations for men and women: in both cases, the brother is sent away for an education while the sister stays closer to home; in both cases the brother seeks vengeance on the man he blames for his father's death, while the sister's response is more complex—and in both cases the brother's hostility is heightened by the other man's influence over the sister. Maggie's hidden passion for Stephen reveals itself when she is "borne away by the tide" with him, as Ophelia's passion for Hamlet (as most Victorians would have read it) reveals itself in her madness.

All these plot elements are related to social and literary conventions of women's subordination, but throughout the novel Maggie argues with the conventions as Ophelia does not. The narrator too argues with those conventions in many ways: when Maggie is explicitly compared to a tragic hero, it is Hamlet, not Ophelia—and yet in a way that demythologizes Hamlet by imagining him "with a reputation of sanity, notwithstanding many soliloquies, and some moody sarcasms towards the fair daughter of Polonius, to say nothing of the frankest incivility to his father-in-law" (353). In this passage, which questions the aphorism "Character is destiny," the narrator emphasizes how Hamlet's fate is shaped by a plot written for him—a condition apt to be regarded as female rather than as male. If the passage puts Maggie in the tradition of the tragic hero, it also mocks that tradition by suggesting tragic heroes are not really as heroic as they have been thought. Hamlet is an especially interesting character to evoke here because he was the most culturally honored Shakespearean hero in the nineteenth century, the hero most often acted by women, and the hero most associated with ambivalence and intense inner life, traits so characteristic of Maggie.[54]

The Mill on the Floss at times invites reading not only in relation to tragic tradition, but also in relation to the tradition of the history play. The narrator claims that the novel registers historical change, portraying "young natures . . . that in the onward tendency of human things have risen above the mental level of the generation before them, to which they have been nevertheless tied by the strongest fibres of their hearts [,representing] the suffering, whether of martyr or victim, which belongs to every historical advance of mankind" (238). This tragicomic view of history resembles one way of reading the sequence of Shakespeare's history plays beginning with *Richard II,* and Stephen himself makes a joke that aligns his contrast with Philip with the contrast between two rivals for England in that play. The wrist warmers Maggie is selling at the bazaar, says Stephen, "must be intended for imaginative persons who can chill themselves on this warm day by thinking of the frosty Caucasus. . . . You must get Philip to buy those" (379). Stephen is quoting Henry Bolingbroke's words when his father, John of Gaunt, advises him to use his imagination to reconcile himself with his exile: "O, who can hold a fire in his hand / By thinking of the frosty Caucasus" (1.3.294–95). It is this very day, a little later, that Stephen shows himself unable to chill his own hot passion for Maggie as he kisses her naked arm. Like Bolingbroke, Stephen is a determined, unreflective man of action. He associates his own desires with both progress and evolution and tries to take possession of Maggie somewhat as Bolingbroke takes possession of England. In contrast, Philip, like Richard, is a man of imagination, and from one point of view both are practically ineffective and give up too easily.

Philip is not simply a man of imagination but also one of sympathy, however, and at two crucial points he is associated with the cultural image of Shakespeare himself. When Lucy hears Maggie's story of her relationship with Philip, she responds, "Ah, now I see how it is you know Shakespeare and everything, and have learned so much since you left school" (340). When Philip's last letter is signed in "a hand in which her name had been written long ago, in a pocket Shakespeare which she possessed" (441), this memory connects the sympathy he shows her, more than any other man in the book, with the sympathetic Shakespeare. The plays are among the books Philip gave her, as he tried to enlarge her world beyond the confines of her asceticism.

Philip—and Shakespeare—are not enough for Maggie. Neither one can keep her from her disastrous relationship with Stephen, since he appeals to her sexually as Philip does not. Indeed, it is with Stephen that Maggie's literary images of love come to life and she feels "the half-remote presence of a world of love and beauty and delight, made up of vague, mingled images from all the poetry and romance she had ever read, or had ever woven in her dreamy reveries" (338). In contrast, when she sums up her relationship with Philip, she tells Lucy, "You see, I am like Sir Andrew Aguecheek—*I* was adored once!" (340). This comparison to a ridiculous minor character, with no chance of succeeding in courtship, is a self-deprecating joke, part of Maggie's attempt to disable herself as a rival for Stephen. But it also suggests how distant her relationship with Philip is from her images of love—it may even suggest that it is *he* who is like Sir Andrew Aguecheek. Here the novel is, in one sense, meditating on the inadequacy of sympathy as a guide for Maggie.[55]

But in a larger sense, the novel is arguing—sometimes very explicitly—for a kind of sympathy that includes an awareness of sexual desire. As in her description of Caterina, Eliot wants to promote compassion for a character with passion. Sympathy may not be enough as an ethical guide, but the novel suggests that lack of sympathy, as shown in Stephen, in Tom, and in the town of St. Oggs, is worse.

In a sense, the two antagonists of *Richard II* both win on their own terms. Henry gets the kingdom and Richard gets the role of martyr, along with better poetry and the center of the stage. In *The Mill on the Floss,* neither Stephen nor Philip does as well. Maggie rebels against Stephen's plans to marry her, and the novel's structure makes her fate far overshadow Philip's. By contrast to the male-centered world of Shakespeare's histories or tragedies, *The Mill on the Floss* puts a woman's agency and consciousness, however confused, at the center. Maggie dies, unlike Ophelia, while she is actively trying to save her brother's life, having chosen to put family love higher than any other, although her imagination and passion draw her to a larger world. At the end of the novel, Tom finally appreciates her choice "with a certain awe and humiliation" (458), and Stephen and Philip both remember in her "their keenest joy and keenest sorrow" (459). There is one female character in Shakespeare who transgresses the sexual laws of her society, stages her own death scene, and dominates the imagination of the survivors— Cleopatra. But the generic and social dislocation that only an Egyptian queen can create in Shakespeare, Eliot produces through a middle-class woman. Like many of the possible comparisons between *Mill on the Floss* and Shakespeare, this one emphasizes the contrast between Eliot's vision and his.

Later Eliot and Shakespeare

Although I have been arguing that Eliot simultaneously claims and criti- cally transforms Shakespeare, Eliot and her friends in their letters rarely compared Eliot and Shakespeare in order to identify Shakespeare's limi- tations. But they did not compare the two in order to suggest Eliot's limitations, either. When she was working on *Romola,* Lewes recom- mended that she shorten the background research that he—as well as many later readers—regarded as excessive and instead rely on what he had long felt she shared with Shakespeare—"that wonderful intuition with which genius throws itself into all forms of life. Why is it that Shakespeare makes us believe in his Romans? Certainly not from any of those 'solid achievements' which would have made him a valuable contributor to Smith's Dictionary of Greek and Roman Biography, and earned the respect of the 'Saturday Review'" (*GEL* 3:420). By impli- cation, both Shakespeare and Eliot have more talent and value than such scholars. Charles Bray employed the Eliot/Shakespeare analogy to defend the people who were trying to locate the originals of Eliot's characters. But Eliot objected to Bray's argument—"I fail to see any parallel. . . . I am not yet an 'archäological' subject" (*GEL* 3:163–64)— and did her research in spite of Lewes's urging. Her use of the Shake- speare identification was selective; for example, she used the "popular Shakespeare" in persuading her translator to use colloquial language in

the French version of *The Mill on the Floss:* "Even in his loftiest tragedies—in Hamlet, for example—Shakespeare is intensely colloquial.
One hears the very accent of living men" (*GEL* 3:374).

And her use of his plots continued to be revisionary. In *Silas Marner,*
for example, she writes a story in which, as in *The Winter's Tale* and in
Pericles, a daughter is reunited with a long-lost father—but here the
daughter rejects the father of blood and affirms the father who adopted
her.[56] In *Romola,* a father almost as learned as Prospero has raised a
daughter in innocence similar to Miranda's of a world outside books,
but the marriage that Bardo arranges for Romola is disastrous.[57] The
treatment of varieties of fatherhood in these and other Eliot novels,
such as *Felix Holt,* can be seen, among other things, as meditations on
kinship in literary tradition; in whichever context, they emphasize the
fallibility of many fathers and the necessity for combining choice with
loyalty.

Nevertheless, using Shakespeare as a model sometimes led Eliot, like
the romantic poets discussed by Jonathan Bate, to writing that few critics have found successful, especially in her poetic drama, *The Spanish
Gypsy.* Like Coleridge in *Osorio* and Wordsworth in *The Borderers,* Eliot
may have had difficulties here partly because the closeness of Shakespeare's genre to hers was inhibiting.[58] Eliot struggled with *The Spanish
Gypsy* for several years before and after writing *Felix Holt*; she even
studied Shakespearean versification and other Renaissance poetry with
the aim of improving her poetry writing. The greatest legacy of this
work, ironically, may have been what it contributed to her last three
novels. At this point Eliot had found the genre and the setting in country and in century where she could do her best work, and her writing
began to use more poetic technique not in its genre but in the structure
of imagery.[59]

She also found another technique to remind readers of her connection to literary tradition—the chapter epigraph. Though they had
earlier been used by writers as different as Ann Radcliffe, George
Crabbe, and Walter Scott, epigraphs were new in her work. Those in
Felix Holt contribute importantly to the number of verbal Shakespearean
allusions: it contains more than any other Eliot novel.[60] Epigraphs mark
quotations off from the narrative voice; at the same time they ask the

reader to think about the many possible ways the text can be relevantly appropriated. Thus they both mark the author's presence and encourage the reader to think about how the author is rewriting. As Susan Lanser notes, Eliot's use of epigraphs "mediates the tension in her work between a semantics of indeterminacy and a syntax of authority."[61] The largest single number of attributed epigraphs in these novels comes from Shakespeare, yet three times that number are anonymous, and almost certainly Eliot's own; she makes herself, as Lanser says, "her own most quoted sage."

In a letter written long before her novels, the woman who would become George Eliot wrote, "I wish you thoroughly to understand that the writers who have most profoundly influenced me—who have rolled away the waters from their bed raised new mountains and spread delicious valleys for me—are not in the least oracles to me." Of Rousseau, her example here, she wrote, "It is simply that the rushing mighty wind of his inspiration has so quickened my faculties that I have been able to shape more definitely for myself ideas which had previously dwelt as dim 'ahnungen' [presentiments] in my soul—the fire of his genius has so fired together old thoughts and prejudices that I have been ready to make new combinations" (*GEL* 1:277). Her attitude toward past writing already had that independence that Lewes argued for in his "Principles of Success in Literature" (1865)—the past "is our Ancestry, and not our Life."[62]

Many other nineteenth-century novelists used Shakespeare in distinctive ways—Scott, Thackeray, and Dickens, especially. Scott transforms Isabella into Jeanie Deans in *The Heart of Midlothian;* Thackeray rewrites Beatrice in Beatrix of *Henry Esmond;* a variety of Dickens novels transform Hamlet's quest and Lear's relationship with Cordelia.[63] These examples, and George Eliot's early fiction, suggest that Eliot had a gender-related greater interest in engaging with Shakespeare in her presentations of female passion; further contrasts might well be drawn. Critics have been writing about these novelists' uses of Shakespeare for years, however. That one male writer can use an earlier male writer's work as a starting place for creativity has often been observed. I am trying to show that women novelists have transformed Shakespeare's work, in acts more complicated than some feminist criticism's alternatives of rebellion or "immasculation," acts that complicate the supposedly mutually exclusive categories of identifying with men or identifying with women.[64] This is true in different ways of Jane Austen, Charlotte Brontë, and George Eliot. It is most obvious in Eliot, and the evidence is most abundant in her last three novels.

With her pseudonym, her accomplishments within a largely male intellectual world, and her interest in male heroes such as Adam Bede, Silas Marner, and Tertius Lydgate, George Eliot has often been placed as a male-identifier. On the other hand, more recent critics have traced her affinities with women writers in her own time and before.[65] As Elaine Showalter notes, the woman writer "confronts both paternal and maternal precursors,"[66] and it is part of Eliot's achievement that she can draw on identification with both sides. Furthermore, she can make new combinations. Just as her male pseudonym, among other things, recalls a famous woman writer, George Sand, her use of Shakespeare draws primarily on his female characters, male characters sometimes considered feminine, such as Hamlet and the sonnet speaker, and his associations with that ambiguously gendered quality of sympathy.[67] For Eliot, as in Judith Butler's analysis of Monique Wittig, "the very notion of 'identification' reemerges . . . as immeasurably more complex than the uncritical use of that term [male-identified] suggests."[68]

Chapter Four

Felix Holt

IN THE HETEROGLOSSIA of each of Eliot's last three novels, the elements in dialogue include language associated with several different Shakespearean genres, all used partly for social criticism. In *Felix Holt,* this combination of languages is part of what contributes to the critical controversy about Felix himself. The most fully developed intertextuality in this novel associates Felix himself with two tragic heroes, Hamlet and Coriolanus, and allows the reader to see Felix's alienation from his society as admirable; on the other hand, the admirability of both these tragic characters has often been challenged, and the novel sometimes encourages us to see Felix's limitations, both in its echoes of their lines and when it recalls the more relativizing worlds of Shakespeare's histories and comedies. Felix's presence, however, also casts a critical light on places where other characters show a manipulative ambition like that found in the history plays or an interest in aristocratic social life like that found in the comedies. The novel pays more attention than most of Shakespeare's tragedies or histories to the experiences of women; this both contributes to interrogating qualities shared by Felix and the male tragic hero, or Harold and the male history hero, and in Mrs. Transome creates a new kind of hero, in whose plot manipulative ambition and interest in aristocratic social life turn out to have tragic consequences.

The uses of Hamlet and Coriolanus in *Felix Holt* will lead us to the political discourse of the nineteenth century, where Shakespeare, as discussion of *Shirley* has recalled, was hotly contested. On the one hand, the conservative Walter Bagehot wrote, "You will generally find that when a 'citizen' is mentioned [in Shakespeare], he does or says something absurd."[1] On the other hand, the ex-shoemaker and Chartist journalist Thomas Cooper included portions of *Hamlet* in the adult classes he taught and in 1842 played the title role in a production to raise money for his legal defense.[2] Beginning in 1852, the Leicester Domestic Mission Men's Class held a celebration of Shakespeare's birthday every year, attended by an overwhelmingly working-class audience. Even though the class was founded to pacify workers, it also contributed to appropriating Shakespeare for radical culture. "In 1866, a working man, A. Garland, introduced the celebration with a prologue he had written himself, in which he declared:

> I have a right, a kindred right I claim,
> Though rank nor titles gild my humble name,
> Tis from his class, the class the proud discard,
> For Shakespeare was himself the people's bard."[3]

While it is unlikely that George Eliot knew of this event, in the same month she finished volume 2 of *Felix Holt the Radical*. In this novel she appropriates both Hamlet, a hero frequently used for the radical side, and Coriolanus, one more often claimed by conservatives (and attacked as conservative by Hazlitt). Felix's attack on Esther's pretension to "fine ladyism" echo those of Hamlet's speeches that Mary Wollstonecraft used in *Vindication of the Rights of Woman* to criticize the fine ladies of her day; Esther's alternatives resemble Wollstonecraft's constructions of women's choices.[4] Furthermore, like William Bridges Adams, an early nineteenth-century radical journalist writing close to the same time as the events recreated in the novel, *Felix Holt* associates Coriolanus's unconventionality, integrity, and criticism of public irrationality with a radical political position.[5] Felix himself is much like Adams's view of what Coriolanus would be like if he were living in the nineteenth century with a good education. The novel's language gives Esther too some of Hamlet's vision and Coriolanus's unconventionality and also borrows from the sonnets and *Measure for Measure* in developing her relationship with Felix. Women play a larger role than typically in most of the Shakespearean genres recalled but a smaller one than in the romantic comedies; this qualification registers also the emphasis on

Esther's submission to Felix for moral leadership, with which the novel draws back from its feminist potential.

Felix Holt and Radical Uses of Shakespearean Tragedy

The title character of *Felix Holt the Radical* is "heir to nothing better than a quack medicine" (46), whose manufacture he has renounced; although he talks like an intellectual he chooses to stay associated with the working classes as a watchmaker and to educate other workers and their children. Written during the struggle for the Second Reform Bill, extending the vote further, and set during the struggle for the First, the book gives a critical view of electoral politics, especially on the radical side. Blackwood, himself rather conservative, could say, "I suspect I myself am a radical of the Felix Holt breed" (*GEL* 4:246) and wrote that the novel's "politics are excellent and will attract all parties" (4:247). Thus it has a problematic relation to George Eliot's project of extending literary sympathy to classes previously excluded. In spite of the fact that artisans such as watchmakers were centrally involved in the developing working-class culture of this period, and the wide-ranging intellectual interest of that culture, Felix is shown not in relation to other artisans, but rather, when among workers, with miners; how much literary sympathy workers receive here is ambiguous at best.[6]

One of the most explicit and surprising appropriations of Shakespeare in Eliot is her identification of the radical Felix with Coriolanus, so associated—as discussion of *Shirley* has shown—with scorn of the people. The novel makes this link most clearly through chapter 30's epigraph from Menenius's description of Coriolanus, chapter 27's epigraph from one of Coriolanus's speeches, and a passage in chapter 30 where Felix argues with an activist working man who appropriates Menenius's Fable of the Belly. The epigraphs emphasize the tragic hero's hatred of compromise, whether with power or with custom. The one for chapter 30 reads:

> His nature is too noble for the world:
> He would not flatter Neptune for his trident,
> Or Jove for his power to thunder. His heart's his mouth:
> What his breast forges, that his tongue must vent;

And being angry, doth forget that ever
He heard the name of death.

(3.1.254–59)

The chapter after the epigraph, however, like the Shakespearean passage preceding Menenius's description, shows the hero refusing to flatter not only the powerful but also the poor. The working man with
whom Felix argues says, "We are the belly that feels the pinches, and
we'll set these aristocrats, these great people who call themselves our
brains, to work at some way of satisfying us a bit better" (247). Felix
disagrees with this speaker's demand for suffrage because he believes
the workers aren't yet ready for political power; out of a hundred working men who had a vote, he says, seventy would be drunken or stupid.
Yet, he claims, as Coriolanus would not, "I want the working men to
have power" (249).

While Shakespeare presents enough opposing perspectives on
Coriolanus that Brontë's Caroline, as we have seen, assumed that the
play would show Robert the error of Coriolanus's pride and his own,
Eliot, on the whole, idealizes Felix.[7] Robert criticizes workers because of
his own narrowness; Felix does so, the novel suggests, because of theirs.
Furthermore, his criticism of working people claims the authority of his
choice of their lot over social mobility. The narrator portrays listeners
looking to him admiringly, "unconsciously influenced by the grandeur
of his full yet firm mouth, and the calm clearness of his grey eyes"
(248–49). The description removes him from personal interest, giving
him instead "the look of habitual meditative abstraction from objects of
merely personal vanity or desire, which is the peculiar stamp of culture,
and makes a very roughly-cut face worthy to be called 'the human face
divine'" (248).[8] Through all his errors of judgment, the novel emphasizes Felix's humanitarian motives. When Esther defends him in court,
she concludes, "His nature is very noble [echoing that epigraph]; he
is tender-hearted; he could never have had any intention that was not
brave and good" (376). And everyone believes her. While Brontë opposed the viewpoints of the Coriolanus figure and the moral educator
who argues for sympathy, Eliot has paradoxically combined them.

Felix's own words about himself frequently associate him with another Shakespearean character more congenial for radical appropriation. He identifies himself as melancholy (220), a word often used of Hamlet in the nineteenth century, and quotes the assessment of himself by a phrenologist: "his large Ideality . . . prevents him from finding anything perfect enough to be venerated" (60). Both heroes can be self-critical in extravagant, abstract terms that don't suggest realistic perspective: Hamlet says to Ophelia, "I am very proud, revengeful, ambitious, with more offenses at my beck than I have thoughts to put them in, imagination to give them shape, or time to act them in" (3.1.125–28). To Esther, Felix says, "It is just because I'm a very ambitious fellow, with very hungry passions, wanting a great deal to satisfy me, that I have chosen to give up what people call worldly good" (222). Both Hamlet and Coriolanus have many lines attacking compromise, and Felix's attitude could be compared to both of them when he says: "I'm determined never to go about making my face simpering or solemn, and telling professional lies for profit" (222).

Hamlet's attack on a reigning king, not to mention his complaints about "Th' oppressor's wrong, the proud man's contumely, / . . . The insolence of office" (3.1.72,74), make a plausible basis for his appeal to radicals and to working men like Charles Cooper in the nineteenth century. In *Aurora Leigh,* Elizabeth Barrett Browning's Lord Howe says of Romney Leigh,

> he, Prince Hamlet, weds a pretty maid
>
> . . . .
>
> By symbol, to instruct us formally
> To fill the ditches up 'twixt class and class.[9]

Eliot had already associated Hamlet with Maggie in *The Mill on the Floss;* her echoes of his language in characterizing a radical hero are not surprising.

Eliot's association of Felix with Coriolanus, however, is more paradoxical, and it is much more surprising to find that an earlier author had also imagined a radical Coriolanus. In "Coriolanus No Aristocrat," an article written in 1834, shortly after the passage of the Reform Bill debated in the historical period portrayed in *Felix Holt,* William Bridges Adams claimed that if then alive, Coriolanus "would have been a heart-whole leader, in the great cause of human nature, which has been espoused by those who are best described as philosophic radicals" (43). This article appeared in the *Monthly Repository*, a Unitarian-turned-secular journal that continued until 1838, in time for Lewes to place his first two essays there, and three years before Mary Ann Evans, as she then called herself, made her first Unitarian friends, the Brays and the Hennells.[10] Adams, writing under the pseudonym of Junius Redivivus, is more qualified about Shakespeare's Coriolanus than Eliot is about Felix, but some of the terms of his qualifications suggest Felix: "Oh, Marcius, Marcius [Coriolanus's name early in the play], had you been a philosopher, you had been perfect. You would then have pitied the poor people, and would have known that their vices are the result of their physical misery" (47). Adams, like Eliot, emphasizes the relevance to his England of Coriolanus's protest against the Roman electoral system: "Coriolanus is bitterly satirical, when he alleges as a reason why they should elect him, that he has the 'customary gown.' In England a man tells the electors that he has the customary *money;* and that is as germane to the purpose" (198). Like Eliot, Adams emphasizes the description of Coriolanus as noble, in a moral sense, "not a class sense"; quoting the other passage that Eliot uses for a chapter epigraph, he emphasizes Coriolanus's critical view of custom, to show that, rather than being an "aristocratic defender of vested abuses," he has "sound radical principles, equally applicable to all abuses" (199). Of Coriolanus's criticism of the people, Adams says, "were it in England even now, it would be, alas, but too true! The only remedy for it is education" (198). This is Felix's view as well.

Coriolanus was one of the Shakespearean plays most explicitly discussed in political terms in the nineteenth century; its meaning was contested, but people did not necessarily find their own views in the play. As we have seen, Hazlitt disagreed with what he saw as its dramatic moral, that "those who have little will have less, and . . . those who have much shall take all that others have left"; he used this play as proof that "the language of poetry naturally falls in with the language of power."[11] Adams calls the view that the play's bias is aristocratic an "ancient Tory fallacy" (423) but notes its prevalence: "The modern English Tories have made him [Coriolanus] all their own, and have been accustomed to liken their leader to him. . . . His Grace of Wellington has occasionally figured in the print shops in a Roman garb making scorn of sundry plebeian leaders, attired as 'unwashed artisans' " (142). On the other hand, Macready's 1838 production presented the people in a way that earned the respect even of the Tory journal *John Bull:*

> It is not merely a coward crowd before us, but the onward and increas-
> ing wave . . . of men who have spied their way to equal franchise and
> are determined to fight their way to the goal. There is no mistaking
> the struggle for power that has begun. It is not noble against serf, but
> against freeman. The illusion is still further maintained by their dress.
> They are no longer the mere *tunicatus popellus,* who have hitherto cari-
> catured the Roman commonalty. In many there is an approximation to
> the toga; and the squalor . . . is altogether done away with.[12]

When Eliot recalled *Coriolanus* in a novel that deals with class relations and the Reform Bill, she was participating in a literary/political
dialogue already under way, but like Adams, in claiming Coriolanus
himself and not just the balance of sympathies in the play for the radical side, however construed, she was apparently reinterpreting the play
drastically. The *Monthly Repository* is not one of the sources listed in
her journal as part of research for *Felix Holt;* however, it is tempting to
believe that through Lewes and through the Hennells and the Brays,
to whom she often quoted Shakespeare in her letters, she would have
heard about Adams's reinterpretation of Coriolanus. Whether she did or
not, the echo points to intellectuals' interest in appropriating a Shakespearean tragic hero as an image of integrity in politics and therefore
indicates a certain ambiguity in their relation to the people he scorned.
Adams claimed, "he does not scorn them because they are plebeians,
but because they are base plebeians" (47). Analogously, Felix says, "I
want to be a demagogue of a new sort; an honest one, if possible, who
will tell the people they are blind and foolish, and neither flatter them
nor fatten on them" (224). As Peter Coveney notes, Felix suggests
George Eliot's belief, expressed in her essay "The Natural History of
German Life," that it is a "miserable fallacy that high morality and refined sentiment can grow out of harsh social relations, ignorance and
want."[13] This attitude, however, makes the political implications of
Felix Holt's radicalism hard to distinguish from conservatism.

To be sure, Eliot is trying to show the potential for heroic acts outside royalty and aristocracy, and Felix is very explicit about the dignity of his class: "I have the blood of a line of handicraftsmen in my veins, and I want to stand up for the lot of the handicraftsman as a good lot" (224). Nevertheless, the novel doesn't show much potential for a working-class community to improve its conditions—the trade union man who speaks before Felix is dismissed as having an expression of "mere acuteness and rather hard-lipped antagonism" (248).[14] Analogously, Adams wishes that the First Plebeian would boldly face up to Coriolanus and say, "A plebeian is a man!" (46), but he is unable to see possibilities for appropriation in the plebeians as Shakespeare wrote them.[15]

The political views of the *Monthly Repository* in general, and the views its editor William Johnson Fox still held after it folded, agreed with Felix's and Eliot's in many respects. "From 1844 to 1846, Fox devoted his Sunday evenings to delivering popular lectures to large audiences of the working classes in the National Hall in Holborn. . . . Fox . . . saw more for them to hope for in mass education than in a trades union organization."[16] Eliot had received his collection *Hymns and Anthems* from Sara Hennell in 1843 (*GEL* 1:160) and borrowed his *Lectures Addressed Chiefly to the Working Classes* in 1852 (2:52). "Human nature" is an important term for both Felix and the *Repository,* and in both cases explorations of human behavior are cast in rational, scientific terms.[17] Like Felix's father, Fox's father had been, among other things, a weaver—an occupation shared by many radical leaders; unlike Felix, Fox became a bank clerk and a minister and an editor, but in the 1840s he wrote "a long series of popular and effective 'Letters on the Corn Laws,'" signed "A Norwich Weaver-Boy," in the Anti–Corn Law *League*.[18] He died in 1864, the year before Eliot began *Felix Holt.*

Knowledge of Fox and the *Monthly Repository* inclines one to qualify views such as Simon Dentith's that Felix's "Radicalism is of a kind that was never seen in heaven or earth. It is a specifically anti-political kind of Radicalism, which is attached to no real historical movement whatsoever."[19] In the 1830s, under the leadership of Fox and Adams, the *Repository* was identified with the Radical party, and Felix often thinks and talks with their kind of radicalism, though he has no real intellectual companions in the novel.[20] While the novel identifies organized radicalism with Harold Transome, what was left of Fox's audience would have been able to place Felix's ideas; on the other hand, identifying Felix explicitly with Fox and the *Monthly Repository* group might have waved too much of a red flag before some of the readers Eliot was trying to reach. As it was, according to Frederic Harrison, "the religious people, the non-religious people, the various sections of religious people, the educated, the simple, the radicals, the Tories, the socialists, the intellectual reformers, the domestic circle, the critics, the metaphysicians, the artists, the Positivists, the squires, are all quite convinced that it [the novel] has been conceived from their own point of view" (*GEL* 4:285). If they argued over its politics, perhaps doing so made it seem even more Shakespearean.

Gender and *Felix Holt*'s Uses of Shakespeare

Felix Holt is also connected both with Shakespeare and with the ambiguities of nineteenth-century radical thought in its treatment of women's lives and Felix's attitude to them. Felix's criticism of Esther paraphrases Hamlet's criticism of women. Is this attack misogynistic, or, since, as I shall note, Mary Wollstonecraft borrowed Hamlet's lines in her criticism of women in her society, is it feminist? Eliot herself wrote a review of *Vindication of the Rights of Woman* the year before she began writing fiction, and she praises Wollstonecraft for stressing the bad effects of women's oppression much as Eliot would stress the bad effects of class oppression in "The Natural History of German Life," written soon after, and in *Felix Holt* much later.

> Unfortunately, many overzealous champions of women assert their actual equality with men—nay, even their moral superiority to men—as a ground for their release from oppressive laws and restrictions. They lose strength immensely by this false position. If it were true, then there would be a case in which slavery and ignorance nourished virtue, and so far we should have an argument for the continuance of bondage. . . . Both Margaret Fuller and Mary Wollstonecraft have too much sagacity to fall into this sentimental exaggeration. (*Essays*, 205)

Some recent feminists, however, have seen this "sagacity" of Wollstonecraft's as showing internalized misogyny, just as Susan Wolfson has seen it in Wollstonecraft's use of Hamlet and other critics have seen it in Eliot.[21] How does Felix's attack on Esther's attitude at the beginning fit with the treatment of gender in the novel as a whole?

The most obvious set of literary echoes occurs at their first meeting, when Felix criticizes Esther for some of the same attitudes Hamlet attacks in Ophelia after being betrayed, as he thinks, by both her and his mother. Mocking women in general for face painting and other sorts of pretense, Hamlet says, "God hath given you one face and you make yourselves another. . . . You nickname God's creatures, and make your wantonness your ignorance" (3.1.145–148).[22] Felix sounds, perhaps, rather like the sarcastic nontragic Hamlet imagined in *The Mill on the Floss,* but he also insults a whole class of women in one, and emphasizes pretense, especially in language: "O, your niceties—I know what they are. . . . They all go on your system of make-believe. 'Rottenness' [Hamlet's view of "something . . . in the state of Denmark"] may suggest what is unpleasant, so you'd better say 'sugar-plums,' or something else such a big way off the fact that nobody is obliged to think of it. . . . A fine-lady is a squirrel-headed thing, with small airs and small notions, about as applicable to the business of life as a pair of tweezers to the clearing of a forest" (152–53).

Mary Wollstonecraft, in *Vindication of the Rights of Woman,* quotes the same passage in Hamlet echoed here, as well as another making a similar point. While criticizing the education of women, she says, "they dress, they paint, and nickname God's creatures—Surely these weak beings are only fit for a seraglio!—Can they be expected to govern a family with judgment?"[23] Specifically attacking *Dr. Gregory's Thoughts on the Education of Daughters,* she mocks his emphasis on fashions and says, "Women are always to *seem* to be this and that—yet virtue might apostrophize them, in the words of Hamlet—Seems! I know not seems!— Have that within that passeth show!" (99; *Hamlet* 1.2.76, 85).

Esther's first appearance shows the concern for surface that Hamlet, Wollstonecraft, and Felix all criticize—most vividly in her covering up the bust of the religious leader George Whitfield to hide his squint.[24] She is a snob who sees Felix as coarse and is disappointed that he is a watchmaker. But she makes a neat ironic hit at his verbal bullying when she says, "If I had ever met the giant Cormoran, I should have made a point of agreeing with him in his literary opinions" (62). Right after this line, the narrator tells us that she has "that excellent thing in woman, a soft voice," but to this echo of Lear's masculinist praise of Cordelia is added "with a clear fluent utterance." She is a paradoxically talkative Cordelia, a comic heroine in a context full of allusions to tragedies.

At the beginning, Esther is a woman of playfulness and spirit as well as of excessive concern for style; the novel poses the question of how she can maintain the first two qualities while dropping her interest in appearances. In juxtaposing her with Felix, this novel can be seen as rewriting *Jane Eyre*'s story of Rosamond Oliver and St. John Rivers (it is rewritten again, I will argue, in *Middlemarch*) or, as in *Daniel Deronda,* bringing together figures based, to some degree, on Eliot's favorite Shakespearean characters, Rosalind and Hamlet.[25] The characterization of Esther lacks the verbal allusions to Rosalind found in the other novels, but she is apparently, like Rosalind, a kind of princess out of place, and her playfulness, charm, and worldliness resemble qualities of Rosalind, Rosamond, and Gwendolen. In allowing Felix both to educate Esther and to marry her, *Felix* is, arguably, the most conservative of the last three Eliot novels. It is also, in this respect as in some others, more conservative than *Shirley,* since Caroline begins with a social conscience and Esther needs to learn hers from Felix.

Initially Felix, like Hamlet, is opposed to marriage. In addition to the generic conflict (there are few happy marriages in tragedies, except when they end with joint suicides), critics have attributed Hamlet's attitude to immaturity, to the specific requirements of his moral duty, or to his criticism of his society, among other causes. These are also possible explanations for Felix's opposition to marriage. He phrases his rejection this way: "I'll never marry, though I should have to live on raw turnips to subdue my flesh. I'll never look back and say, 'I had a fine purpose once—I meant to keep my hands clean and my soul upright, and to look truth in the face; but pray excuse me, I have a wife and children—I must lie and simper a little, else they'll starve'" (66). In her review of Wollstonecraft, Eliot had described the cost of marriage to men in a way that anticipates Felix's position, predicts Lydgate's frustration, and associates them both specifically with cultural restrictions on women. "The precious meridian years of many a man of genius have to be spent in the toil of routine, that an 'establishment' may be kept up for a woman who can understand none of his secret yearnings, who is fit for nothing but to sit in her drawing-room like a doll-Madonna in her shrine. No matter. Anything is more endurable than to change our established formulae about women" (204–5).

The plot of *Felix Holt* gives Esther two opposing alternatives similar to women's choices as constructed by Wollstonecraft: life with Harold, in a world of privilege associated with the world Hamlet attacks, and with Shakespeare's history plays (and, as in Wollstonecraft, with the life of the prerevolutionary French monarchy); and, on the other hand, life with Felix, in a world of moral integrity associated with Hamlet, Coriolanus, Shakespeare's sonnets, and *Measure for Measure.* Esther discovers that she is entitled to the Transome estate and has the chance to marry Harold Transome, who is used to living with privilege and expects his wife to "do nothing but to sit in her drawing room." This would seem the culmination of her early desires, but she ultimately rejects Harold and the estate, both because of the education that Felix has given her and because of the unhappiness that she can see in Mrs. Transome. In the Transome world, as in the world of Shakespeare's history plays, language of chivalry and homage often masks underlying selfishness and political manipulation.[26]

Throughout *Felix Holt,* Harold Transome voices the commonplace and restrictive view of women that Wollstonecraft attacks: that women "must always be protected, guarded from care, and all the rough toils that dignify the mind" (Wollstonecraft, 149).[27] When he returns to take over the family estate, he says to his mother, "You've had to worry yourself about things that don't properly belong to a woman. . . . You shall have nothing to do now but be grandmamma on satin cushions" (20).

Furthermore, as in Wollstonecraft, Harold's condescending attitude toward women is distanced by association with the Orient: in the very scene of his return to his mother, he says, "I hate English wives; they want to give their opinion about everything. They interfere with a man's life" (20), and later on, we are told, he is wary of Western women, preferring "a slow-witted large-eyed woman, silent and affectionate, with a load of black hair weighing much more heavily than her brains"

(292).[28] Nevertheless, at the time that he thinks this, he is beginning to consider the possibility of marrying Esther, largely as a way of saving his inheritance. His condescending attitude to her is placed with an epigraph from Shakespeare's *Henry VI, Part 1:* "She's beautiful; and therefore to be wooed; / She is a woman; therefore to be won" (317; 5.3.78–79). These are Suffolk's words about Margaret of Anjou, whom he wins for himself and marries to the unworldly Henry VI to help himself politically.[29] The political and dynastic nature of Harold's interest in Esther is further emphasized by the epigraph to chapter 36, in which he confides his hopes of marrying her to his mother: "Are these things then necessities? / Then let us meet them like necessities" (285). These are the words that Henry IV, whose name Harold's may echo, uses when he plans to counter the increasing strength of the rebels (*Henry IV, Part 2* 3.1.92–93).[30]

Harold's attitude toward women is rather close to that of most men in Shakespeare's histories. He expects them to be passively exchanged; yet, like Margaret, like Mrs. Transome, and finally like Esther, they can subvert that exchange. In both *Felix Holt* and Shakespeare's history plays, women are expected to be, as bearers of children, transmitters of the bloodline of inheritance, but they can also destabilize it.[31] The epigraphs to chapter 9 (100), where Mrs. Transome foresees the future conflict between Harold and Jermyn, recall this structural point of anxiety by appropriating lines from two women in history plays: Constance in *King John* and Isabella in *Richard II.* The first epigraph is Constance's self-description when she hears of a political marriage that threatens her son's possibility of becoming king: "A woman, naturally born to fears" (3.1.15); the second is Isabella's speech when the rebellion that will lead to her husband's deposition is beginning:

> Methinks
> Some unborn sorrow, ripe in fortune's womb,
> Is coming towards me; and my inward soul
> With nothing trembles.
>
> (2.2.10–12)

Both of these epigraphs contain birth imagery, which is foregrounded when spoken by a female character even if it does not directly refer to her own giving birth;[32] thus they reinforce the hint that Mrs. Transome's anxiety about Harold has in part to do with her secret knowledge about the circumstances of his conception. Although Isabella is a very minor character, Constance was a popular role on the Victorian stage, especially renowned as a mother who grieves over the loss of her son. Anna Jameson's description of her as "a grand impersonation of pride and passion, helpless at once and desperate," could well apply to Mrs. Transome, although she loses not her son but her hopes for him.[33] In the same passage, Jameson compares Constance to a "mother-eagle": Eliot calls Mrs. Transome "eagle-like" both in the first description of her (14) and in the description of how she first appears to Esther (308).

Eliot read *King John* just after she began writing *Felix Holt* (*GEL* 4:195). She might have chosen it while considering the relevance of earlier English political battles to her novel; earlier in the century it had been very popular as a patriotic play, and one of the first lectures given by F. D. Maurice in his 1852 attempt to begin a Working Men's College was on *King John* as an aid in understanding English history.[34] But one of the other important intersections between play and novel is the issue of illegitimacy, frequently discussed in Shakespeare's plays but only here, in *Lear, Titus Andronicus, Measure for Measure,* and *Much Ado about Nothing* presented as reality rather than as anxiety. *King John* begins as *Felix Holt* ends, with a son learning of his illegitimacy. But his mother, Lady Faulconbridge, is given little responsibility or point of view to articulate (though she has more than the absent adulterous mothers in *Lear* and *Much Ado*); she was seduced by King Richard the Lion-Hearted, and the Bastard, admiring Richard, is glad to hear it. In *Felix Holt,* in contrast, an adulterous woman's perspective is presented in great detail, and the son introduced to a father he hates. Indeed, it is part of the subversive force in Eliot's use of Shakespeare here that in creating and framing the adulterous mother, Mrs. Transome, she uses words associated with *King John*'s faithful mother, Constance, rather than with the very minor Lady Faulconbridge.

Mrs. Transome's adultery with Jermyn is part of her regretful memory throughout the novel, and the past becomes increasingly vivid; the terms in which she remembers it recall Wollstonecraft's description of how women's upbringing has involved a "specious homage" that has tended to make women rather "alluring mistresses than affectionate wives and rational mothers" (Wollstonecraft, 7). "This man, young, slim, and graceful, with a selfishness which then took the form of homage to her, had at one time kneeled to her and kissed those hands fervently; and she had thought there was a poetry in such passion beyond any to be found in everyday domesticity" (335). Like Wollstonecraft, Eliot's narrator attributes the misery of such women as Mrs. Transome in part to her limited education, which enabled her to read "the lighter parts of dangerous French authors" and to "express herself with propriety on general subjects" but failed to give her "a perennial source of interest in things not personal" (27–28).

When Eliot repeatedly contrasts Mrs. Transome as she is in age with the young woman she was, especially by evoking the youthful portrait on the wall, she echoes Wollstonecraft's argument that an education aimed at making women merely accomplished makes them "useless when the short-lived bloom of beauty is over" (142). Mrs. Transome illustrates Wollstonecraft's view of rich women: "the unfolding mind is not strengthened by the practice of those duties which dignify the human character—They only live to amuse themselves, and . . . they soon only afford barren amusement" (Wollstonecraft, 9).

The language that describes the relationship of Harold and Esther repeats the language that describes the relationship of Jermyn, Harold's father, and Mrs. Transome and likewise echoes the words Wollstonecraft uses to describe relationships that she criticizes—"Chivalry" and "homage" (323). The graceful and romantic attention he pays her contrasts markedly with Felix's rude criticism. At the beginning of the novel Esther longs for such homage as well as for the possibility of gratifying cultivated tastes that more money would bring. But by the time she first goes to visit the Transomes, she has already formed a serious attachment to Felix.

Many Shakespearean associations contrasting with the history-play and chivalric language of her relation to Harold help to construct Esther's change of values and her relationship with Felix. When she discusses Felix's nobility with Harold, he says, "I am conscious of not having those severe virtues that you have been praising. . . . a woman would not find me a tragic hero" (352). She agrees and says that Harold belongs in "genteel comedy," not Shakespearean comedy. In chapter 27, which describes one of the longest private conversations between Felix and Esther, the language recalls not only the tragic heroes whose association with Felix we have already discussed but also Shakespeare's sonnets as well as one of his most problematic comedies. I shall discuss the Shakespeare allusions in this chapter—a kind of parallel to the "*Coriolanus*" chapter in *Shirley*—in detail because they bear such a heavy weight in constructing the relationship between Felix and Esther that will be her alternative to marriage to Harold.

The sonnet epigraph—"To hear with eyes is part of love's rare wit"—is a slight misquotation of one of Eliot's favorite sonnets; her use of it elsewhere will be discussed in the chapter on *Middlemarch*. [35] At the beginning of the chapter it suggests Felix's sensitivity to Esther's agitation after hearing her mother's life story. But it also has relevance to the interest that Esther shows Felix as he tells her of his ideals and to the possibility of a relationship between the two that comes silently to both of them as "their words were charged with a meaning dependent entirely on the secret consciousness of each" (225).

The second epigraph, one of the many Coriolanus allusions, was used by Adams in his defense of Coriolanus as a radical:

> Custom calls me to't
> What custom wills, in all things should we do't?
> The dust on antique time would lie unswept,
> And mountainous error be too highly heaped
> For truth to over-peer.
>
> (2.3.117–21)

Esther is consciously going against custom in walking with Felix, which "might be a subject of remark—all the more because of his cap, patched boots, no cravat, and thick stick. Esther was a little amazed herself at what she had come to" (220). But the major opposition to custom in the chapter is Felix's determination to give up the social mobility so available to him—what he calls "the push and the scramble for money and position" (221).

The custom that Coriolanus's lines originally denounce is the custom of appearing in the marketplace in a toga to ask votes from "Hob and Dick"—he doesn't like a custom that subordinates him, temporarily, to the common people. Felix, on the other hand, is criticizing a custom that would distance him more from the common people; yet he would still distance himself from them morally. This is the scene in which he imagines himself as an honest demagogue who will tell the people they are blind and foolish.

Other allusions in the scene also present him as both a tragic hero and a moral leader. Felix says, "I am a man who am warned by visions" as he explains why he thinks they won't "walk together or sit here again" (224).[36] His word "visions," especially associated with a duty to give up Esther, recalls Hamlet's vision of his father's ghost, although instead of the past, Felix says, "we are saved by making the future present to ourselves." Also transforming Hamlet, Felix emphasizes the need for another—Esther—to have "such a vision of the future that you may never lose your best self. . . . nothing but a good strong terrible vision will save you" (224). Esther does, we are told, have such a vision when she sees Mrs. Transome's present as like her own future:

> With a terrible prescience which a multitude of impressions during
> her stay at Transome Court had contributed to form, she saw herself
> in a silken bondage that arrested all motive, and was nothing better
> than a well-cushioned despair. . . . The dimly-suggested tragedy of this
> woman's life, the dreary waste of years empty of sweet trust and affec-
> tion, afflicted her even to horror. It seemed to have come as a last vision
> to urge her towards the life where the draughts of joy sprang from the
> unchanging fountains of reverence and devout love. (390, 393–94)

While Felix is the leader in going against custom and seeing visions, Esther can join him in these activities of tragic heroes. What they lead her to is the generic conclusion of comedy—marriage—but with more moral weight.

Appropriately, he links himself to another Shakespearean figure who is a moral guide in a play that could be described as beginning like a tragedy but ending like a comedy. After wishing Esther to be "the woman whose beauty makes a great task easier to men instead of turning them away from it" (224), he continues in words very close to those of the Duke in his commission to his deputy Angelo at the beginning of *Measure for Measure*. "Spirits are not finely touch'd / But to fine issues," says the Duke (1.1.36–37); Felix says, "I am not likely to see such fine issues; but they may come where a woman's spirit is finely touched." As a character who claims a social concern and takes a humble position, partly in order to educate, Felix has some affinities with the Duke. In his disguise as friar, the Duke becomes a kind of spiritual adviser to Isabella, and at the end of the play he proposes marriage to her. Marriage between the Duke and Isabella, according to critical consensus, receives little psychological preparation in the text, unlike marriage between Felix and Esther, and at the beginning, Isabella, a novice in a convent, is very different from Esther, but both women follow the men's guidance, and both can be seen as taking on more social responsibility. Notably, both at the end make public pleas that another person receive mercy (in both Renaissance and nineteenth century the most acceptable kind of public speech for a woman). Eliot's acquaintance Anna Jameson compared Isabella to St. Theresa, and Felix evokes the same saint in thinking of a woman who might understand his ideals: "Women, unless they are Saint Theresas or Elizabeth Frys, generally think this sort of thing madness, unless when they read of it in the Bible" (225).[37] We will find both St. Theresa and the same *Measure for Measure* passage alluded to again in relation to Dorothea.

In this pivotal chapter 27, then, the relationship of Esther and Felix appears in turn as a heterosexual version of the "marriage of true minds" of the sonnets, a rewriting of Hamlet's and Coriolanus's relationships with women giving the woman more potential for active heroism, and a rewriting of the relation between the Duke and Isabella in which the two parties are presented as similar in age and rank (and in which they use religious imagery instead of wearing religious habits). Unlike *Shirley*, in which Robert Moore is fixed as a Coriolanus figure until the end, and Caroline's role in the chapter where they discuss Shakespeare is mainly to criticize his attitude toward his workers, *Felix Holt* here uses language from three Shakespearean genres—tragedy, sonnet, and comedy—to construct the relationship between Felix and

Esther and transforms each of the Shakespearean texts suggested to give more attention to women.

Nevertheless, it is significant that *Measure for Measure* is the comedy most clearly alluded to in *Felix Holt;* that generically unusual play (later in the nineteenth century classified as a problem play and now frequently referred to as a problem comedy) is unusually male-dominated for its genre. Esther has less power than do the women of most Shakespearean comedies. When Anna Jameson imagines putting Hamlet in the same play with one of her female "characters of intellect," they overshadow him: "Rosalind would have turned him over with a smile to the melancholy Jaques; Beatrice would have laughed at him outright."[38] In contrast, Esther, faced with this transformed tragic hero, stops laughing rather soon. At the beginning of chapter 27, she can still tease Felix about his melancholy somewhat as Rosalind teases Jaques; at the middle of the chapter she can criticize him by saying, "You talk to me like an angry pedagogue" (224)—a phrase Lewes used to describe a poorly played Hamlet[39]—but by the end of the chapter she has lapsed into an emotionally forced silence. When he visits her on the election day, he asks, "don't parry what I say" (262), and moved by his "expression of painful beseeching," she drops the parrying mode of conversation that she has shared with such comic heroes as Beatrice.

In *As You Like It, Twelfth Night, The Merchant of Venice,* and *Love's Labour's Lost,* the men must recognize their errors—most obviously in not seeing through the women's disguises, but also by implication in other matters; twentieth-century critics have often seen the women educating the men. Likewise, Beatrice in *Much Ado* regains her ability to criticize Benedick, and he himself admits that he was wrong when he vowed never to marry, saying, "Man is a giddy thing" (5.4.106). In this novel, in contrast, though the final description of Felix does not tell us whether he is still trying to educate others as aggressively as earlier, his few apologies are all fairly early in the book—before the crucial chapter 27.[40] Esther, on the other hand, abandons much of her own system of values to accept Felix's and is emphatic both to herself and to him about his moral superiority. At the beginning he says to her, "If a woman really believes herself to be a lower kind of being, she should place herself in subjection: she should be ruled by the thoughts of her father or husband" (108). At the end she says, "I am weak— my husband must be greater and nobler than I am" (397). Felix does talk differently to Esther by now, not like the "angry pedagogue." He has of course learned that she has changed, so that marriage to her will not be the hindrance to his vocation he once thought—but this learning on his part is a tribute to Esther's greater education. He will still be the moral leader and can still speak pedagogically to others, as at his trial. Darcy, Rochester, Robert Moore, and even Knightley acknowledge more of their own limitations and show themselves more influenced by the heroines at the end of their novels.

The Shakespearean comedy in which a woman talks most at the end about her earlier errors and the change in her behavior is *The Taming of the Shrew*.[41] One of the most telling of the similarities between this play and *Felix Holt,* conflicting with the predominant ideology of *Vindication,* is the association of a normative womanhood with submission and weakness. After some time of friendship with Felix, the narrator says of Esther, "The consciousness of her own superiority amongst the people around her was superseded, and even a few brief weeks had given a softened expression to her eyes, a more feminine beseechingness and self-doubt to her manners" (205). Compare the rhetoric of Kate's last speech:

> Why are our bodies soft and weak and smooth
>
> .   .   .   .
>
> But that our soft conditions and our hearts
> Should well agree with our external parts?
> (5.2.167, 169–70)

When Felix for the first time loses his self-possession with Esther, after he asks her to stop parrying his words, she enjoys Felix's behavior as "signs of her power," but this joy is partly because of the rarity of power to "Esther, like a woman as she was—a woman waiting for love, never able to ask for it" (262). George Eliot had noted in her book review, discussed earlier, that Shakespeare's women very often do express their love first, but Esther lacks such verbal and social power.

There are some countermovements to this emphasis on woman's

weakness in Esther's plot. For example, in chapter 27 Esther's complaint about her lack of choice serves as a hint to Felix that her values are actually closer to his than he had thought. Esther continues to talk like a comic heroine in her scene with Harold, and the conversation in the last chapter when she tells Felix that she has given up Harold and the money combines seriousness and playfulness. She says, "You don't know how clever I am," teases Felix about improving his French accent, and even moves him to joke self-mockingly about her admiration of him: "If you take me in that way I shall be forced to be a much better fellow than I ever thought of being" (397–98). As some critics of *Taming of the Shrew* have seen playful pretense in Kate's last speech, a reader might see Esther taking a joking tone when she says, "I am weak."[42] Unlike Kate, she certainly does not claim physical weakness: there are final echoes of Wollstonecraft's discourse: when Felix says, "You are such a delicate creature," Esther responds, "I am very healthy. Poor women, I think, are healthier than the rich."

Nevertheless, the larger structure of the Esther-Felix plot coheres with the presentation of Esther, unlike Wollstonecraft's model woman, as a "relative creature."[43] The narrator writes, in a seemingly nonprescriptive way, "In the ages since Adam's marriage, it has been good for some men to be alone, and for some women also" (551). The passage continues, however, "But Esther was not one of these women: she was intensely of the feminine type, verging neither towards the saint nor the angel." Like Blanche, whose marriage to the Dauphin of France is arranged, in *King John,* to bring peace, she is, says the narrator, " 'a fair divided excellence, whose fulness of perfection' must be in marriage" (551). Blanche's marriage failed in its political aim but, according to Anna Jameson, brought domestic happiness instead.[44] For Esther too, the allusion may hint, marital happiness is more likely than public influence. Even when emphasizing Esther's growth beyond the limiting view of women deplored by Wollstonecraft—"She was created to be his toy, his rattle" (Wollstonecraft, 34)—the imagery keeps Esther submissive to Felix: "This bright, delicate, beautiful-shaped thing that seemed most like a toy or ornament—some hand had touched the chords, and there came forth music that brought tears" (376).[45] During the trial, the narrator says, "In this, at least, her woman's lot was perfect: that the man she loved was her hero; that her woman's passion and her reverence for rarest goodness rushed together in an undivided current" (375). Such a union is what Dorothea Brooke and Gwendolen Grandcourt long for; in what, from a feminist perspective as well as many others, seems the greater artistry of *Middlemarch* and *Daniel Deronda,* it is not accessible.

A feminist perspective also points to *Felix Holt*'s limitations in treating workers and the question of how their lot is to be improved.[46] In the "political" part of the book, both Esther and Mrs. Transome are absent for a long time: the trade union speaker says, "The greatest question in the world is, how to give every man a man's share in what goes on in life" (246). Felix says, "Hear, hear," and no one wonders what a woman's share might be. This is not simply a generic use of "man"; the speaker goes on to say, "It isn't a man's share just to . . . haggle about your own wages and bring up your family to be ignorant sons of ignorant fathers" (247). Dorothy Thompson has shown that there were working women involved in early nineteenth-century radical politics; some of them are mentioned in Samuel Bamford's *Passages in the Life of a Radical,* which Eliot read as background for *Felix Holt.*[47] Working women's involvement lessened as the century went on, but as *Felix Holt* was in progress, middle- and upper-class women, including some of George Eliot's friends, were agitating for the vote.[48] The analogy between women and workers might well have been in the minds of some nineteenth-century women. It had been made explicitly by Charlotte Brontë, as we have seen, as well as by Wollstonecraft, who wrote, "Women ought to have representatives, instead of being arbitrarily governed. . . . But . . . they are as well represented as a numerous class of hard-working mechanics, who pay for the support of royalty when they can scarcely stop their children's mouths with bread" (147). But Sally Shuttleworth has shown that in the 1860s the analogy could well be used to support a conservative political position, and Bonnie Zimmerman has argued that it is so in *Felix Holt.*[49]

"God was cruel when he made women" (316), says Mrs. Transome, and George Eliot in her own letters wrote that women seemed to have "as a fact of mere zoological evolution . . . the worse share," yet she went on to say that this provided the way for "a sublimer resignation in woman and a more regenerating tenderness in man" (8:402). In a related passage in *Felix Holt* she moved from describing Esther's power over Mr. Lyon to decrying "the narrowness of a brain that . . . looks to no results beyond the bargains of today; that tugs with emphasis for every small purpose, and thinks it weakness to exercise the sublime power of resolved renunciation" (69). By implication, this is one of the many judgments on Mrs. Transome. The novel's imagery conflates the narrowness of self-centeredness with the narrowness of private life and offers submissive resignation as a solution to both.

Are the options for women only narrowness or resignation? In George Eliot's copy of Wollstonecraft's *Vindication*, the one sentence that Eliot both underlined and marked in the margin reads as follows: "Restrained from entering into more important concerns by political and civil oppression, *sentiments become events, and reflection deepens what it should, and would have effaced, if the understanding had been allowed to take a wider range*" (Wollstonecraft, 183).[50] Reading *Felix Holt* with this passage in mind, we might agree with Gillian Beer that "George Eliot intensifies the private/public split so that it is shown as the matter of tragedy, not good order."[51] But although Mrs. Transome's life is shown as tragic, Esther and Felix are given the traditional comic solution of marriage, and the novel encourages the expectation that Esther's choice, so different from Mrs. Transome's, will guarantee her happiness. *Middlemarch* and *Daniel Deronda,* in contrast, take characters past the comic ending and show how married life differs from their expectations.

In her essays, Eliot had criticized those who argued for the rights of either women or the poor on the grounds of their moral superiority; in this context she felt it was important not to romanticize the results of oppression. In glorifying women's capacity for submission, as she does in some letters and in portraying Esther, she *was* romanticizing such results, but in her portrayal of Mrs. Transome she showed that not all women fit this idealized image. Ironically, in the message Felix Holt gives to workers, the main way Eliot is writing as a woman is in directing male workers to acquire virtues traditionally associated with women.[52] In the election plot, *Felix Holt* has less radicalism than *Shirley,* where Caroline gives the message of compassion and forbearance more forcefully to Robert than to working men; in the Felix-Esther plot there is something of the same contradiction of attitudes as in *Shirley.* At its most conservative point, Esther is silenced and Felix Holt the radical Coriolanus is indistinguishable from a Tory Prospero: Felix says, "while Caliban is Caliban, though you multiply him by a million, he'll worship every Trinculo that carries a bottle" (226).

Felix Holt claims Shakespeare for a kind of radicalism that is so "philosophic," in Adams's term, that it is equivalent to the "position" of many-sidedness that Blackwood delightedly found in the novel. Similarly, with regard to gender, *Felix Holt* appropriates some Shakespearean lines and themes to give more attention to women but subordinates Esther to Felix in marriage in a way reminiscent of the more conservative strains in Shakespearean comedies rather than of their emphasis on (at least temporary) female power and freedom. The myth of the universal Shakespeare may have been useful to Eliot as she constructed a novel that would seem to take a neutral position in its own time. Although there are points in the novel where I can imagine Eliot "writing back" against a male dominance that would constitute itself with reference to Shakespeare, as in the way she gives Esther "a clear fluent utterance," ultimately her uses of Shakespeare, including the echoes of the same passages of *Hamlet* that Wollstonecraft uses, combine several different understandings of gender, and don't take a unified position, either feminist or antifeminist.

"Feminist" is a twentieth-century term, however, and it is worth remembering how many nineteenth-century women who struggled for women's rights also combined several different understandings of gender. Even Bessie Rayner Parkes, who had insisted on calling her friend Miss Evans instead of Mrs. Lewes and led the efforts to open new jobs to women, wrote, "Do we wish to see the majority of women getting their own livelihood; or do we wish to see it provided for them by men? Are we trying to assist the female population of this country over a time of difficulty; or are we trying to develop a new state and theory of social life? . . . I feel bound to say that I regard the industrial question from a temporary point of view. . . . we are passing through a stage of civilisation which is to be regretted, and . . . her house and not the factory is a woman's happy and healthful sphere."[53]

Published the year following Parkes's essay, *Felix Holt* has a similar caution in its framing of Esther with a marriage similar to those which provide conservative conclusions for Shakespearean comedies. Yet in the presentation of Mrs. Transome, we can read greater daring, comparable perhaps to protests such as that by Florence Nightingale, "Why have women passion, intellect, moral activity—these three— and a place in society where no one of the three can be exercised? . . . The family? It is too narrow a field for the development of an immortal spirit, be that spirit male or female."[54]

Chapter Five

Middlemarch

MORE EXPLICITLY than any of Eliot's earlier novels, *Middlemarch* meditates on the two themes of sympathy and marriage, and more frequently than any of her earlier novels it engages with the treatment of these themes in Shakespeare's sonnets and comedies and puts attitudes associated with these different genres in dialogue with each other. The complex conversation of this novel with Shakespeare, like its complex conversations with Milton and Wordsworth, provides a way for Eliot to be, as Margaret Homans writes, "at once original and deferential."[1] Evoking Shakespeare's female characters early in the presentation of Rosamond, Dorothea, and Mary, *Middlemarch* both extends Rosalind's critiques of marriage, and of Petrarchan attitudes toward love, and uses Shakespeare's sonnets to emphasize that the marriage difficulties of its characters go beyond those of the comic world.[2] Sympathy is both an attitude the narrator is urging toward the characters and an attitude whose presence or absence in those characters—often associated with Shakespeare's sonnets—the narrator analyzes. But the emphasis on Dorothea's final self-assertion and the limitations of her "happy ending" make feminist points that few, if any, critics of Eliot's time could apply to Shakespeare.

Sonnets, Comedies, and Tragedies

Eliot's journal and notebooks indicate two extensive readings of Shakespeare's sonnets during the time when *Middlemarch* was taking shape.

Her journal entry for August 1, 1869, reads, "Yesterday, sitting in Thornie's room, I read through all Shakspeare's sonnets."[3] Thornton, Lewes's twenty-five-year-old son, was back from South Africa with tuberculosis, and Eliot at this time was nursing him, taking notes, and writing *Middlemarch*. On July 19 she wrote an introduction to *Middlemarch*, on July 23, according to her journal, she "Meditated characters," and on August 2, "Began *Middlemarch*."[4] Thornie's illness increased; he died in October. Eliot's grief slowed her work on the novel, and her journal and note taking stopped until spring 1870. When she returned to writing, she took six pages of notes on Shakespeare's sonnets, including some lines chosen for their pauses, others for their "trivial" conceits, the first line of the twenty-four sonnets she considered fine, and a few other entries.[5] One reads:

> Some of the sonnets are painfully abject. He adopts language which might be taken to describe the miserable slavery of oppressed wives: for example,
>
> 57   "I am to wait, though waiting so be hell
>   Not blame your pleasure be it ill or well."
>
> Again,
>
> 56   Being your slave what should I do but tend &c
>   . . . .
>   Nor dare I chide the world-without end hour
>   Whilst I, my sovereign, watch the clock for you."[6]

These comments, and other sonnets she liked, show that Eliot was both interested in and ambivalent about the emphasis on sympathetic identification in the sonnets.[7] On the one hand, she thinks of wives' slavery, knowing that wives in particular are expected to be self-sacrificing and, unlike the mothers of young children but like the speaker in these poems, often asked to sacrifice for someone who is absent most of the time. On the other hand, she praises other poems of sympathetic identification, such as the one sonnet of which she copies eight lines, calling it "an exquisite utterance of love":

> For all that beauty that doth cover thee
> Is but the seemly raiment of my heart,

> Which in thy breast doth live, as thou in me:
> How can I then be elder than thou art?
> O therefore, Love, be of thyself so wary
> As I, not for myself, but for thee will;
> Bearing thy heart, which I will keep so chary
> As tender nurse her babe from faring ill.
>
> (*Notebooks,* 212; Sonnet 22)

The imagery of this sonnet, in which the speaker is older than the addressee and is compared to a nurse (even if an infant's nurse rather than a sick person's), could have reminded Eliot with particular vividness of her reading of the sonnets in Thornie's room. Another line she praises as "vigorous," and later uses in her letters to empathize with others' joys in their growing children (7:16 and 7:158), is about the imaginative identity of parent and child: "And see thy blood warm while thou feel'st it cold" (Sonnet 2). "Some of these self-merging sonnets," she writes after quoting from "Being your slave," "gain a fine meaning by a mystical application: as . . . 'Sin of self-love possesseth all mine eye'" (Sonnet 62). Developing the ambivalence in Eliot's reading of the sonnets, *Middlemarch* presents both positive views of sympathy and negative views of its degeneration into miserable slavery—both attitudes sometimes linked to sonnet allusions.

Eliot's use of Shakespeare's sonnets in *Middlemarch* needs to be distinguished from her use of sonnet conventions, even though in her notebook she writes that most of Shakespeare's "sonnets are artificial products, governed by the fashion of sentiment which had probably grown out of the imitation of the Italian poets." She criticizes "writers who set out with the notion that Shakespeare was in all things exceptional, & so never think of comparison with contemporaries even when the occasion is thrust upon them" (*Notebooks,* 213). Nevertheless, Eliot's tendency in *Middlemarch* is to criticize the sonnet *tradition* while giving authority to lines from Shakespeare's sonnets. *Middlemarch* generally mocks the sonnet tradition for its unrealistic, Petrarchan idealization of a distant beloved. Such mockery is part of Shakespeare's own technique in the comedies, on which *Middlemarch* also draws, and thus the uses of allusions from the different genres in *Middlemarch* are closely intertwined. In both genres, Shakespeare writes about lovers' idealization and the presence or absence of shared feeling, and George Eliot shares those interests. In the sonnets, however, the impact of disillusionment is much greater, and Eliot sometimes uses lines from the sonnets to emphasize the problems created in part by social pressures toward marriage analogous to those typical of comic plots. On the other hand, at the end Dorothea acts like an assertive heroine from the comedies rather than like the self-abnegating speaker of the sonnets.

Like Shakespeare's comedies, *Middlemarch* criticizes cultural attitudes toward marriage by including several parallel courtships and by allusions to literary tradition. Rosalind declares that the romantic versions of the legends of Troilus and Leander are "all lies. Men have died from time to time, and worms have eaten them, but not for love" (4.1.96–98). In the "Prelude," the narrator notes that women's lives are really much more varied "than anyone would imagine from the sameness of . . . the favourite love-stories in prose and verse" (2). Unlike the typical comedy, *Middlemarch* moves past marriage contracts to show their consequences and spells out the suffering that Rosalind gaily predicts when she says, "Men are April when they woo, December when they wed. Maids are May when they are maids, but the sky changes when they are wives" (4.1.140–42).

Shakespearean comedies present a world where courtship, marriage, and family are the main concerns, where love at first sight can cohere with suggestions of rational understanding, where love and money do not finally conflict. They contain criticism of these comic assumptions—Touchstone's "loving voyage," says Jaques, "Is but for two months victuall'ed" (5.4.190–91)—but those criticisms are *contained* in another sense as well. *Middlemarch* echoes Touchstone's image, making it more ominous, in analyzing Dorothea's marriage—"Having once embarked on your marital voyage, it is impossible not to be aware that you make no way and that the sea is not within sight" (228). *As You Like It* includes Rosalind's complaints about "this working-day world," but throughout most of the play she is allowed to be in a holiday humor (1.3.12). In contrast, early in her letters George Eliot called "working-day world" her "favorite little epithet" (1:44),[8] and she makes Caleb Garth warn explicitly, "Young folks may get fond of each other before they know what life is, and they may think it all holiday if they can only get together, but it soon turns into working-day, my dear" (252–53). Even Fred has to go beyond the world of comedy to learn how to deal with the problem of "the working-day world showing no eager need whatever of a young gentleman without capital and generally unskilled" (543). The characters' awareness of living in a working-day world is often marked by sonnet allusions.

Instead of centering on the relationship of a comic woman and a tragic man, as in *Felix Holt, Middlemarch* juxtaposes one such couple with others characterized by varying degrees of comedy, tragicomedy, and tragedy. Mary Garth, who takes "life very much as a comedy in which she had a proud, nay, a generous resolution not to act the mean or treacherous part" (307), is more like a Shakespearean comic heroine than any other character in the book; she keeps Fred at verbal distance while they discuss love, and the bonds of their relationship seem to help them grow. When they discuss the issue of how well lovers know each other, Fred says, questioningly, "I suppose a woman is never in love with anyone she has always known—ever since she can remember; as a man often is" (135). Her response is "Let me see. . . . I must go back on my experience. There is Juliet—she seems an example of what you say. But then Ophelia had probably known Hamlet a long while" (135). Mary and Fred are old friends, and like the heroines in Shakespeare's comedies, Mary knows her lover's limitations and tells him about them. She would never die for love as Juliet and Ophelia do; her calling them part of her experience deflates the ideals of romantic love, somewhat like Rosalind's claim that Leander died of a cramp (4.1.93) or the mockery of the Shakespearean passages that compose Catherine's curriculum in *Northanger Abbey*. But Mary leads a less charmed life than the traditional heroine of a comedy. Mary is, as Mrs. Vincy notes, "without lilies or roses" (629). Her "inventory" (111) of Lydgate's features makes almost the same joke about descriptions that Olivia makes when she tells Viola that her beauty "should be inventoried, and every particle and utensil label'd to my will" (*Twelfth Night* 1.5.240–42); but unlike Olivia, Mary is neither beautiful nor vain enough to make the joke about herself. And though she would never kill herself for love, her relationship with Fred has sacrificial aspects of a more everyday sort.

Fred is a charming, occasionally foolish, irresponsible, and emphatically young hero, rather like the young men of Shakespeare's comedies. But Fred's need for reform is stressed more than usual in Shakespearean comedy, and a sonnet epigraph underlines the fact that in all these qualities he resembles the young man of the sonnets as well.[9] The epigraph of chapter 24, "The offender's sorrow brings but small relief / To him who wears the strong offence's cross" (236) is a slight misquotation of Sonnet 34 ("lends but weak relief"), one of the earliest sonnets to accuse the young man of bad treatment. These lines are among the most direct reproaches among the sonnets. Eliot singled them out in her *Middlemarch Notebooks* as being "fine lines" (212); they summarize one of the themes that link her novels with the tragic genre, the ineradicable effects of people's actions.[10] They introduce a chapter in which Fred, having lost money through imprudence, goes to the Garths to borrow some to repay his other debts, discovers their own financial difficulties, and feels "for the first time something like the tooth of remorse." Beginning to use "exercise of the imagination on other people's needs, . . . at this moment he suddenly saw himself as a pitiful rascal who was robbing two women of their savings" (244). Because the novel is not simply a comedy, this recognition is painful; because it is not simply a tragedy, Fred can reform. By making Fred and Rosamond brother and sister, George Eliot emphasizes the fact that they begin as companion portraits in charming immaturity. While recollections of Shakespearean comedy point up their charm, allusions to the sonnets emphasize the selfishness that Fred confronts in himself as Rosamond never does.

While Mary herself introduces her relation to Shakespeare's women with a joke, for Rosamond the narrator encourages the comparison by way of her teacher, Mrs. Lemon, who praises her for superficial accomplishments. We are told, "probably if Mrs. Lemon had undertaken to describe Juliet or Imogen, these heroines would not have seemed poetical" (94). These two figures of devoted love seem to have had a special moral status as heroines for the Victorians; when Anna Jameson most explicitly uses Shakespeare to critique her own society, she complains that the kind of education women are receiving produces "precocious roses of the hot-bed . . . who are models of manner, . . . who sneer at sentiment, and laugh at the Juliets and the Imogens."[11]

As the novel proceeds, Rosamond's contrasts to such Shakespearean heroines become more and more obvious; her name may even resonate with the "precocious roses of the hot-bed." Beyond the conventional association of the rose and female beauty, the name Rosamond calls up a long history of literary love, back to *The Romance of the Rose* and Chaucer's poem "To Rosemound," in which he compares himself to Tristram, the famous lover whose name Lydgate bore in an early version of the novel.[12] A Rosamund, mistress of Henry II, is the speaker in Samuel Daniel's "The Complaint of Rosamund."[13] Victorians were interested in her; she appears, for example, in Tennyson's poems "A Dream of Fair Women" and "Rosamund's Bower" and in Burne-Jones's painting *Rosamund and Eleanor,* now at the Yale Center for British Art, which depicts the visit of Henry's jealous wife.[14] Even more like Rosamond Vincy is the Rosamond Oliver of *Jane Eyre,* whom St. John Rivers gives up, calling her "truly the Rose of the World," because, as her name suggests, she is too worldly to be a good missionary's wife.[15]

Rosamond Vincy's role in the novel includes an interplay between these contrasting allusions and allusions to Shakespeare's Rosalind, herself named to suggest the *Romance of the Rose* tradition. The images that Eliot uses to evoke what Lydgate sees in Rosamond—"that distinctive womanhood which must be classed with flowers and music" (161)—overlap with images that Anna Jameson uses to evoke Rosalind, for example "sweet as the dew-awakened blossoms," "like a delicious strain of music."[16] She has the conventional beauty of the Rosamunds and of the Rosalind in Orlando's imagination, and the ability to dominate and manipulate of the Rosalind we see on stage, without self-awareness and without the sympathy that the Victorians, in particular, saw in her.[17] Like Rosalind she puts all her companions in the shade; like Rosalind she quickly falls in love and thinks of marriage, and like Rosalind she claims her man with a more literal kind of chain. At the moment when Rosamond and Lydgate become engaged, she is holding "some trivial chainwork" and nervously drops it when Lydgate rises to go. He stoops to pick it up and then finds himself "very near to a lovely little face set on a fair long neck which he had been used to see turning about under the most perfect management of self-contented grace. . . . He did not know where the chain went" (294).

The needlework that becomes a chain is more than a random verbal echo of the chain that Rosalind gives Orlando in *As You Like It*. In both texts the chain is an appropriate emblem for marriage, its solidity an ironic contrast with the spontaneity of the moments when Rosalind shows the frank passion that Eliot had noticed in her earlier essay and Rosamond is "as natural as she ever was at five years old." For all the satirical comments Rosalind and Touchstone make, however, *As You Like It* celebrates Rosalind's union with Orlando. On the one hand, while both characters are, as Rosalind calls herself, "out of suits with Fortune" (1.2.236), comic conventions assure that this will not prevent or shadow their marriage. Orlando, like Tertius Lydgate, is the youngest of three sons, but his lack of inheritance is magically remedied. On the other hand, before their marriage, he and Rosalind, disguised as Ganymede, talk about their expectations of the future in a way that Lydgate and Rosamond never do. George Eliot has made her plot more realistic and her dominating female character less so and has subtracted the friendly dialogue that Shakespeare added to romance. Thus the *Middlemarch* chain scene is a rewriting in which a marriage does not begin or end "as you like it." Lydgate learns his role: "an engaged man, whose soul was not his own, but the woman's to whom he had bound himself" (295). These conventional images tighten upon Lydgate just as Rosamond's conventionality does. The narrator says of this couple, "Each lived in a world of which the other knew nothing" (162), and this lack of knowledge determines Lydgate's lifetime of frustrated ideals.

Lydgate has a larger mind and, as his name hints, seems to belong more in the genre of tragedy or history—the fifteenth-century Lydgate wrote *The Falls of Princes,* and his namesake begins with the idealism of the tragic or epic hero. But while many readings of those heroes take their condescension to women for granted, George Eliot explicitly makes Lydgate's attitude to women part of his "spots of commonness" (147) and thus analogous to the "tragic flaw" of a leading nineteenth- and early twentieth-century interpretation of tragedy. Lydgate, at the beginning of the novel, feels an intellectual passion for medical discovery, but never thinks that a woman might share this enterprise, as Mary Wollstonecraft would have urged him to think. When he first meets Dorothea, he puts her in the category of women who "are too ignorant to understand the merits of any question, and usually fall back on their moral sense to settle things after their own taste" (92). He is interested in women to the extent that they can serve him as adornments—just the opposite of Felix Holt's attitude. Before meeting Rosamond, he had loved an actress named Laure, who in name and in the predominance of his imagination over reality in their relationship recalls Petrarch's Laura. His enjoyment of Laure's singing echoes the comparison of music to "the sweet sound ["south" in some editions] / That breathes upon a bank of violets" by Orsino, in *Twelfth Night* (1.1.5–6), who uses music to feed fresh his long-distance love for Olivia: "His only relaxation was to go and look at this woman, just as he might have thrown himself under the breath of the sweet south on a bank of violets for a while" (148).

Before marriage, Rosamond as well is described in terms that echo Shakespearean descriptions of lovers. When she is upset because Lydgate is staying away, the narrator borrows "lightness" from Polonius's description of Hamlet's madness as resulting from Ophelia's rejection (2.2.148), "leanness" from the "lean cheek" in Rosalind's description of the stereotypical unhappy lover (3.2.364), and "effects of passion" from the conspirators' invention of lovesickness in Beatrice (*Much Ado* 2.3.108) to locate Rosamond's feelings: "Anyone who imagines ten days too short a time—not for falling into leanness, lightness, or other measurable effects of passion, but—for the whole spiritual circuit of alarmed conjecture and disappointment, is ignorant of . . . a young lady's mind" (293). The narrator here, somewhat like Rosalind, is making fun of the conventional exaggerations of love-melancholy, but nevertheless emphasizes that Rosamond's love, more destructively than that of many characters in Shakespearean comedy, is narcissistic and self-contained.

After their marriage we see the consequences of their mutual ignorance. In the epigraph to chapter 58, Eliot quotes part of bitter Sonnet 93, one of those that express disillusionment with the fair young man whose beauty has been described with words similar to those in which other sonneteers praised their ladies:

> For there can live no hatred in thine eye,
> Therefore in that I cannot know thy change:

> In many's looks the false heart's history
> Is writ in moods and frowns and wrinkles strange;
> But Heaven in thy creation did decree
> That in thy face sweet love should ever dwell;
> Whate'er thy thoughts or thy heart's workings be,
> Thy looks should nothing thence but sweetness tell.

These lines devastatingly match Rosamond's condition in the crisis of the chapter, which uses similar imagery. While the narrator observed that "perhaps Lydgate and she had never felt so far off each other before," still, "Rosamond had no scowls and had never raised her voice," and as Lydgate prepares to tell her of his financial troubles, "her delicate neck and cheek and purely-cut lips never had more of that untarnished beauty which touches us in spring-time and infancy and all sweet freshness" (579–80).

This sonnet begins with two lines that Eliot omits: "So shall I live, supposing thou art true / Like a deceived husband." These lines depend upon a general cultural suspicion of women even as they express the discovery that a man is equally untrustworthy. Women's deceptiveness did not loom as large in nineteenth-century ideologies of gender as it did in the Renaissance, but the dynamics in the Lydgate-Rosamond marriage show some of the cultural conditions that generate it as both a belief and a female strategy.

Middlemarch never juxtaposes Lydgate with any particular Shakespearean tragic hero as Felix Holt is linked with Hamlet and Coriolanus. The novel gives him initial stature more by linking him with great scientists and by suggesting that his is a kind of heroism that literature has not yet explored. Nevertheless, the words of one Shakespearean tragic hero are associated with him late in the novel. In the chapter that begins with the sonnet epigraph just discussed, at the point where Lydgate is trying to warn Rosamond against horseback riding during pregnancy, she asks him to fasten her hair, and the narrator parenthetically interposes, "To such uses do men come!" (570). After he meditates on Yorick's skull, musing that this will be the end both of "my lady . . . , let her paint an inch thick," and of Alexander the Great, Hamlet exclaims, "To what base uses we may return, Horatio!" (5.1.202). On the surface the echo, if heard (perhaps more likely in a chapter with a Shakespearean epigraph), seems to be a joke, but the thoughts of death, vanity, and defeated ambition in this Shakespearean passage are relevant: fastening Rosamond's hair, Lydgate becomes identified with Alexander's decaying corpse. The allusion may hint at affinities between Lydgate's condescension to women and Hamlet's hostility to women, but at the same time it suggests the narrator's sympathy to Lydgate as the novel is showing how Rosamond is provoking hostility.[18]

In spite of Lydgate's greater aspirations, both he and Rosamond share attitudes toward love with comic characters; Dorothea's attitude toward love, more unconventional, receives something of the grandeur of a tragic error. Although Dorothea's marriage to an elderly scholar echoes a plot situation frequently used to begin farces and fabliaux, in describing it Eliot evokes a play in which Shakespeare turned a similar situation into tragedy, a play that, showing the alienation of a recently married couple, has been described by Carol Thomas Neely as "a terrifying completion of the comedies"—*Othello*.[19] The comparison becomes explicit when the narrator moves to the mind of Sir James Chettam: "Nevertheless, while Sir James said to himself that he had completely resigned her, since with the perversity of a Desdemona she had not affected a proposed match that was clearly suitable and according to nature [marriage to him]; he could not yet be quite passive under the idea of her engagement to Mr. Casaubon" (66). This is based on

> Not to affect many proposed matches
> Of her own clime, complexion, and degree;
> Whereto we see in all things nature tends.
> (*Othello* 3.3.236–38)

While Sir James is criticizing her here, and is too conventional to see grandeur in Desdemona's choice of Othello, his comparison still suggests something of his continued idealization of her; if she is perverse, it is with the perversity of a tragic heroine, and he has an inkling that some disaster awaits her. Different as are the passionless Casaubon and Othello, there are surprising similarities in Dorothea's and Desdemona's attitudes to marriage. Both women are devoted to their unlikely lovers, who are somewhat older, and not physically attractive in conventional terms. Like Desdemona, Dorothea could have said that she sees her husband's "visage in his mind" (1.3.255). Both are eager to dedicate themselves and to accompany their husbands, whether to battle in Cyprus or to research in Rome. While romantic idealism links their characterization, perhaps subliminal echoes (the number of syllables, the beginning and ending with the same letters) link their names as well.

The social relations of the sexes as portrayed in novel and play, however, provide most of the similarities between the two couples. Both works contrast all-male worlds, attractive and exotic to the women, with a domestic world, strange to the men. Crucially, both men are egotists somewhat uncertain of their position, and any interest their wives take in other men, even in the altruistic interest in which neither Desdemona nor Dorothea sees any cause for suspicion, is threatening to them. Thus persisting similarities in their societies' gender arrangements join the marital experience of the passionate Othello and the cold Casaubon. In both societies women are groomed to please their husbands and to take pleasure in their husbands' achievements, and even an extraordinary woman is more likely to envision a life of helping an extraordinary man than one of initiating work for herself. The coldness, age, and physical weakness that make Casaubon less glamorous than Othello also make him less likely to kill his wife, but there are still tragic elements in their marriage. Of Casaubon's lot, the narrator says, "everything is below the level of tragedy except the passionate egoism of the sufferer" (413), and, with less qualification, Dorothea's unhappiness exemplifies "that element of tragedy which lies in the very fact of frequency" (189).

As these quotations show, meditations about genre as well as Shakespearean allusions in *Middlemarch* frequently suggest a desire to expand genres or to play one genre against another. If in some respects it, like *Othello,* can be seen as a comedy that turns into tragedy, in other respects it can be compared to *Measure for Measure,* which provides a comic resolution for characters that seem potentially tragic, and it recalls that play at several points. The epigraph to chapter 66 is taken from one of Angelo's early speeches defending his harshness in enforcing the law: " 'Tis one thing to be tempted, Escalus, / Another thing to fall." These lines apply to the chapter first to distinguish Fred, who struggles with the temptation to gamble, from Lydgate, who is gambling heavily with what Fred sees as "strange unlikeness to himself" (661). But they also associate Lydgate with Angelo, in the combination of his initial self-righteousness—recalled in Fred's opinion "that he was a prig, and tremendously conscious of his superiority" (661)—and his corruptibility. Angelo's final punishment, in this play that strains at the limits of comedy, is a marriage he has tried to evade. Perhaps this memory is relevant to the way Lydgate's marriage also becomes his punishment.

The presentation of Dorothea even more clearly evokes *Measure for Measure,* particularly Anna Jameson's influential reading. In comparing Dorothea to Saint Theresa, the prelude names the same saint to whom Jameson likened Isabella, a novice at the beginning of the play.[20] Dorothea is frequently compared to a nun, particularly in her marriage to Casaubon; the order Isabella joins is that of St. Clare, the saint after whom Ladislaw's friend names his portrait of Dorothea. Like Isabella, Dorothea shows a moral idealism that differentiates her from most women in her society, even though it involves a high valuation of some virtues they are expected to have.[21] In considering Dorothea's life, Eliot twice echoes lines from *Measure for Measure* to which she also alludes in *Felix Holt:* "Spirits are not finely touch'd / But to fine issues" (1.1.36–37). As she longs to see Will after Casaubon's death, the narrator says, "Life would be no better than candle-light tinsel and daylight rubbish if our spirits were not touched by what has been, to issues of longing and constancy" (527), and the final paragraph begins, "her finely-touched spirit had still its fine issues" (825).

The Duke, who engineers much of the plot and finally (surprisingly) proposes to Isabella, says the original of these lines, and Felix echoes them; but in *Middlemarch* the narrator says them, not Will. This novel, unlike *Felix Holt* or *Measure for Measure,* denies its heroine a moral guide.[22] Dorothea has tried one, Casaubon; indeed, what she says about him at the beginning—"I should wish to have a husband who was above me in judgment and in all knowledge" (40)—echoes some of Esther's final words about Felix and in its dramatic irony suggests the more feminist perspective of this novel. Both with regard to Will's limitations and with regard to the limitations of private life, *Middlemarch* sets qualifications on how we can idealize Dorothea's final situation.

In Shakespearean comedy and tragicomedy, no epilogues defend the significance of characters' "unhistoric acts" (825) as the narrator of *Middlemarch* defends those of Dorothea. Shakespearean comedy may be seen as a counterworld to history, assuming its own domestic values self-validating;[23] but the Elizabethans had not developed as explicit an ideological association of women with private life as would the Victorians. In *Middlemarch,* written in a culture that increasingly dichotomized the domestic and the public, the narrator's insistence that Dorothea's impact goes beyond her own household hints at how confining Victorian women could find this dichotomy.[24]

The chief respect in which Dorothea's marriage to Will *is* idealized in a way that links it to Shakespearean comedy is in its mutuality, described in terms of understanding and listening.[25] In an early letter to Maria Lewis, Mary Ann Evans, as she was then known, had hit upon the key Shakespearean passage about the need for mutuality, discussed in chapter 3 of this book, which occurs as a comment on the most incompatible marriage in *As You Like It.* She aligns her feelings with Wordsworth's description of joy in nature, but her concern is more with response, or lack of it, from human beings. She wrote, "O how lusciously joyous . . . to feel one's 'heart leap up' after the pressure that Shakspeare so admirably describes, 'When a man's wit is not seconded by the forward child understanding it strikes a man as dead as a large reckoning in a small room.' The poor Clown's distress that his Audrey was not poetical is a type that is reacted daily under a thousand circumstances" (*GEL* 1:71; *As You Like It* 3.3.10–12). In spite of Rosalind's disguise (and perhaps in some ways because of it), she and Orlando respond to each other, as do other Shakespearean couples such as Orsino and Viola or Beatrice and Benedick. Similarly, in *Middlemarch* the interchanges between Dorothea and Will, as between Fred and Mary, promote much more mutual understanding before marriage. Mary is described as an audience that demands Fred's best—in effect "the theatre of all [his] actions" (237)[26]—and Will contrasts markedly to the unresponsive Casaubon: Dorothea and Will share "young delight in speaking to each other, and saying what no one else would care to hear" (534).

Two different kinds of contrast to this mutuality are presented in terms of sonnet conventions. We are told that, in marriage, Casaubon expected to "receive family pleasures and leave behind him that copy of himself which seemed so urgently required of a man—to the sonneteers of the sixteenth century" (272). This motif is actually a distinctive feature of Shakespeare's first seventeen sonnets, not a conventional one, but Eliot, like many other readers, found those sonnets so tedious—"a wearisome series"[27]—she probably preferred to think the theme conventional. In her allusions to it, she reinforces the emphasis on Casaubon's egoism and his lack of concern for Dorothea. The hypothetical woman is present in those seventeen sonnets only as a vial or womb; Dorothea is present to Casaubon's mind as "a blooming young lady—the younger the better, because more educable and submissive" (272). Casaubon shows some of the attitudes that created the "oppressed wives" of whom the sonnets reminded Eliot when he says to Dorothea, "The great charm of your sex is its capability of ardent self-sacrificing affection, and herein we see its fitness to round and complete the existence of our own" (50).

Will is satirized more gently by associating him with sonnet tradition; he is both attracted to and dissatisfied by the Petrarchan/sonnet convention of addressing a distant, idealized beloved, mocked by Shakespeare especially in *As You Like It.*

> What others might have called the futility of his passion, made additional delight for his imagination; he was conscious of a generous movement, and of verifying in his own experience that higher love-poetry which had charmed his fancy. Dorothea, he said to himself, was for ever enthroned in his soul; no other woman could sit higher than her footstool; and if he could have written out in immortal syllables the effect she wrought within him, he might have boasted after the example of old Drayton, that—
>
> > Queens hereafter might be glad to live
> > Upon the alms of her superfluous praise.
>
> > (460–61)

Yet this is not truly enough for him; after these meditations he manages to see her in church (where Petrarch had his first glimpse of Laura), and the agitation that this causes them both deflates his ability to make "a sort of happiness for himself out of his feeling for Dorothea" (460).[28] He feels, "This was what a man got by worshipping the sight of a woman" (464). Poetic as Will is, here his frustration resembles that of Sir James Chettam, who gives up the uninterested Dorothea for the responsive Celia because "he had no sonnets to write" (61). The narrator, however, describes Sir James's continuing affection for Dorothea with an echo of Sonnet 54—one of three in Eliot's notebook list of fine sonnets that are marked with a plus sign—which says of sweet roses, "Of their sweet deaths are sweetest odours made": "But he had a chivalrous nature (was not the disinterested service of woman among the ideal glories of old chivalry?): his disregarded love had not turned to bitterness; its death had made sweet odours" (279).

Will tries writing poetry about the "frugal cheer" (462) of his love with something of the air of Orlando or Silvius, and perhaps Eliot's presentation of him as a poet activates, parodically, the Shakespeare allusion in his first name. But perhaps just as relevant are other meanings of his name, which contribute to many of the puns in the sonnets. Will feels that he must give up his will, largely because of Casaubon's will; similarly Dorothea feels that she must give up her Will and her will. Consideration of Dorothea's struggle will take us to larger questions about Eliot's use of the idea of sympathy as presented in the sonnets.

Sympathy and the Sonnets

Like the sonnets, *Middlemarch* is full of real and fantasy triangles, and at several significant points in the novel, characters, like the speaker of the sonnets, must deal with feelings of exclusion and jealousy. This is a setting for the conflict between self-centeredness and concern for others that was one of George Eliot's major subjects. In portraying both Sir James's and Will's struggles with jealousy, Eliot's perspective is gently ironic—neither one can overcome selfishness as much as he thinks he can. But with two other characters the struggle toward identification with the others in the triangle goes further. Farebrother's giving up his own aspirations to court Mary because of Fred's love for her is a domesticated parallel to the sonnet speaker's self-abnegation; the bond between the mature, fatherly older man and the charming youth, and the love they share for a witty dark woman without conventional beauty is a bowdlerized version of the triangular story the sonnets suggest. It is part of the bowdlerization that Farebrother maintains his self-sacrifice, which leads to happiness for Fred and Mary.

But the intensity of Dorothea's struggle after seeing Will with Rosamond is closer to that of the sonnets. Will may struggle with his frustration over Dorothea, but he does not really endure disillusionment with her; she does, though mistakenly, with him. In her mistaken belief about Will, Dorothea suffers as does Shakespeare's sonnet persona. He tries to suppress his feelings in sympathetic identification with the friend and the mistress who have betrayed him. The description of the two images of Will that tear Dorothea apart (775) recalls the fluctuation of the sonnet persona between two images of the young man, as well as the pain of Othello and Troilus at being torn between two images of the woman they love. The narrator explicitly compares Dorothea to Hamlet at this point when she answers Celia's questions by saying, "Oh, all the troubles of all people on the face of the earth," making Celia uneasy at "this Hamlet-like raving" (765). Dorothea turns outward from absorption in her own suffering to concern for the others involved, and her action, arousing a responsive generous moment in Rosamond, helps her to find out the truth that vindicates Will. In this passage George Eliot dramatizes a move out of self-concern and toward sympathy, one of the themes in the sonnets that meant the most to her.[29] Yet, unlike the sympathy of the sonnets, Dorothea's sympathy opens her to learning of Will's love for her and thus brings its own reward. Much as the novel evokes the sonnets, it here suggests a critique, or at least an ambivalence, about the self-sacrificing sympathy voiced in some of them. Significantly, the chapter in which she finally declares her love to Will is given an epigraph not from Shakespeare but from Donne's "The Good-morrow."

Sympathy is not enough for Dorothea to learn. She has been associated with sympathy from the beginning of the novel, when she wants to build cottages for the poor and then to devote herself to Casaubon. In one of her first conversations with Will, he charges her with "the fanaticism of sympathy" (252) when she says, "It spoils my enjoyment of anything when I am made to think that most people are shut out from it." It is true that the narrator distinguishes her fantasies of devoting herself to Casaubon from the more realistic ability to conceive "that he had an equivalent centre of self, whence the lights and shadows must always fall with a certain difference" (243) and marks her limitations and growth with regard to this more realistic sympathy, associated once with an image from *Macbeth:* "Pity, that 'newborn babe' which was by-and-by to rule many a storm within her, did not 'stride the blast' on this occasion" (316).[30] But practical sympathy for Casaubon—or even the practical sympathy for Rosamond that she shows later—does not complete the novel's presentation of Dorothea's moral development. She must also learn the strength of her own personal desire for Will and must act to keep him from leaving her at the end.[31] Instead of the self-abnegating musings of the sonnet speaker, or the silence of Isabella, she speaks with an assertiveness closer to that of a comic heroine or perhaps to the lines of Mariana in *Measure for Measure*—"I crave no other nor no better man" (5.1.431). And yet the plot has put her in a situation in which this assertive act is also self-sacrifice—for marrying Will means giving up her inheritance from Casaubon. While her self-assertion calls into question the self-denying sympathy associated with the sonnets, nevertheless the economic cost of the marriage to her also critiques the happy endings of Shakespeare's comedies, where the heroines do not have to choose between money and love. Furthermore, the finale returns to imagery of self-sacrifice when it suggests widespread regret that Dorothea should have been "absorbed into the life of another, and be only known in a certain circle as a wife and mother" (822).

The year during which George Eliot began planning *Middlemarch* and read the sonnets in Thornie's room is also a year in which her letters are full of references to her "growth of a maternal feeling" (5:5) and "unused stock of motherly tenderness"—though, as she says in the same letter, "I profoundly rejoice that I never brought a child into the world" (5:52).[32] In *Middlemarch*, women's relations to somewhat irresponsible men, like Mary's to Fred and Dorothea's to Will, are described in motherhood imagery as well as in language from the sonnets.[33] Celia's behavior as a new mother shows that the novel does not equate literal maternity with sympathy.[34] Nevertheless, two discourses of sympathy converge explicitly when one of the sonnet lines she had described in her notebooks as "fine" describes the sympathy that permits Mrs. Vincy to put aside her prejudice against Mary when Fred, in his sickness, longs to hear about her. "No word passed his lips; but 'to hear with eyes belongs to love's rare wit,' and the mother in the fulness of her heart not only divined Fred's longing, but felt ready for any sacrifice in order to satisfy him" (260).[35]

The reader may feel a bit of exaggeration in the melodramatic terms in which Mrs. Vincy thinks of speaking about Mary as a sacrifice, but any suggestion of parody is countered by the emphasis on Fred's sickness in this scene, which uncannily recalls—with a less ominous ending—Eliot's reading of the sonnets in Thornie's sickroom.[36] The coalescence here of the theme of identification in the sonnets with the attitude of maternal sympathy suggests how George Eliot was able to present her own writing as both womanly and Shakespearean, as part of what Homans calls her "strategies for making [her] peace with [her] culture."[37] For Eliot, the idea of sympathy mediated between her culture's ideal of womanhood, associated at its highest with maternity, and her culture's ideal of art, associated at its highest with Shakespeare. As other authors' uses of the term discussed in chapter 1 show, sympathy could be gendered as feminine or considered as beyond gender; this may make it a concept particularly interesting—though also problematic—for women, and there are other marks perhaps associated with gender, as well as with specifics of her particular situation, in Eliot's continued interest in the sonnets.

Barber and Wheeler find "the poems of abasement and farewell . . . unsatisfying" and ask, "Are any of them ever anthologized?"[38] In her list of "fine" sonnets, which numbers about twenty-four, Eliot selects at least three of them, 71 ("No longer mourn for me when I am dead"), 90 ("Then hate me when thou wilt; if ever, now"), and 93 ("So shall I live, supposing thou art true"), the one appropriated as an epigraph to describe Lydgate's relationship to Rosalind.[39] The emphasis on a close relationship of identification was an aspect of the sonnets that particularly interested Eliot, who often referred to herself and Lewes as "my double self" and used a similar phrase in writing to friends about themselves and their husbands (*GEL* 4:118, 5:159). Like the speaker in the sonnets she was involved in a relationship which was not legally marriage, although she called it so.[40] She took George Lewes's last name in her social life and his first name (though it was also, importantly, George Sand's) in her writing life. Not having the ritualized conventions and public acceptance that would surround a legal marriage, Eliot had to think more about what marriage really meant to her.[41]

Later she would inscribe the manuscript of *Daniel Deronda* "To my dear Husband, George Henry Lewes," with a copy of most of Sonnet 29, one of the three sonnets she marked with a plus sign in her notebook list of fine sonnets:

> Wishing me like to one more rich in hope
>
> . . . .
>
> Desiring this man's art and that man's scope,
> With what I most enjoy contented least.
> Yet in these thoughts myself almost despising,
> Haply I think on thee,—and then my state
> Like to the lark at break of day arising
> From sullen earth, sings hymns at heaven's gate;
> For thy sweet love remember'd such wealth brings,
> That then I scorn to change my state with kings.[42]

Her choice of this sonnet marks an affinity not simply because of the emphasis on identification with the beloved but also because of its articulation of discontent with the self. In this context it is also interesting that she made notes on changes in Shakespeare's apparent confidence in his poetry—fluctuation between "this powerful rhyme" and "these poor rude lines."[43] Lack of self-confidence was a difficulty with which Eliot repeatedly had to cope. Early in her writing career, Lewes described her to her publisher as in need of someone to whisper, "You see, George, you really are not a confounded Noodle!" (*GEL* 3:31). This trait did not disappear.

At some time later than her first writing in her notebooks for *Middlemarch,* in a different color of ink, she concluded, "Nevertheless, I love the Sonnets better and better whenever I return to them. They are tunes that for some undefinable reason suit my frame."[44] Part of the undefinable reason, I suggest, is that Eliot found in the sonnets a psychology similar to her own—an interest in the presence of the other closely connected with discontent about the self. There is a startling resemblance between this passage and a more recent appreciation of Shakespeare's sonnets by Maya Angelou: "I found myself and still find myself, whenever I like, stepping back into Shakespeare. . . . 'When in disgrace with fortune and men's eyes, / I all alone beweep my outcast state. . . .' [she goes on to quote Sonnet 29, the same one quoted by Eliot in the dedication of *Daniel Deronda*]. Of course he wrote it for me; that is a condition of the black woman. Of course, he was a Black woman. I understand that. Nobody else understands it but I *know* that William Shakespeare was a black woman."[45] Peter Erickson argues that Angelou loves this sonnet because "the lower-class position of many black women" corresponds to the position of the speaker as he addresses a young man above him on a class hierarchy; while this is a relevant factor, a reader can translate position in a class hierarchy to position in a gender hierarchy as well. Even though Eliot was a famous novelist when she inscribed this dedication, some aspect of her psychology corresponded to the sense of power differential. One line in Angelou's speech, which I did not quote earlier, however, suggests more sense of effort about her identification with Shakespeare—"Whenever I like, I *pull* him to me [italics Angelou's]"—and exemplifies the relevance of race in reader psychology.

Like Angelou's, Eliot's responses to the sonnets, and to Sonnet 29 in particular, could be placed in the context of the psychological theories of Nancy Chodorow and Carol Gilligan, who have found ease of identification with others more characteristic of women than of men.[46] On the other hand, both in her *Notebook* and in *Middlemarch* Eliot observes ways in which requiring women to be sympathetic can be oppressive, and thus her writings can be taken as a critique of some uses of these writers. While Dorothea's development parallels Gilligan's view of women's moral development as moving first to care for others and then including care of self as well, Eliot emphasizes the injustice of the social constraints on Dorothea's choices.[47]

In her Shakespearean references in *Middlemarch*, Eliot makes fun of the sonnet convention somewhat as Shakespeare does in *As You Like It,* but then she opposes to the comic worldview an attitude of greater seriousness associated with the sonnets she considers fine. In other words, poetic idealization of women is played off against comedy, which is in turn countered by a world in which questions of sympathy and betrayal, transcending conventional gender roles, are most important. Reading Shakespeare as a woman, she identified with the female characters, such as Rosalind, who mock sonnet conventions, including the idealization of the distant beloved; and in *Middlemarch* she makes fun of conventional sonneteers. Still, she also identified with the attempts at sympathetic love she found in the sonnets she loved most, a love that was congruent both with her culture's ideals for women and with her own ideal for the artist, and in *Middlemarch* she called on that identification as well. Yet seeing this ideal as something she could fulfill as a writer helped authorize her to portray women as acting to follow personal desires and to move her readers to sympathize with them.

Much more here than in her earlier novels, Eliot suggests approaches to Shakespeare congruent with those of feminist criticism. She draws on both *As You Like It* and *Othello* for a critique of marriage related to the social construction of gender, and goes beyond both of them, showing varieties of unhappiness in marriage less dramatic than wife murder. While she uses the sonnets especially for their ideal of sympathy, she knows that this ideal can be imposed on women to keep them subordinate, and finally she shows Dorothea seeking her own will and her own Will with some of the frankness that Eliot had long ago found in Shakespeare's heroines. And if the novel, like Shakespeare's comedies, ends with a marriage that subordinates its most interesting female character, it is unlike any of the comedies, but like recent feminist criticism, in the explicit record of protest: "Many who knew her, thought it a pity that so substantive and rare a creature should have been absorbed into the life of another, and be only known in a certain circle as a wife and mother" (822). Even though Eliot cut, after the first edition, her complaint about "modes of education which make a woman's knowledge another name for motley ignorance" (824n), there is much in *Middlemarch* to resonate with the view that Anna Jameson claimed her essays on Shakespeare's women would show, that "the condition of women in society, as at present constituted, is false in itself, and injurious to them,—that.the education of women, as at present conducted, is founded in mistaken principles, and tends to increase fearfully the sum of misery and error in both sexes."[48]

Chapter Six

Daniel Deronda

U. C. KNOEPFLMACHER NOTED in 1961 that "*Daniel Deronda*, Eliot's last work of fiction, is the most consciously Shakespearean of all her novels."[1] Knoepflmacher points to "a deliberate process of imitation on the part of the novelist" and suggests that she incorporates "the playwright and his works into the novel itself as an original means of characterization and differentiation."[2] The Shakespearean allusions in *Daniel Deronda* gain resonance when we can situate them in a context both personal and cultural. Gwendolen's identification with Rosalind looks back to Eliot's own past and allusions to Eliot's in her earlier writing; however, Eliot stresses the contrast between Rosalind's plot in *As You Like It* and Gwendolen's in *Daniel Deronda* and identifies the possibilities of women's experience that do not fit into Shakespeare's comedy. In her characterization of Deronda himself, she emphasizes his wide-ranging sympathy—important both in her culture's image of Shakespeare and in her own aesthetic—and, critiquing the concept in a different way than in *Middlemarch*, relates it to irresolution, important in her culture's image of Hamlet. In its two plots, *Daniel Deronda* may be described as contrasting a realistic rewriting of *As You Like It* with a romantic rewriting of *Hamlet*.[3] In these rewritings, Shakespeare provides materials to use in exploring Victorian ideals of womanhood and womanly qualities, ideals that she partly shared and partly criticized, as well as materials to use in her attempt, as an author, to transcend the limitations her culture associated with her gender. In contrast, although the novel deals with Judaism, it gives very little attention to Shakespeare's treatment of it in *The Merchant of Venice*.

Rosalind, Hamlet, and Shakespeare

By the end of her career, descriptions of the impression she created in person as well as in her novels often resemble the Victorian image of Shakespeare. When Lewes contrasts Shakespeare with Goethe, for example, he writes, "He uttered no moral verdict; he was no Chorus preaching on the text of what he pictured. Hence we cannot gather from his works what were his opinions."[4] Cross's summary at the end of his *Life and Letters* makes a similar point: "And it was this wide sympathy, this understanding of so many points of view, that gained for her the passionate devotion not only of personal friends, but also of literary admirers from the most widely sundered sections of society. . . . This many-sidedness, however, makes it exceedingly difficult to ascertain, either from her books or from the closest personal intimacy, what her exact relation was to any existing religious creed or to any political party."[5]

To the reader of *Daniel Deronda*, this description may recall not only the Victorian image of Shakespeare but also the initial presentation of Daniel himself, and it is significant that his many-sided sympathy has its drawbacks. In his characterization, Eliot treats her ideal of compassion in a self-conscious way. Partly because of the link between aesthetic many-sidedness and inactivity, nineteenth-century critics often identified Shakespeare with Hamlet; Daniel has something of what they saw in both. Indeed, an 1876 reviewer called him "Hamlet without a grievance."[6]

Like Rosalind, Hamlet interested George Eliot throughout her career, but while the greatest concentration of allusions to *As You Like It* in Eliot's correspondence is early, her allusions to *Hamlet,* the second largest group overall, increase as time proceeds. Any cultured Victorian probably knew this play well, but Eliot's interest in it can be related to her particular situation within her culture. I suggest that she often sees *Hamlet* from a woman's viewpoint, in several different ways.

In *The Mill on the Floss,* her narrator turns a cold demythologizing eye on its hero and takes critical note of his attitude toward Ophelia.

"Hamlet, Prince of Denmark, was speculative and irresolute, and we have a great tragedy in consequence. But if his father had lived to a good old age, and his uncle had died an early death, we can conceive Hamlet's having married Ophelia and got through life with a reputation of sanity notwithstanding many soliloquies, and some moody sarcasms towards the fair daughter of Polonius, to say nothing of the frankest incivility to his father-in-law."[7] We have seen the way that the allusions to *Hamlet* in *Felix Holt* also critique Hamlet's words to Ophelia.

In contrast, the narrator of *Middlemarch* refers to Hamlet differently: when Dorothea returns with a "triumphant power of indignation" from the visit in which she sees Rosamond with Ladislaw, and moans, "Oh, all the troubles of all peoples upon the face of the earth," Celia is "uneasy at this Hamlet-like raving" and asks, "Dear me, Dodo, are you going to have a scheme for them?"[8] This association in Celia's mind suggests that Eliot finds in Hamlet the universal sympathy she sees in his creator, a quality congenial to the self-image of an idealistic Victorian woman, if not to the pragmatic Celia.

In Hamlet, Eliot chose a hero whose manhood is often questioned by himself and others. David Leverenz, who writes that Hamlet is, "as Goethe was the first to say, part woman,"[9] has shown how often characters describe him using female imagery: Claudius calls his grief "unmanly" (1.2.94), and Hamlet associates his powerlessness with that of a whore or a drab. According to Bernard Grebanier, starting with Sarah Siddons in 1775, more than fifty women have played Hamlet, many in the nineteenth century. Like Eliot, they were interested in transcending the limits usually set on women, but their particular focus on Hamlet, like hers, I would argue, resulted from seeing him as a figure who also crossed the bounds of gender.[10] Both sides of the dominant critical view—emphasis on his lack of action and on his excess of feeling—might make him easy for women to identify with, in a society where their actions were limited and feelings were heightened for other reasons. Many male critics of the nineteenth century used words such as "sensitivity," with feminine associations, to apply to Hamlet. What is unusual—and foreshadowing Deronda—in the *Middlemarch* passage is the implied association of Hamlet with sympathy—a word or concept harder to find in nineteenth-century descriptions of Hamlet.[11]

Hamlet is the one Shakespearean character for whom Eliot tells us directly a character of hers is named: "A College Breakfast-Party" begins with "Young Hamlet, not the hesitating Dane, / But one named after him."[12] Flanked by characters named for Horatio, Rosencrantz, Guildenstern, and Fortinbras—their parents clearly destined them all for the same college—he is "held inert / 'Twixt fascination of all opposites . . . Having no choice but choice of everything." Speculative and irresolute indeed! He asks a priest:

> I crave direction, Father, how to know
> The sign of that imperative whose right
> To sway my act in face of thronging doubts
> Were an oracular gem in price beyond
> Urim and Thummim lost to Israel.
> That bias of the soul, that conquering die
> Loaded with golden emphasis of Will—
> How find it where resolve, once made, becomes
> The rash exclusion of an opposite
> Which draws the stronger as I turn aloof.[13]

Ruby Redinger comments on the poem: "She herself had known well the Hamlet-road of quest and questioning."[14] It was published in 1874, an incidental project while she was writing, in her last novel, about another character whose "sensibility and reflectiveness had developed into a many-sided sympathy, which threatened to hinder any persistent course of action."[15] This blending of Hamlet characteristics with the Shakespeare characteristic most associated with "female" values is one of the main ways that *Daniel Deronda* shows Eliot reading and revising Shakespeare from a woman's point of view.

The two main characters in *Daniel Deronda* are, in different ways, rewritings of these two Shakespearean figures Eliot found so interesting—Rosalind and Hamlet. The identification of Gwendolen with Rosalind is the most explicit, although, as Knoepflmacher observes, the effect is ironical.[16] It is partly because George Eliot loves the frank passion that she sees in Shakespeare's women (and stressed in her Girardin review, discussed in chapter 3) that she recalls them so emphatically in the creation of a character as far removed from frank passion as Gwendolen. On a festive day in the forest, "It was agreed that they were playing an extemporized 'As you like It': and when a pretty compliment had been turned to Gwendolen about her having the part of Rosalind, she felt the more compelled to be surpassing in liveliness" (135). Gwendolen has Rosalind's charm, commanding personality (except with Grandcourt), and love of role-playing, but like Rosamond she lacks the affection toward others that is one of the most salient characteristics of Rosalind in Eliot's allusions to her. When Gwendolen says to Anna, "You are a dear little coz" (50), she echoes Rosalind's words to Celia and recalls the relationship that Eliot enjoyed evoking in her early letters. But Gwendolen lacks Rosalind's easy sisterly communication and thus seems more isolated.

Victorians who emphasized Rosalind's sympathy, including the actress Helen Faucit, a friend of Eliot, had moved the character "from an eighteenth century hoyden, a comic breeches part, into the sentimental 'womanly woman.' "[17] In one particularly important scene, Rosalind, disguised as a boy, is accosted by Orlando's brother Oliver, who explains that Orlando has saved him from a starved lioness and flourishes a cloth stained with his brother's blood. At this sight Rosalind faints, revealing the depth of the feeling under her disguise. She tries to cover up this emotion, however, by claiming that she was acting: "I pray you," she says to Oliver, "Tell your brother how well I counterfeited" (4.3.165–66). Faucit wrote that here the audience "must be made to feel the tender, loving nature of the woman through the simulated gaiety by which it is veiled."[18] Anna Jameson exclaimed about the "depth of love in her passion for Orlando, . . . half betrayed in that beautiful scene where she faints at the sight of the kerchief stained with his blood."[19] The frequency of such comments makes it likely that many readers might remember it in two contrasting scenes where Gwendolen tries to disguise her feelings.

Early in *Daniel Deronda,* Gwendolen acts in a Shakespearean tableau: she plays Hermione in the statue scene from *The Winter's Tale.* When Paulina calls for music and Herr Klesmer, the musician, plays a chord on the piano, a panel flies open to reveal a dead face, and Gwendolen is terrified. Obviously her terror is not an intended part of the performance, but Herr Klesmer pretends it is: he twice praises it as a "bit of *plastik*" (54, 55). In both scenes, self-possessed characters are momentarily shocked out of their poise. Rosalind's shock comes from her feeling for Orlando, and she has enough aplomb to invent a quick excuse for herself. Gwendolen's shock stems from a more primitive fear of death; she is not resourceful enough to invent an excuse and is so self-deceived that she thinks Herr Klesmer really means the praise of her acting that he offers.

But if Gwendolen's fear is heartfelt, Eliot shows her acting soon afterward. Her uncle Gascoyne tells her about her cousin Rex's fall on a riding expedition from which Gwendolen has returned with great success. Gwendolen's response is: "'Oh, poor fellow! he is not hurt, I hope?' with a correct look of anxiety, such as elated mortals try to superinduce when their pulses are all the while quick with triumph" (68). Gascoyne is carefully watching Gwendolen to determine what she feels about his son; when he explains that Rex has put his shoulder out and is bruised, "Gwendolen, instead of any such symptoms as pallor and silence, had only deepened the compassionateness of her brow and eyes, and said again, 'Oh, poor fellow! it is nothing serious, then?'" As he deliberately emphasizes the incongruity of his description, Gwendolen gives up attempts to look sympathetic and bursts into laughter. Comparison with Rosalind, who can't help fainting when she hears about Orlando's injury, emphasizes Gwendolen's lack of feeling for Rex and by extension for other people in general. As Bonnie Zimmerman has shown, many details place Gwendolen as a type of the "new woman" of the 1860s and 1870s, the "Girl of the Period," whose highest priority, in the critical view of Eliza Lynn Linton, was fun.[20]

Gwendolen's most disastrous act is a further contrast to Rosalind. Rather than choose a husband she loves, as Rosalind does with the frankness Eliot praises in her essay on Girardin, Gwendolen marries Grandcourt. To others, this appears the climax of a romantic courtship: on the day of the forest party, for example, the earl interprets Grandcourt's lateness as if it belonged to a character like Orlando—"a lover so absorbed in thinking of the beloved object as to forget an appointment which would bring him into her actual presence" (134–35). When Gwendolen is asked whether she has met him on a walk, she replies, recalling Orlando's activities in Arden, "No. . . . And we didn't see any carvings on the trees either" (138).

What she has seen shows how much darker the world of *Deronda* is than the world of Shakespeare's comedy, even when both are dealing with marriage. In the play, infidelity is something to be laughed at ("Wilt thou have me?" "Ay, and twenty such," 4.1.11–12), and the emphasis is on cuckoldry—the husband's perspective on a wife's behavior. In the novel, infidelity is male as well as female, results in children, and has more serious consequences for women: Gwendolen meets Lydia Glasher, who has left her husband for Grandcourt and has then been rejected by *him*. In *As You Like It,* realism is making fun of Petrarchan convention; here the inadequacy of literature goes deeper: "Gwendolen's uncontrolled reading, though consisting chiefly in what are called pictures of life, had somehow not prepared her for this encounter with reality" (140).

The inadequacy of Gwendolen's reading is analogous to the inadequacy of the Shakespeare quotations learned by Catherine in *Northanger Abbey,* but Eliot is criticizing Gwendolen more, while Austen's target is mainly cultural uses of Great Passages. As Knoepflmacher has observed, Gwendolen has read Shakespeare without understanding.[21] In the *Winter's Tale* tableau, she changes the staging from Shakespeare's text so that she will be paid the tribute of a kneeling Leontes. "This awakened Hermione is to maintain the remoteness and detachment of the carved figure."[22] The scene interests her because of the opportunity of appearing in a statuesque pose in her Greek dress. Elsewhere she quotes—slightly misquotes—Othello's lines about Desdemona (3.3.92–93) only to make fun of her suitor's lack of expression: "If he had to say, 'Perdition catch my soul, but I do love her,' he would say it in just the same tone as, 'Here endeth the second lesson'" (49). (It is ironic that after this dismissal of Mr. Middleton she marries a man whose emotionless manner is much more ominous.) She often sees life in terms of theater but without understanding the demands of either. "She had never acted—only made a figure in *tableaux vivans* at school; but she felt assured that she could act well," and she wondered "whether she should become an actress like Rachel, since she was more beautiful than that thin Jewess" (48). In calculating her chances for success, she uses arguments that recall Sarah Siddons's description of Lady Macbeth as "fair, feminine, nay perhaps even fragile": "I think a higher voice is more tragic: it is more feminine; and the more feminine a woman is, the more tragic it seems when she does desperate actions" (48).[23] Though these lines hint something of Gwendolen's future in this book, at this point she knows nothing of tragedy or desperation. For her the plays exist mainly as opportunities for actresses to be seen.[24] She knows them as part of what George Eliot calls "the sort of culture which combines Shakespeare and the musical glasses" (*GEL* 5:174; corrected 8:352).

The allusions to *As You Like It* suggest a doubleness in the way Eliot takes a woman's viewpoint on Shakespeare at this time: she enjoys his representation of women who could combine power and love and recalls it to criticize Gwendolen, but she associates Gwendolen's illusions about her power as a wife with Gwendolen's interest in the power of Shakespeare's women, and thus, more explicitly than in *Middlemarch,* she criticizes a reading of the comedies to foster romanticism about marriage as well as illusions about women's power.

Gwendolen has less feeling for others and more ambition than her culture's ideal of woman. Eliot juxtaposes her with Daniel, who has more feeling and apparently less ambition than his culture's idea of man. The narrator makes it explicit that Daniel transcends traditional gender expectations—he is "moved by an affectionateness such as we are apt to call feminine, disposing him to yield in ordinary details, while he had a certain inflexibility of judgment, an independence of opinion, held to be rightfully masculine" (295).

In a different way from the associations of Gwendolen and Rosalind, the *Hamlet* allusions in this novel also show Eliot reading Shakespeare as a woman. Like Hamlet, Gwendolen and Daniel in turn each receive a "ghastly vision" (137) and "a new guest who seemed to come with an enigmatic veiled face, and to carry dimly-conjectured, dreaded revelations" (152). These images can be linked with Brontë's use of preternatural images from *Hamlet* and *Macbeth* to suggest Rochester's mystery. Both Gwendolen's literal visitor, Mrs. Glasher, and Daniel's metaphorical one, the idea of his illegitimacy, carry secret messages connected with another's sexual behavior. For both characters, Eliot is rewriting Hamlet's ghostly visitation, except that the message in *Deronda* is presented as the wrong done to women and children rather than, as in *Hamlet,* the wrong that inspires disgust with women.

Daniel is like the Victorian Hamlet and the Hamlet of "A College Breakfast-Party" because of his "reflective hesitation" (164). He returns to England after studying on the continent "questioning whether it were worth while to take part in the battle of the world" (169). Like Hamlet he has a Polonius-like foil in Sir Hugo. When he asks permission for his continental studies, Sir Hugo says, with both the superficiality and the interest in selfhood in Polonius's famous speech to Laertes: "For God's sake, keep an English cut, and don't become indifferent to bad tobacco! And—my dear boy—it is good to be unselfish and generous; but don't carry that too far. It will not do to give yourself to be melted down for the benefit of the tallow trade; you must know where to find yourself" (168). But unlike Hamlet's "incivility" to Polonius, as *The Mill on the Floss* calls it, Deronda maintains a tolerant affection for his uncle.

Deronda is given an Ophelia as well as a Polonius. He meets his future wife for the first time as she is on the point of drowning herself. The willows in the background recall the setting of Ophelia's drowning as described by Gertrude—a frequent subject for painting and other allusions in the nineteenth century.[25] It is as if Eliot's rewritten Hamlet must reverse the course of the original in dealing with women and so become even more idealized. Shakespeare's Hamlet moves from disgust with his mother—"Frailty, thy name is woman" (1.2.146)—to rejection of Ophelia—"If thou wilt needs marry; marry a fool, for wise men know what monsters you make of them" (3.1.138). Deronda, seeing Mirah's misery, thinks, "Perhaps my mother was like this one" (175), and saves her from drowning.

Deronda is more like Hamlet and like the Shakespeare of the sonnets in his intense involvement with male friendship. At the university he gives up much of his own study time to help his friend Hans Meyrick (whose Holbein associations and classical interests link him to the humanist cult of friendship exemplified also by Erasmus and Thomas More), but he longs for a friend to whom he can confide more about himself, toward whom he feels more of an equality. His friendship with Mordecai, who communicates mystical visions of Zionism, is presented in language echoing the idealizing sonnets, without their tensions or disillusionment. When they are about to have their first conversation, the two have "as intense a consciousness as if they had been two un-declared lovers" (462). With cross-gender imagery like that in the son-nets, including some discussed in the previous chapter, Mordecai has "something of the slowly dying mother's look when her one loved son visits her bedside" (462) and says to Daniel, "It has begun already—the marriage of our souls" (698).[26]

In general, Daniel's Shakespearean associations idealize him. While with Gwendolen we repeatedly find less sympathy than her Shake-spearean prototype, with Daniel we find more. And although he learned about illegitimacy from "having read Shakespeare as well as a great deal of history" (151–52), he is emphatically more compassionate than the Shakespearean characters who presumably contributed to his image of the bastard—he is "the reverse of that type painted for us in Faulcon-bridge and Edmund of Gloster" with their "coarse ambition for per-sonal success" (437). In contrast with Gwendolen, he reads with em-pathy: forgetting "his own existence in that of Robert Bruce" (154), he gives "ardour" to the "imaginary world in his books" (152). There is no hint that he has the moral ambiguity of that accomplished Shake-spearean reader, Jane Austen's Henry Crawford. The narrator repeat-edly attributes to him "many-sided sympathy," with strongly virtuous connotations. This trait does not idealize him in every respect, how-ever; rather than the problem of deception, it causes the higher-level moral problem of his frequently analyzed inaction. Like the revision of Hamlet's disgust with women into Deronda's "interest in the fates of women" (174), this rewriting suggests Eliot's nineteenth-century woman's perspective, but here, as in *Middlemarch,* that perspective is somewhat ambivalent about sympathy, aware of the ways it can be problematic, a point to which I shall return later.[27]

Nevertheless, preeminence in sympathy links Deronda not only to Hamlet but to the Victorian idea of Shakespeare. Eliot calls it "an ac-tivity of imagination on behalf of others" (162) and gives an explicitly Shakespearean reference point for this sympathy: "Grandcourt held that the Jamaican negro was a beastly sort of baptist Caliban; Deronda said he had always felt a little with Caliban, who naturally had his own point of view and could sing a good song" (303–4).[28] Although he is not a poet, the imagery presenting him often compares him to one; the narrator calls his "meditative interest in learning how human miseries are wrought . . . as precocious in him as another sort of genius in the poet who writes a Queen Mab at nineteen" (163).

Reading Shakespeare with Eliot's passion, imagining others' sorrows as she saw her own art as doing, Daniel becomes identified not only with Hamlet but also with Eliot's own public image. Consider, for example, the account of a meeting with Eliot late in life that her childhood friend Mary Sibree Cash wrote to Cross: "It touched me deeply to find how much she had retained of her kind interest in all that concerned me and mine, and I remarked on this to Mr. Lewes. . . . When I added, inquiringly, 'The power lies there?' 'Unquestionably it does,' was his answer; 'she forgets nothing that has ever come within the curl of her eyelash.'"[29] Compare these descriptions of Daniel: "What he felt was a profound sensibility to a cry from the depths of another soul; and accompanying that, the summons to be receptive instead of superciliously prejudging. Receptiveness is a rare and massive power, like fortitude; and this state of mind now gave Deronda's face its utmost expression of calm benignant force" (463); "His eyes . . . were of a dark yet mild intensity, which seemed to express a special interest in every one on whom he fixed them, and might easily help to bring on him those claims which ardently sympathetic people are often creating in the minds of those who need help" (304). At times, Eliot writes of problematic elements in her own sympathy in terms similar to the problematic elements in Daniel's: "my weaknesses all verge towards an excessive tolerance and a tendency to melt off the outlines of things" (*GEL* 5:367).

Critics have found a number of autobiographical elements in Gwendolen's early life. Many of the passages I cite here suggest ways in which Daniel is also a projection of Eliot's own experience. Eliot links them both with Shakespearean figures important to her: the novel's Shakespearean dimension is closely related to its personal dimension because Shakespeare was so much a part of Eliot's personal mythology. Eliot's letters and her narrators' voices speak of maturity as a conversion from self-concern to sympathy. But both self-concern and sympathy, as Eliot imagined them in Gwendolen and Daniel, possess the intense feeling that Eliot associated with Shakespeare. Daniel gently urges to Gwendolen the conversion that Eliot enacted, indeed, self-dramatized, in her own life: "I suppose our keen feeling for ourselves might end in giving us a keen feeling for others, if, when we are suffering acutely, we were to consider that others go through the same sharp experience" (420).[30] But Eliot did not either write or act only out of sympathy, and neither can Daniel. Instead of the universal identification so often credited to Shakespeare at that time, he takes on a very particular Jewish identity.[31] And as part of that identity choice, he marries Mirah, who can join him in struggling for a Jewish nation, and rejects Gwendolen.

The conclusions of both plots in *Daniel Deronda* rewrite literary tradition. Gwendolen's expectations that Daniel will stay in her life as, at least, a mentor, coalesce with novelistic and comic conventions that, like a Mr. Knightley or a Felix Holt, having educated her, he will marry her. But there is no comic ending for Gwendolen. She is left in an openness and uncertainty that recalls something of Deronda's situation near the beginning.[32] Now she is compared to Hamlet more explicitly than he ever was, and with the emphasis on the sympathy felt by her and by Hamlet as coming from self-accusation: "There is a way of looking at our life daily as an escape, and taking the quiet return of morn and evening—still more the star-like out-glowing of some pure fellow-feeling, some generous impulse breaking our inward darkness—as a salvation that reconciles us to hardship. Those who have a self-knowledge prompting such self-accusation as Hamlet's, can understand this habitual feeling of rescue. And it was felt by Gwendolen" (740). Alternatively, she is "a melancholy statue of that Gwendolen whose laughter had once been so ready when others were grave" (717; see also 748), a reversal of the scene of Hermione's statue brought to life, which she enacted earlier. But this too suggests openness rather than closure, especially when she insists, "I am going to live" (751).

A passage in *Clerical Life*, discussed in chapter 3 of this book, declares a character's astronomical ignorance irrelevant to talent for loving, but by the time she wrote *Daniel Deronda* Eliot had become much more ambitious about the scope of her fiction. Reversing her emphasis, she begins chapter 32 with an epigraph that implies that writing about Daniel's love in relation to his intellectual worldview is rewriting the great love stories of history in another way: "In all ages it hath been a favourite text that a potent love hath the nature of an isolated fatality, whereto the mind's opinions and wonted resolves are altogether alien: as, for example, . . . Romeo in his sudden taking for Juliet, wherein any objection he might have held against Ptolemy had made little difference to his discourse under the balcony. Yet all love is not such, even though potent; nay, this passion hath as large scope as any for allying itself with every operation of the soul: so that it shall acknowledge an effect from the imagined light of unproven firmaments, and have its scale set to the grander orbits of what hath been and shall be" (332).

Daniel chooses to commit himself to making a Jewish nation in terms that, as Bonnie Zimmerman has noted, idealize Judaism as the "heart of mankind, . . . the core of affection" (492)—a drastic revision of the associations it has in *The Merchant of Venice*.[33] His final vocation tries to break down the public/domestic dichotomy in a visionary image of public life. Daniel's valuation of Judaism for its transmission of emotion is rather like the valuation that Eliot places on "that exquisite type of gentleness, tenderness, possible maternity suffusing a woman's being with affectionateness, which makes what we mean by the feminine character" (*GEL* 4:468). Thus, in his membership in an oppressed group as well as in his temperament, Daniel's viewpoint is close to what Eliot sees as a woman's, and this is an important part of Eliot's identification with him.

Eliot's "Notes on the Spanish Gypsy and on Tragedy in General" emphasizes the role of hereditary conditions in tragedy, using as main examples Othello and the Virgin Mary, designated because of her heredity for a fate different from "the ordinary lot of womanhood."[34] But that "ordinary lot," or what remains of it even for an atypical woman, is itself a hereditary condition in a different sense.

Eliot herself had dealt with the conflict between the ideal of female domesticity and her interest in accomplishing something in the larger world. Her discovery of herself as a fiction writer coincided with her discovery that her own life had given her subject matter in the lives of women as well as the lives of her former neighbors, whose provinciality had seemed a burden to her. Her attitude toward being a woman eventually came to be, in some respects, rather like Deronda's attitude toward being a Jew: ultimately she gloried in defining herself as "wife" and "mother" and wrote to other women in ways that assumed much more community with them in these roles, as in others, than contrast.[35] Though not as activist as Deronda's, her sense of solidarity involved an interest in social change: Gillian Beer has recently shown her familiarity with the "writing and actions of the women's movement."[36] It is tempting to say that her novels had become the woman's homeland she could create, but she did not want, either literally or metaphorically, a separate land for women. In a letter to her activist friend Mrs. Nassau John Senior, she writes, "On one point I have a strong conviction, and I feel bound to act on it, so far as my retired way of life allows of public action. And that is, that women ought to have the same fund of truth placed within their reach as men have; that their lives (i.e. the lives of men and women) ought to be passed together under the hallowing influence of a common faith as to their duty and its basis" (5:58). Much of *Felix Holt, Middlemarch,* and *Daniel Deronda* shows the effects of women's lack of this same fund of truth.

Though Eliot had early found Shakespeare's female characters models of frank passion, they did not exhaust the plots of women's lives, as her portrayal of Gwendolen emphasizes.[37] To mediate between private and public roles, like many Victorian women, Eliot used the concept of sympathy, as she moved from the interested correspondent and good listener, the translator and anonymous journalist, to the internationally known sage whose novels dealt with events in world history. She also behaved somewhat as Carolyn Heilbrun urges contemporary women to do and reinterpreted male literary figures for her own purposes.[38] The romantic and Victorian Hamlet, with his concern for the world's wrongs and his contemplative nature, was a suggestive model, though imperfect. Identifying with the romantic and Victorian Shakespeare, whose writing was motivated by sympathy, merged these strategies. But could sympathy really mediate between the particularity of Eliot's womanhood and the universality sometimes attributed to Shakespeare? Perhaps Daniel's choice of a *particular* identity (though one considerably romanticized) signals Eliot's awareness of the impossibility of undesirability of *universal* sympathy. Both because she felt that "woman has something *specific* [emphasis mine] to contribute"[39] to art and literature, and because he had written so many years previously, Shakespeare was the kind of model who left her much of her own to say, somewhat as Daniel leaves Gwendolen to find her own work.

Yet in another sense *Daniel Deronda* shows Eliot trying to be more universal than Shakespeare. His treatment of Judaism had seldom disturbed English anti-Semitism and was easily appropriated by it. She, however, wrote Harriet Beecher Stowe that *Deronda* was an effort "to treat Jews with such sympathy and understanding as my nature and knowledge could attain to. Moreover, not only towards the Jews, but towards all oriental peoples with whom we English come in contact, a spirit of arrogance and contemptuous dictatorialness is observable which has become a national disgrace to us. There is nothing I should care more to do, if it were possible, than to rouse the imagination of men and women to a vision of human claims in those races of their fellowmen who most differ from them in customs and beliefs" (*GEL* 6:301–2). As she used the ideal of writing as sympathy to authorize the portrayal of women who did not necessarily show sympathy, she used the ideal of writing as sympathy to authorize the portrayal of Jewish culture in its specificity.[40]

Lewes considered *The Merchant of Venice* a "great tragedy" sometimes mistakenly acted as "a brutal melodrama,"[41] but Eliot made no attempt to rewrite Shylock sympathetically: indeed Lapidoth, Mirah's father, seems a deliberate reversal, even in a negative characterization, for he is a spendthrift and a gambler instead of a miser.[42] Victorians vividly remembered Shylock's grief at Jessica's selling her father's turquoise ring for a monkey: Mirah, unlike Jessica, is loyal to her father and has great attachment to family keepsakes. On the other hand, Gwendolen pawns her father's turquoise so she can gamble and, in the novel's first portrayal of anti-Semitism, thinks "these Jew pawnbrokers were so unscrupulous in taking advantage of Christians unfortunate at play!" (15). Eliot gives the Christian characters of her novel some behavior like that which her society criticized in Jews of the play and gives her Jewish characters some behavior her society admired in the Christians of the play: Mordecai and Daniel speak the language of idealized friendship similar to that used by Antonio and Bassanio and with less possibility of ironic undercutting. The only record in Eliot's journal of her reading *The Merchant of Venice* was in Berlin in 1854, very close to the time she saw Lessing's protolerance play *Nathan der Weise,* about which she wrote, "In England the words which call down applause here would make the pit rise in horror" (*GEL* 2:185).[43] While in extending sympathy to characters who are outsiders because of class and sex Eliot could sometimes draw on allusions to Shakespeare, in extending sympathy to Jews she created many characters whose Jewishness is presented in completely different terms from those his plays give.

In *Daniel Deronda* Eliot was rewriting Shakespeare in several ways. Gwendolen's story ends more sadly than Rosalind's because of Gwendolen's own limitations as well as because of the greater harshness of the world where Eliot places her. Daniel, on the other hand, sometimes seems a Hamlet idealized enough to represent Eliot's own ego ideal. In Gwendolen's plot she both critiques some cultural uses of Shakespeare's women and suggests how to rewrite their stories for her own time; in Daniel's plot she claims both Shakespeare and Hamlet as figures with which she could identify partly because of their possession of qualities that she associated with women. Her interest in women as a distinct and diverse group, sharing many social restrictions, predominates in the realistic mode of Gwendolen's plot; her interest in culturally feminine values predominates in the idealizing mode of Daniel's plot, even in its occasional ambivalence about the diffuseness of his sympathy. Comedy revised toward realism, tragedy revised toward romanticism—this description of the two plots may help to account for the disjunction many readers have felt between them. Yet one of the novel's most powerful moments comes when Daniel confronts the mother who gave him up, and gave up Judaism, to pursue her career. Here the plot transcends the dichotomy between realism and romanticism to confront, for both characters, the limits of sympathy.[44] Ironically, when Alcharisi describes her choice of opera over motherhood, she uses an image suggestive of Coleridge's "myriad-minded" Shakespeare, described in chapter 1:[45] "I was living a myriad lives in one" (584). The sympathy with which an artist creates is here opposed to the sympathy with which a woman cares for a child, although elsewhere, I have been arguing, Eliot often tried to link these qualities.

By associating Daniel's identity and vocation with a particular ethnicity, which when discovered ends his resemblance to Hamlet, the novel interrogates both the ideal of universal sympathy that initially characterized Daniel, and the possibility of applying that ideal to Shakespeare, much as it questions the Rosalind fantasy that contributed to Gwendolen's disastrous marriage. More explicitly than any of Eliot's other novels, *Daniel Deronda* writes back against some popular Victorian uses of Shakespeare, but it is an affectionate critique. The fantasies the novel criticizes are fantasies that Eliot's own letters and essays sometimes indulge.

Eliot was conscious of the fact that the reminder of earlier artists' work could be oppressive. On May 18, 1860, she wrote to Blackwood from Florence, "As for me, I am thrown into a state of humiliating passivity by the sight of the great things done in the far past—it seems as if . . . my own activity were so completely dwarfed by comparison that I should never have courage for more creation of my own" (3:294). Nevertheless, her own imaginative creativity put her knowledge, love, and ambivalence about Shakespeare to work to promote her own writing rather than inhibit it. Nor did her interest in Shakespeare keep her from reading writers closer to her own time and appropriating some of them in her work as well: Ellen Moers has shown her use of such women writers as Jane Austen, Charlotte Brontë, George Sand, and Harriet Beecher Stowe; Gillian Beer has added Geraldine Jewsbury and Fredrika Bremer.[46]

Of course, none of Eliot's works has as its strongest effect promoting a new way of seeing Shakespeare as an end in itself; none of them is as unified by appropriation as, for example, Jean Rhys's *Wide Sargasso Sea* is unified by its rewriting of *Jane Eyre*. Eliot's novels create their own imaginative worlds; nevertheless most of them place themselves explicitly in a system of literary references. Her allusions to Shakespeare, along with those of many other Victorian writers, helped to maintain his importance in the English literary tradition, but she also contributed to shaping what his meanings would be for her own time. While she was not a typical Victorian woman, she negotiated with her culture's ideas both about gender and about Shakespeare, in her interest in female characters, in male characters' attitudes to them, and in sympathy. This description omits many aspects of her novels. But it should suggest something of how Eliot reimagined a literary tradition that she could claim as her own.

Eliot and Late Twentieth-Century Feminist Criticism

Much twentieth-century feminist Shakespeare criticism also tries to claim a literary tradition rather than to analyze the terms of women's exclusion from it.[47] As I have discussed Eliot's appropriation of Shakespeare, I have of course made my own appropriation of Eliot, but I have also discovered ways in which her approach to Shakespeare differs greatly from my own or from that of contemporary feminist criticism in general. Eliot was concerned about gender, but the terms in which she wrote about it differ in many respects from ours. The most obvious contrast is, of course, between fiction and professionalized literary criticism—and accordingly the closest and least ambiguous convergences are between Eliot's nonfictional writings and feminist criticism published in the early 1980s or before, especially some of the exploratory work later described as liberal feminist criticism.

One early use of Shakespeare and Eliot together in criticism, so remarkable that it must be mentioned here, is that of Anna Julia Cooper in *A Voice from the South.*[48] Cooper, an educator who has some claim to be the first black American feminist or womanist critic, uses both Shakespeare and George Eliot (paraphrasing a sentence in chapter 50 of *Adam Bede*) as allies against racism. Protesting against a racially biased exclusion from an art school, she writes, " 'Tis only sympathy, another name for love,—that one poor word which, as George Eliot says, 'expresses so much of human insight'—that can interpret either man or matter. It was Shakespeare's own all-embracing sympathy, that infinite receptivity of his, and native, all-comprehending appreciation, which proved a key to unlock and open every soul that came within his radius."[49] Cooper begins the first half of her book of social and literary criticism, dealing more with gender, with an epigraph from Eliot's poem "How Lisa Loved the King," and she begins the second part of the book, dealing more with race, with an epigraph from *Felix Holt*—

the sentence beginning "The greatest question in the world is how to give every man a man's share in what goes on in life."

Though more recent feminist Shakespeare critics use Eliot, when they do, much differently from Cooper, Eliot's writings on Shakespeare in the *Leader,* in her journals, and in her early letters, discussed in chapter 3, often foreshadow late twentieth-century feminist criticism. Her comments on the assertiveness of Shakespeare's women in love fit very easily with the approach to Shakespeare in Juliet Dusinberre's *Shakespeare and the Nature of Women,* or my own *Love's Argument;* indeed, both of us quote her.[50] In her continued fascination with *As You Like It,* she resembles feminist critics of several different schools.[51] Her appropriation of the friendship of Rosalind and Celia hints at points developed in Carole McKewin's "Counsels of Gall and Grace: Intimate Conversations between Women in Shakespeare's Plays" and in the discussions of female bonds in Carol Thomas Neely's *Broken Nuptials in Shakespeare's Plays.*[52] Her criticism of the treatment of Silvia in *Two Gentlemen of Verona* could come from almost any feminist today.

In contrast, Eliot's interest in Hamlet and in the *Sonnets,* and her favorable treatment of Coriolanus, discussed in chapter 4, have few companions among late twentieth-century feminist critics. When considering *Hamlet,* they have often turned attention to Ophelia or to Gertrude;[53] when discussing its hero, or Coriolanus, their perspective has been much more explicitly critical than Eliot's. Most feminist critics have paid little attention to the *Sonnets.*[54] Eliot is more apt to see their language, and aspects of Hamlet's situation, as appropriable by women; judging from her use of epigraphs from *Coriolanus* in *Felix Holt,* she is more interested in maintaining the nobility of the tragic hero. In her interest in combining comic and tragic perspectives in the same novel, often juxtaposing a woman recalling a Shakespearean comic heroine with a man recalling a Shakespearean tragic hero, her rewritings could be compared to Linda Bamber's *Comic Women, Tragic Men,* which continually meditates on the relation between these genres.[55]

On the other hand, Eliot's novels, as opposed to her essays, letters, and journals, are often ambiguous about what judgment of a Shakespearean figure they imply. Modern feminist readers disagree about how much *Felix Holt* tries to idealize its hero; many of the points of characterization that could be seen as either idealized or criticized are resemblances to Hamlet. When Eliot's last fictional Hamlet, Deronda, lacks the suspicion of women manifested by his original and also by Felix, perhaps this indicates that she does read this aspect of Shakespeare's Hamlet critically.[56]

A similar ambiguity arises with regard to Eliot's treatment of *As You Like It* in *Daniel Deronda*. While Eliot's earlier interest in Rosalind would seem to group her with critics who take an affirmative view of this play, or with cultural materialists such as Catherine Belsey and Jean Howard who find liberating moments in it, does Gwendolen's disastrous marriage, anticipated by comparisons with *As You Like It,* mean that by the time of writing this novel she, like Clara Claiborne Park and Peter Erickson, read *As You Like It* thinking sadly of its end as a loss of female power? If, as I have suggested earlier, her reading of *As You Like It* here is ambivalent, Eliot anticipates several different strands of feminist critics in the way she uses it.

What of the relation to feminist critics today of Eliot's image of Shakespeare himself, her association of him with sympathy? Current Anglo-American feminist Shakespeare criticism cannot use this image unproblematically. Having earlier found Keats's view of Shakespeare's "negative capability" attractive for some of the same reasons I see it as attractive to nineteenth-century women novelists, when I wrote my own book on Shakespeare I tried to qualify this view in my conclusion, and wrote of his plays as giving an *illusion* [emphasis added] of presenting all sides of human relationships."[57] Even Germaine Greer, whose *Past Masters* volume on Shakespeare emphasizes his contribution to English tolerance and pluralism, and who speaks of his "myriad-mindedness" in a section called "Negative Capability," says, "Hazlitt goes too far when he claims that Shakespeare could follow every human faculty and feeling 'by anticipation, intuitively, into all their conceivable ramifications.'"[58] And for the many feminist critics who have written about how the plays' perspectives can be located with regard to gender, class, color, and colonialism, there would be no danger that their image of Shakespeare could be confused with Hazlitt's in this respect.[59]

Sympathy itself, as either an aesthetic or an ethical ideal, has also been questioned by many feminists though not by all.

Yet an image of Shakespeare very similar to the romantic one appears in a recently translated essay by the French theorist Hélène Cixous: "There have been poets who let something different from tradition get through at any price—men able to love love; therefore, to love others, to want them; men able to think the woman who would resist destruction and constitute herself as a superb, equal, 'impossible' subject, hence intolerable in the real social context. . . . There was that being-of-a-thousand-beings called Shakespeare."[60] And although one could argue that Cixous is freer to appropriate Shakespeare than Anglo-American feminist critics because he does not belong to her national canon, and she can draw on long-standing French associations of Shakespeare with liberty, this explanation does not hold for the one astounding recent appropriation of Shakespeare discussed in chapter 5. It is partly because Shakespeare *does* belong to her national canon that Maya Angelou, thinking of "When in disgrace with fortune and men's eyes," says, "Of course he wrote it for me. . . . I *know* that William Shakespeare was a black woman."[61]

The best analogues to Eliot's uses of Shakespeare, however, are those in the work of other English and American women novelists. The next chapter will show that several, in the twentieth century, have been much closer to Eliot than to contemporary feminist critics in their interest in Hamlet and in the sympathetic Shakespeare, though for others Eliot may have replaced Shakespeare. Then the last chapter will turn to more recent novels that engage with Shakespeare in a more global, interracial, and experimental context.

Chapter Seven

Uses of Shakespeare
by Twentieth-Century
Women Novelists

THE MOST IMPORTANT KINDS of novelistic engagements with Shakespeare I found among nineteenth-century women can be divided into three: first, using his cultural association with sympathy, second, rewriting his characters and plots with significant differences, and, third, developing characters' cultural and political location in part through their attitude toward Shakespeare. Since the nineteenth century, women novelists have continued to engage with Shakespeare, but their modes of engagement are changing. The association of Shakespeare with sympathy persisted among some Anglo-American women novelists through the midcentury and was emphatically developed by Iris Murdoch in 1959, but is much less frequently invoked by more recent women writers. Some of them still consider the sympathetic imagination as important for art, but they have substituted George Eliot for Shakespeare as their model; others, like Angela Carter, have broken with the aesthetic of sympathy.

In contrast, the second kind of use continues. Women novelists are still rewriting Shakespeare's plots, but now, even more clearly than Eliot, they often emphasize those plots' inadequacies as cultural myths about women. The third use, often combined with the second, becomes especially important in novels that include self-conscious exploration of

Shakespeare appropriations as examples of cultural hybridity. Several very recent such novels will be discussed in chapter 8; here I will focus, rather, on novels associated with modernism and the second wave of feminism, which engage with Shakespeare as part of a continuous, if argumentative, tradition in which George Eliot forms a bridge.

The novelists from whom I choose my examples in these two chapters include Virginia Woolf, Iris Murdoch, Margaret Drabble, and Angela Carter, from England; Margaret Atwood, from Canada; Willa Cather, Gloria Naylor, and Jane Smiley, from the United States, and Nadine Gordimer, from South Africa. I am not claiming that this group is representative of twentieth-century women novelists in involvement with Shakespeare: I have chosen them because they are among the ones *most* interested in revisioning his works and his image.[1] But I will not discuss their rewritings in as much detail as I have Eliot's. With the exception of Woolf's, their novels are less engaged with his works and his image, and two books already in print or forthcoming deal with Woolf's uses of Shakespeare in detail.[2] Rather, I present these chapters as a kind of extended epilogue to consider nineteenth-century women novelists' ways of using Shakespeare as they have continued and as they have changed.

These novelists by no means belong to a single school. My survey should dismiss the notion that an author's engagement with Shakespeare inevitably marks her as politically and aesthetically conservative and unconcerned with women's issues. Some novelists, like Murdoch, link themselves with Shakespeare by way of nineteenth-century novel theory and write a character-centered novelistic style drawing in part on nineteenth-century models; others, like Woolf, invoke a modernist Shakespeare and write more experimentally. Some, like Carter, play on various associations between Shakespeare and gender-crossing, especially recalling the boy actors in the original productions and the disguised heroines of the comedies; others, like Atwood, frequently remember Shakespeare's tragedies and give them different endings. Some use Shakespeare primarily in exploration of male psychology, assume many masculine personae, and seem to be outside feminism's sphere of influence; others refer most to his portrayal of women or invoke his male characters to give them explicit criticism from a feminist point of view. Still others combine several of these apparent opposites or, like Drabble, move from one side to the other at various stages of their career.

Cather, Woolf, and Murdoch

In this chapter I will discuss two groups of women novelists and contrast their attitudes to Shakespeare. The aesthetic theory of the earliest writers to be discussed, Cather, Woolf, and Murdoch, contributes to and draws on literary modernism. Many modernists were particularly interested in the image of the writer as invisible, detached from personality, in a way that could easily be linked with the Shakespeare of Hazlitt and Keats discussed in chapter 1—the "camelion poet" who was "every thing and nothing."[3] Cather, Woolf, and Murdoch all, at some point, imagine the ideal writer as having sacrificed personal bias, but they are more apt than most male modernists to use words like "sympathy" and "love" with regard to the writer's, and Shakespeare's, attitudes.

For closely related reasons, they praise George Eliot much more than do most male modernists. Cather, even when dubious about many women writers, praises Eliot for being able to "lay all her own traditions aside and at will confine herself to those simple, elementary emotions and needs that exist beneath the blouse of a laborer, as well as under the gown of a scholar."[4] She remained interested in Eliot later in her life; her emphasis on the landscape of her childhood in fiction may be compared to Eliot's, as her Rosamond in *The Professor's House* may be compared to Rosamond Vincy and her use in *My Ántonia* of a male narrator coded as androgynous may be compared, especially, to the narrator of Eliot's early works.[5] Murdoch attributes to Eliot a "godlike capacity for so respecting and loving her characters as to make them exist as free and separate beings."[6] Woolf, though writing novels stylistically much more different from Eliot's than were Cather's or Murdoch's, praised her, as many have, for her sympathy for her characters but also in more distinctive terms for plucking "the strange bright fruits of art and knowledge" while not renouncing "her own inheritance—the difference of view."[7] As Alison Booth has shown in *Greatness Engendered: George Eliot and Virginia Woolf,* "George Eliot seemed to define the broadly 'human' role Virginia Woolf adopted for herself."[8]

But while Eliot was important for each of these three writers, especially for Woolf, their works and their biographies include many more references to Shakespeare.[9] Often, as with Cather's androgynous male narrator, the same element in their novels can be seen in relation to both predecessors, with Eliot serving, somewhat as Brontë and Austen did for her, as a kind of model of how a woman can use Shakespeare. The similarity of attitudes toward Shakespeare of these very different women, and their echoes of nineteenth-century concerns, show how attention to literary periodicity and to literary schools needs to be supplemented with an emphasis on gender.

Cather, Woolf, and Murdoch maintain the image of the sympathetic Shakespeare and generally rewrite him in modes of tribute more than of contestation. Willa Cather, whose allusions extend the gender and class of those characters given tragic dignity but provide no other marked revision of the tragic plot, is chronologically the earliest of these writers and also the most bardolatrous. In 1894 she wrote, "Perhaps some day the Anglo-Saxon races will realize what Shakespeare did for them, how he dignified their language, exalted their literature and letters above that of all people, and gave them their place among the nations of the earth."[10] Such praise is very much in the tradition of Elizabeth Montagu's and Caroline Helstone's defense of their English Shakespeare against French criticism, with modifications for Cather's own nationality. While exalting Shakespeare, her image of him was quite malleable: "One always fancies if he had been born just a few centuries later he would have been an American."[11]

But Shakespeare did not simply mean Anglo-American racialism or American nationalism to Cather.[12] She was very much like Elizabeth Montagu and Aphra Behn (and the later Sylvia Townsend Warner) in emphasizing that Shakespeare was an actor and in celebrating his accomplishment as a critique of the educational establishment: "that is the great and crowning glory of the stage, its one weapon against the jeers of pedantry, its one high and holy tradition, its justification before the eyes of God, that William Shakespeare was an actor. . . . if Shakespeare

should come to Lincoln I do not think he would be found among those
occupying a chair in any of the universities."[13] And also like Montagu
(and Brontë and Eliot), she saw him as exemplifying the writer's power
of sympathy. In her 1891 essay "Shakespeare and Hamlet," she wrote
that the "great secret of Shakespeare's power was supreme love, rather
than supreme intellect," after speculating that he "read the legend and
felt sorry for the young prince, and as an expression of his sympathy
wrote about him."[14]

Sharon O'Brien, linking Cather's Shakespeare to Keats's and to
Woolf's, notes that such sympathy "corresponds to the selflessness and
empathy traditionally associated with women," an association Cather
makes in her 1895 praise of Sappho and Christina Rossetti for their use
of women's "power of loving."[15] In the section of "Shakespeare and
Hamlet" that moves from Shakespeare to the artist in general, Cather
twice uses metaphors of motherhood for writing: she compares great
artists to "the Doric women who bore the sons of the gods" and attributes environmental influence on the artist to the "law of maternal
impression . . . in the mental as well as in the physical world."[16] In
O'Brien's view, for the young Cather the association of art with sympathy conflicted with an alternative image of art as associated with
virility, exemplified by Kipling, but the model associated with Shakespeare "was closer to Cather's own experience as woman and writer
and contributed more to her reconciliation of identity and vocation."[17]

To qualify O'Brien's views, it is worth noting that Cather's early
writings did not, in general, praise women writers: her 1895 essay contrasts Sappho and Rossetti to other women. In Shakespeare (and in
George Eliot) she found a model who seemed to cross conventional
gender categories as, arguably, she felt she did. In the light of the
interest in Rosalind evident among many women writers, it may be
significant that Cather, who had often worn masculine clothes, chose
"As You Like It" as the title of her newspaper column. Her interest in
Hamlet can also be located along with that of Eliot and the nineteenth-
century actresses discussed in the previous chapter. As Eliot compares
Maggie, Dorothea, and Gwendolen to Hamlet, Cather's essay suggests
his gender-crossing potential by comparing him to Cassandra, given
both prophecy and madness by Apollo.[18]

In a much later novel, Cather directly appropriates the words and plots of Shakespearean men for a female character, old Myra Henshaw. Myra is sick, and unhappy in her marriage, but when taken for an outing by the sea, she eases from her usual bitterness and says, "It's like the cliff in *Lear,* Gloucester's cliff, so it is! Can't we stay here? . . . I'd love to see this place at dawn. . . . That is always such a forgiving time."[19] She consoles herself in her increasing sickness by repeating passages from Shakespeare by heart, "the long declamations from *Richard II* or *King John.* As I passed her door I would hear her murmuring at the very bottom of her rich Irish voice: "Old John of Gaunt, time-honoured Lan-cas-ter" (99). When her illness gets worse, she goes to that cliff at morning to die.

These allusions signify both Myra's ability to find consolation in art and in tradition (the Catholic church of her childhood and the uncle against whom she had rebelled in his lifetime also are important to her at the end) and the novel's rewriting of a Shakespearean tragic plot.[20] Like Lear, Myra can, at one moment, speak of needing forgiveness, and at another moment, rage at those surrounding her; poignantly, she rages most at the husband she married against her uncle's wishes, so that the story also becomes a demystification of *Romeo and Juliet,* a play whose imagery Myra echoes when she says, "People can be lovers and enemies at the same time" (104). Myra has some characteristics often attributed to Lady Macbeth, but she also has articulate awareness of the kind Lady Macbeth is never allowed to voice, except in the confused words of her sleepwalking scene. "I was always a grasping, worldly woman; I was never satisfied. . . . Perhaps I can't forgive him for the harm I did him" (104-5). *My Mortal Enemy* gives the tragic focus on consciousness of error to a female character in a way that Shakespeare never does. Sarah Bernhardt's Hamlet, discussed in the novel, and Eliot's claim of tragic dignity for Maggie Tulliver, are parallel endeavors. Yet as Myra's return to Shakespearean lines invoking the past ("Old John of Gaunt") suggests, this novel emphasizes the integration of a woman into tradition, rather than turning that tradition in another direction.

Virginia Woolf does both. Writing later than Cather and much closer to the women's movement of her society, she developed further an image of writing as imaginative identification. In her diary, she wrote, "I think writing, my writing, is a species of mediumship; I become the person."[21] Other modernists used similar images, but for Woolf, as Maria DiBattista has noted, this view of writing has especially strong links with Keats's discussions of negative capability, intimately connected with his reading of Shakespeare.[22] In *A Room of One's Own* Woolf explicitly saw Shakespeare as a superior writer because of his selflessness: "his grudges and spites and antipathies are hidden from us."[23] Even when, in 1918, she mused about the "majestic" *Paradise Lost,* she noted that it contained "nothing like Lady Macbeth's terror or Hamlet's cry, no pity or sympathy or intuition."[24] Although Woolf saw selfless writing as the ideal for both male and female and envisioned it as involving a transcendence of the writer's biographical specificity, including gender, nevertheless this approach to writing, as to Shakespeare, can be seen as a transformation of her culture's construction of women and its personal impact on her. She described the then dominant image of woman as "The Angel in the House" and described her as "intensely sympathetic. . . . She was utterly unselfish. . . . She was so constituted that she never had a mind or a wish of her own, but preferred to sympathize always with the minds and wishes of others."[25] Woolf rejected this ideal for herself—indeed, said that to write, women needed to kill the Angel in the House—but also maintained it, transformed, in her view of writing as becoming a medium. Phyllis Rose writes, "One of her triumphs as a novelist is that she made this tenuousness of self the basis of her artistic vision and of new literary modes."[26] In this transformation she behaved somewhat like Eliot and the other nineteenth-century women writers who insisted that women's sympathy could be valuable to the society outside the household, but as a modernist Woolf's approach is different.[27] As she imagines killing the Angel in the House, she also erases from her novels the directing voice of the omniscient, understanding narrator. For Woolf, the imagery of selflessness becomes more literal as the idea of identifying with others becomes even more dominant.

Like Eliot, Woolf was fascinated with many of Shakespeare's female characters; when she argued that women have had a more important place in literature than in history, she began with Cleopatra, Lady Macbeth, and Rosalind.[28] Her feminist consciousness, however, which was greater than Eliot's or Cather's because of both historical location— young adulthood close to a successful suffrage movement—and personality, saw problems in his portrayal of women. In 1920 she felt a lack of reality in Lady Macbeth, Cordelia, and Ophelia;[29] in *A Room of One's Own* she commented that Shakespeare's women were shown mainly in relation to men and wondered about the possibility of friendship between Cleopatra and Octavia.[30] Her many literary uses of Shakespeare clearly involve tribute, but they also more often involve feminist rewriting than do Cather's appropriations or even most of Eliot's.

For example, Woolf's second novel, *Night and Day* (1919), playfully revises the treatment of women in *As You Like It*. Like Shakespeare's comedy, it deals with confused courtships among young friends and focuses on a strong, unconventional, and charming young woman. Katherine Hilberry's fiancé, William Rodney, says of her, "And why should she read Shakespeare, since she *is* Shakespeare—Rosalind, you know," and her mother makes the same comparison.[31] Like Rosalind, Katherine criticizes a man's fantasies about her: "You come and see me among flowers and pictures, and think me mysterious, romantic, and all the rest of it. Being yourself very inexperienced and very emotional, you go home and invent a story about me, and now you can't separate me from the poem you've imagined me to be. You call that, I suppose, being in love; as a matter of fact it's being in delusion" (344). This could be a paraphrase of some of Rosalind's speeches, in her Ganymede disguise, such as "Maids are May when they are maids, but the sky changes when they are wives" (4.1.141–42).

George Eliot's Gwendolen points up some of the irony in the comparisons between her and Rosalind when she marries Grandcourt without love and then finds that she does not have the power she expected marriage to bring her; unlike Gwendolen, Katherine refuses to marry someone she is not in love with. More like several of the Austen and Brontë heroines discussed earlier, for a long time she is also uncertain of her feelings for Ralph, the man she finally does marry. What helps to clinch the final double engagement is the behavior of Katherine's mother, the novel's Shakespeare fanatic, who gives the lovers privacy when she goes to Stratford to visit Shakespeare's grave. Like the later

Mrs. Ramsay, she always wants to promote love and marriage, but she also always wants to promote discussion of Shakespeare. Sometimes these goals seem identified, suggesting the constraints of the comic plot, as when on her return from Shakespeare's tomb her words sing "of great poets and the unchanged spirit of noble loving which they had taught."[32]

Although it makes fun of social conventions about appropriate behavior for single women, *Night and Day* lacks the probing analysis of women's situation that *Daniel Deronda* provides. The novels may share a joke about the familiarity of the Rosalind comparison, but the implications are different. It is ironic that jealous and conventional William praises Katherine by identifying her with a female character whose behavior he wouldn't like at all in real life, but Katherine escapes from him with relative ease into a marriage that promises a reasonable amount of happiness. In contrast, Gwendolen's marriage to Grandcourt is a devastating comment on the illusions of power that her identification with Rosalind suggested. On the other hand, in Mary Datchet *Night and Day* gives a more positive picture of a woman who remains single than either *Daniel Deronda* or *As You Like It,* suggesting some of the possibilities for the "new woman" of Woolf's day. Furthermore, the friendship between Katherine and Mary develops with more intensity than any friendship between women in *Deronda*—maybe even more than the relationship between Rosalind and Celia, which so interested George Eliot. On balance, *Night and Day* is both a tribute to Shakespearean comedy and a gently feminist rewriting of it, emphasizing both costs and alternatives for the "compulsory heterosexuality," in Adrienne Rich's term, of the comic ending.[33]

In Woolf's later novel *Orlando* (1928), the title character also pays tribute to Shakespeare, his/her model as a writer, and the very name of Orlando, as well as the novel's play with gender, pays tribute to *As You Like It.* But this novel, in which Orlando literally changes from male to female, leaps well beyond that play's comic plot. It develops more explicitly the critiques of gender roles suggested by some feminist readings of Rosalind's competence in disguise: "Her sex changed far more frequently than those who have worn only one set of clothing can conceive; nor can there be any doubt that she reaped a twofold harvest by this device; the pleasures of life were increased and its experiences multiplied."[34] Furthermore, *Orlando* takes its story past marriage and, as part of its continued allusion to the life of Woolf's friend Vita Sackville-West, refuses an ending that gives up the heroine's multiplicity or engages her in even a ritual of subordination: "She was married, true; but if one's husband was always sailing round Cape Horn, was it marriage? If one liked him, was it marriage? If one liked other people, was it marriage? And finally, if one still wished, more than anything in the whole world, to write poetry, was it marriage?"[35] *Orlando* appropriates the gender-crossing in *As You Like It* into a daring feminist rewriting of the Shakespearean comic plot, highly subversive of conventional laws about sexuality. Perhaps analogously, while showing Orlando's idealization of Shakespeare it pictures him as "a rather fat, rather shabby man" (14) and links him with nameless artists; thinking of obscurity, Orlando muses, "Shakespeare must have written like that, and the church builders built like that, anonymously, needing no thanking or naming" (65). Woolf maintains a Shakespeare myth but uses it, here and elsewhere, to empower rather than disempower less canonical writers.

In 1959, Iris Murdoch articulated an aesthetic theory taking the sympathetic Shakespeare as a model in a way that resembles Eliot's, Cather's, and Woolf's, though with a more dogmatic tone. "Let us start by saying that Shakespeare is the greatest of all artists."[36] What she means by his greatness is that "the pages of Shakespeare abound in free and eccentric personalities whose reality Shakespeare has apprehended and displayed as something quite separate from himself."[37] He is her best example of the artist as "the lover who, nothing himself, lets other things be through him. And that also, I am sure, is what is meant by 'negative capability.'"[38] For Murdoch, even more explicitly than for Cather or Woolf, the essence of art is love, though she defines it in more intellectual terms. "Love is the perception of individuals. Love is the extremely difficult realisation that something other than oneself is real."[39] Thus she deals with the ambiguity about whether the writer's sympathy should be seen as emotional or detached, to which I referred in chapter 1, by using the term "love," usually even more associated with emotions than the term "sympathy," but linking it with the mental effort of seeing reality instead of fantasy, an effort with which George Eliot also concerned herself in her aesthetic theory.

Murdoch, like Cather, both envisions the generic artist as male and associates him with a quality she sees in women: "The artist is indeed the analogue of the good man, and in a special sense he *is* the good man."[40] "Goodness appears to be both rare and hard to picture. It is perhaps most convincingly met with in simple people—inarticulate, unselfish mothers of large families."[41] Although, like Woolf, she praises Shakespeare for exemplifying the selflessness of the ideal artist, unlike Woolf she sees his writing as occasionally showing a personal obsession: "Even *Hamlet* looks second rate compared with *Lear*."[42] On the other hand, unlike Woolf she never explicitly criticizes his presentation of women.

Murdoch has written a number of novels that transfer Shakespearean plot patterns into contemporary settings without making any clear criticism of, for example, the limitations they set on women. It is easy to read these structures as the correlative of the celebration of Shakespeare in her essays on esthetics. Nevertheless, some of her more recent novels suggest feminist critiques of Shakespearean plotting or perhaps of the masculinist elements in traditions of reading Shakespeare. For example, her 1973 novel *The Black Prince* critiques a male egotist's use of *Hamlet*. Bradley Pearson is fascinated by the play and, in a more direct version of Cather's language, says in a tutorial, "it is about someone Shakespeare was in love with."[43] His own self-description echoes a dominant line of Hamlet criticism (and at points the views of his partial namesake, A. C. Bradley)—"I was a bad artist because I was a coward. . . . the grandiose thinker . . . had to coexist in me with a timid conscientious person full of sensitive moral scruples and conventional fears" (116). The student in the tutorial is a much younger woman named Julian, who reveals during its course that she once played Hamlet; this culminating detail moves Pearson to fall in love with her. His fantasies about Shakespeare's autobiographical writing are versions of his own autobiography as well, and his love for Julian is the love of one version of Hamlet for another.[44] Pearson sees his feelings for her expressed in Sonnet 22, the sonnet of tender nurturing concern and identificatory imagery that George Eliot found exquisite, as discussed in chapter 5 ("All that beauty that doth cover thee / Is but the seemly raiment of my heart"). But his attitude to Julian is not merely narcissistic but cruel as well; seeing her in a Hamlet costume moves him to a brutal sexual assault.[45] Claiming to be timid and conscientious, he is actually quite violent toward women—an accusation that has been made against Shakespeare's Hamlet as well.

Murdoch's Hamlet figure, who abuses his student and thinks with disgust of every other woman in the novel, is the opposite of Eliot's sympathetic Daniel Deronda. Pearson's cruelty is so clear that this cannot be a novel of uncritical male identification; rather, as Deborah Johnson has suggested, the male narration is an Irigarayan "acting out or role playing within the text which allows the woman writer the better to know and hence to expose what it is she mimics."[46] Eliot, I have argued, writes as a woman in identifying with a "feminine" man; here Murdoch writes as a woman in making bitter fun of how even a man with many qualities considered "feminine" still has a self-centeredness and even a contempt for women often considered "masculine." Johnson makes an apposite comparison with the way Rosalind and Portia mock male pretense in contemplating their own male disguise.[47]

Murdoch associates male egoists with Shakespearean figures in a number of other novels; for example, in *The Sea, the Sea* the retired director Charles Arrowby is easily comparable to Prospero. Charles's behavior to women, like that of Bradley Pearson, is full of cruelty obvious to most readers at the same time that he believes he is full of love. The allusions to Shakespeare in these novels easily fit with feminist critiques of characters such as Hamlet, Prospero, and Lear, and it can also be seen as a feminist critique that women survive and speak at the end in *The Black Prince,* as they do not in *Hamlet.* But what Murdoch's novels most consistently present is not a feminist critique but a critique of egotism, as we can see by turning to a later, more female-centered work.

In *Nuns and Soldiers* a character named Gertrude marries quickly and surprisingly after her husband's death, "with mirth in funeral and dirge in marriage," as the novel quotes Claudius's description of his marriage to his Gertrude.[48] Murdoch seems to be rewriting Shakespeare from a female perspective in her focus on the experience of the bereaved woman, who in the original play is seen only from her son's point of view.[49] Her Gertrude clearly has greater freedom than Shakespeare's original. The novel makes a pointed refusal of tragedy as it shows Gertrude's choice of ordinary human happiness (with a much younger, much poorer husband). But as the novel then shows the subtle struggle between Gertrude and her friend Anne for the love of their Polish exile friend, always called "the Count," it raises questions about *women's* egotism. *Nuns and Soldiers* interrogates 1960s–1970s feminist attitudes, mocking some minor characters and suggesting ambivalent judgments about major ones. Since the refusal of tragedy occurs quite early, and then the characters have other problems to deal with, one could see this novel as responding not only to Shakespeare but also to 1960s–1970s feminist novels that refuse tragedy, such as those of Drabble, which I shall discuss next.

Drabble and Atwood

British and North American women novelists who came of age as writers in the 1960s and afterward are much more apt than Cather, Woolf, or Murdoch to write novels that explicitly rewrite Shakespeare's plays to suggest different plots for women, and they less often, if ever, invoke the image of Shakespeare as sympathetic when discussing their aesthetic theory. Among these more recent novelists, Margaret Drabble and Margaret Atwood, however, hold views of the relation between sympathy and literature that are similar to those of Woolf and Murdoch—with some significant contrasts—but take George Eliot rather than Shakespeare as their model.

Drabble and Atwood have developed their careers as novelists in a time much marked by an active feminist movement. From the late 1960s on, as Gayle Greene has shown, many women have written novels which very explicitly critique the plots of past literature. In her book *Changing the Story: Feminist Fiction and the Tradition,* describing the interaction between fiction, feminist criticism, and feminist politics, Greene identifies here "a new genre, feminist metafiction," in which "the protagonist looks to the literary tradition for answers about the present, . . . and seeks 'freedom' from the plots of the past."[50]

One of Drabble's novels, *The Waterfall,* centers on a character who takes this approach to Shakespeare. This novel also, and more obviously, signals its rewriting of *The Mill on the Floss* and *Jane Eyre* by the narrator's frequent comparison of her own situation to Maggie's and Jane's. Indeed, the fact that these comparisons are more obvious than the comparisons to Shakespearean tragedy is a sign that female predecessors have greater importance for Drabble than does Shakespeare. But as we have seen, Eliot and Brontë in those novels were themselves rewriting Shakespearean tragedy, and there are places where Drabble shows that she is doing the same. Jane (her character's significant name, echoing Jane Eyre) criticizes her involvement in tragic myth, first with her husband and then with her lover, James. She remembers her first meeting with her husband and says, "I blame Shakespeare for that farcical moment in Romeo and Juliet where he sees her at the dance, from afar off, and says, I'll have her, because she is the one that will kill me."[51] To emphasize how close the novel will come to tragedy, Drabble makes Jane say, "I could die now, quite happily" (183), a paraphrase of Othello's "If it were now to die, / 'Twere now to be most happy" (2.1.187–88), also spoken at a precarious meeting of lovers. (These Shakespearean lines were appropriated without any change by Virginia Woolf when Mrs. Dalloway identifies them with the way she felt, when young, about being with her friend Sally.[52]) Then, even more literarily, James quotes Hamlet, "The readiness is all" (5.2.220). When they have an automobile accident, soon after, Jane thinks, "It would have been so much simpler if he had been dead: so natural a conclusion, so poetic in its justice. The readiness is all, he had said, and a brick had instantly dropped on him from heaven."[53] But she has a different kind of ordeal to face—her own awareness of responsibility, especially in relation to her lover's wife, her cousin and friend Lucy. "Had he died, as all true fictional lovers die, had we both died, then these things would have been evaded forever" (196). At the end, they survive, with a relationship that is no longer either a secret, all-consuming passion or a marriage. "It is all so different from what I had expected. It is all so much more cheerful" (234).

The Realms of Gold (1975) can also be read as a rewriting of Shakespearean tragedy with a happy ending. Near the beginning, when Frances, an archaeologist on a lecture tour, hears news about her lover, she thinks, "Cleopatra had hauled her messengers up and down by the hair when they brought bad tidings. Antony had been reduced to sending his schoolmaster to sue for peace."[54] She quotes to herself Cleopatra's dying speech, "Husband, I come. . . . Now to that name my courage prove my title" (5.2.287). Unlike Cleopatra, she is not imagining meeting him after death but hoping to meet him alive. "It would be like that again, she would have all that again," she thinks, identifying herself with "Cleopatra and grand passion."

For Frances, however, *Antony and Cleopatra* does not carry the thoughts of doom in love that *Romeo and Juliet* suggests for Jane in *The Waterfall*. Frances does not criticize the Shakespearean plot that she finds herself in: she thinks of the lovers' reunion rather than of their death, and she seems to be cheering herself up in making the comparison. Many critics have seen *Antony and Cleopatra* as having affinities with comedy and romance, and Frances's allusions to it are in something of this mode. While it takes longer for her to be reunited with Karel than she expects, explicit references to Shakespearean tragedy vanish from the novel after this early point. At the end, the misunderstanding separating them dissolves rather simply, and so does Karel's inconvenient marriage (and inconvenience is the only dimension of it that has been treated; his wife hardly ever appears in the novel). "Karel's wife went off to the country, as she had often threatened to do, to live in a lesbian commune. . . . [The novel has not shown her threatening to go off to the country or suggested that she might be lesbian.] Invent a more suitable ending if you can" (346). This is narrative contrivance for happy closure, and the last comment shows a self-consciousness that might recall the epilogues of *As You Like It* or *Twelfth Night*, where Feste ends by singing, "That's all one, our play is done, / And we'll strive to please you every day" (5.1.404–5). Drabble herself compares this aspect of the ending with "Shakespearean comedy when characters are forced to marry people they didn't want for the sake of the plot."[55] Unlike Virginia Woolf in *A Room of One's Own*, Drabble does not, in this novel, wonder about how Cleopatra might think about Anthony's wife apart from her sense of competition; but she does imagine an ending in which all three members of the triangle are alive and happy.

But the theme of death lurking in the evocation of *Antony and Cleo-*

patra emerges elsewhere in the novel. Frances's eccentric great-aunt dies of starvation; after her death Frances discovers evidence of her early unhappy love of a married man, his death, and the death of their child. Even more disturbingly, her depressed nephew kills himself and his baby. (In the relation of this event to the main plot, the novel rewrites Septimus's suicide in *Mrs. Dalloway.*) "Death and love. How dreadfully they contradict all culture, all process, all human effort" (342), Frances thinks, but later she comes to accept Stephen's suicide, describing it as the death of a tragic hero: "With a certain admirable determination, he had faced his own nature, and the terms of life and death, and seen what to do. He had had the revelation she had always been denied, which she had glimpsed so often in the distance" (343). In spite of the comic resolution of Frances's love, the novel is a tragicomedy after all with some suffering unavoidable: Frances concludes, "if one can salvage one moment from the sentence of death let us do so, let us catch at it. . . . it is all the living and the lucky can do for the dead, all they can do, given the chance, is to rejoice" (345).

Answering a question from the *New York Times Book Review,* Drabble once described *Antony and Cleopatra* as the work of literature she would most like to have written.[56] *Realms of Gold* can be read as a critique of that play because the novel's adulterous lovers Frances and Karel survive instead of dying, but this is not the main emphasis; perhaps, having written *The Waterfall,* Drabble wanted to pursue a different theme. In *Realms of Gold,* the allusions to *Antony and Cleopatra* both suggest how Frances dramatizes her love for Karel—as when she melodramatically calls him "the only man in Europe" (12)—and also give her some of Cleopatra's glamour as an unusually energetic and achieving woman still in love in middle age. The main way in which the plot of *Realms of Gold* differs from that of *Antony and Cleopatra* and those of many happier love stories, however, is the extent to which it emphasizes its heroine's discovery of connections with many other people besides her lover. Frances confronts death in this way, as she grieves for her great-aunt, and especially for her nephew Stephen and his baby, but she also finds unexpected possibilities for relationship in discovering her cousins Janet and David.

Drabble's later novel *The Radiant Way* (1988) contains many remembered lines from Shakespeare though none as important to the structure as in *Realms of Gold*.[57] In *A Natural Curiosity*, the immediate sequel to *The Radiant Way*, Shakespeare is almost absent. The mutilation of Lavinia, in *Titus Andronicus*, appears as part of a list of violent acts, of which all the others occur during one month in contemporary England.[58] The unhappily married Janice and Edward quarrel "about which of them forgot to set the video for the Channel 4 Titus Andronicus" (254), and their daughter thinks of their quarrel as a "terrible bloody Jacobean marital farce," by implication comparing their marriage to the play. Edward, now a high school drama teacher, was a magical Prospero at twenty and is bitter about not being a star, a minor example of the many lost hopes in the novel. One can read this set of details about the minor characters as suggesting that the Shakespeare of Prospero, and with him triumphant British civilization, is in the past and remembered only by unrealistic dwellers in fantasy, while only the violent Shakespeare of *Titus Andronicus* is relevant to the present. On the other hand, the novel's denouement, like those of Shakespeare's romances, depends on the discovery of a long-lost relative, in this case an actress with "friends in all walks of life," who makes "all things seem possible." Marcia and Edward represent two different images of the theater: as Prospero, Edward had made all the other characters "his puppets" (83)—his colonies?—while Marcia's interest in other people links her with the associations of theater and sympathy found in some eighteenth- and nineteenth-century criticism discussed earlier, as well as, explicitly, with a new multicultural world of "diversity" (292).[59] In *The Waterfall*, *The Radiant Way*, and *A Natural Curiosity*, Shakespeare's plays are a cultural inheritance occasionally remembered by the characters but of dubious relevance. In Drabble's next novel, *The Gates of Ivory* (1991), however, Shakespearean lines appear so frequently and in such a different way that I will discuss the novel in chapter 8 with other examples of cultural hybridity.

In interviews Drabble often relates writing to sympathy, as did Cather, Murdoch, and Woolf: "I think this is important, to make sympathetic in a novel people who are perhaps not immediately real to everybody—to make their worries real to others."[60] Yet unlike those novelists, she does not frequently refer to Shakespeare as her ideal of the author. Instead, speaking of models, she looks to an ancestry specifically among novelists rather than claiming affinities with the theater as Woolf, Cather, and Murdoch—with less theatrical experience—implicitly do in looking to Shakespeare. She calls George Eliot "my ideal novelist . . . she's so inclusive" and writes of her "social conscience" and the breadth it gives *Middlemarch.* [61] The sexist elements in Shakespeare's plays loom larger for her; she was once an understudy with the Royal Shakespeare Company and has recently written about the oppression of repeatedly watching *The Taming of the Shrew* early in her marriage (1960).[62] She was not the only woman to find the play objectionable at that time and to voice her response. Drabble is the first writer discussed here whose reading of Shakespeare and interest in finding a female model were probably much affected by the revival of the feminist movement in the 1960s and 1970s. In addition, by the time of her education, George Eliot and other women novelists were clearly canonical. F. R. Leavis, who had played a major role in establishing Eliot's canonicity, dominated Cambridge when Drabble was there. She was in a historical position to say, "I think I was conscious from a very early age that writing novels was a thing that women did do and had always managed to do best." [63]

Margaret Atwood's novels, like Drabble's, sometimes imagine versions of Shakespeare's tragedies that end not in death but in survival; *Survival,* relevantly, is the title and preoccupation of her thematic study of Canadian literature.[64] But Atwood's novels celebrate the turning of tragedy into tragicomedy less than Drabble's do. For example, in *Life Before Man,* Lesje speculates, in a way reminiscent of the narrator of *The Mill on the Floss* contemplating Hamlet, "How would the Montagues and the Capulets have behaved if Juliet had lived? Juliet, like her [Lesje's] mother, would have become impenetrable, compact, plump, would have drawn herself together into a sphere." [65] Drabble celebrated lovers able to live on in spite of the tragic myths of love and death they evoked; Atwood is more interested in evoking the problems they have as they live on.

In her novel *Cat's Eye* (1989), Atwood's interest in rewriting tragedy envisions a woman's loss of a childhood playmate as analogous to Lear's loss of his one loyal daughter. Elaine, the narrator, is a successful artist whose return to her hometown for a retrospective is dominated by the expectation that she will see the significantly named Cordelia, an expectation filled with anger as well as with regret. "You made me believe I was nothing," she says to the absent presence, using a word that echoes throughout *Lear*.[66] In childhood, the two were both friends and enemies; Cordelia had gained her own sense of identity by dominating Elaine, it seems, but as Elaine grew stronger, Cordelia grew weaker. At their last reunion, Cordelia had begged her for help in getting out of a mental institution, and Elaine refused. Unlike Shakespeare's play, the novel provides no scene of restorative reconciliation; yet unlike Lear, Elaine survives the final loss of her Cordelia.

The Shakespearean name works to raise and dash hopes for a woman who will return and provide nurturance and forgiveness. In Atwood's novel, Cordelia's past cruelty deflated Elaine's early wish for kindness, as Elaine's cruelty later deflated hers. The picture of girlhood that the novel provides emphatically works against the image of feminine sympathy so often associated with Shakespeare's heroines by nineteenth-century readers especially, and so does its picture of womanhood.[67]

Elaine's relation with the feminist movement is highly ambivalent, but the novel is not as clearly hostile to women as such critics as Gayle Greene have suggested. Another possible reading is that the novel is *about* women's alienation from each other. Atwood helps to free it for this interpretation by writing, on the acknowledgment page, "The opinions expressed are those of the characters and should not be confused with the author's." (In the twentieth century this could be taken to be an underlying assumption of the fictional contract, acknowledged only when there is likely to be some such merging because of fictional events similar to well-known historical events or, perhaps, in this case, obvious autobiographical suggestions in the choice of a successful female artist as the narrator.) Elaine's continuing loss of Cordelia can be seen as emblematic of the loss of deep connections to other women apparently required of a professionally successful woman in an individualistic society (a loss that Drabble's novels, such as *A Natural Curiosity,* repair more successfully), and from this point of view, the Shakespearean allusions suggest, in part, that this is a loss as serious as the father-daughter alienation in the tragedy.[68]

Cat's Eye also uses Shakespearean allusions in ways more directly critical of the patriarchy of his world or of cultural uses of him. Cordelia's family is dominated by a tyrannical father. The older two daughters, named Perdita and Miranda after the daughters in Shakespeare's romances who survive separation and reunion, shorten their names and (like Goneril and Regan) negotiate more easily with their father. Their Shakespearean names, we are told, were "Mummie's idea" (33). Mummie is compared to "a bright but willful child," and the names in combination with the father's tyranny make her Shakespearean interest seem sentimental and evasive. Cordelia, who proudly insists on being called by her full name, doesn't have her sisters' skill in handling family relations but also lacks the courage of her namesake. Elaine writes of their family dinner table conversation, "I've seen it many times, her dithering, fumble-footed efforts to appease him. But nothing she can do or say will ever be enough, because she is somehow the wrong person" (264). After this scene, Cordelia's cruelty to Elaine can quite easily be seen as the result of her father's cruelty to her.[69] Shakespeare is further connected with Cordelia's disempowerment as we follow her brief theatrical career. She is props assistant for a *Macbeth* production while in high school and unwittingly sabotages the tragic effect by getting the wrong kind of cabbage for Macbeth's head. While Elaine is learning to paint, Cordelia gets small parts at Stratford, Ontario. Her biggest speech, which she recites to Elaine at their second last meeting, is that of the first nun, in *Measure for Measure*, 1.4.12–13:

> Then, if you speak, you must not show your face,
> Or, if you show your face, you must not speak.
>
> (*Cat's Eye*, 316)

These lines almost describe her limited success in her one Stratford season, where this is the only speaking part she has. Her interest in Shakespeare seems to lead only to further confinement, not to the creativity possible for Elaine.[70]

Atwood's critical treatment of Shakespeare allusions in *Cat's Eye* contrasts interestingly with the Shakespearean appropriations of Margaret Laurence's *The Diviners*, another Canadian novel (published 1974) about a middle-aged woman artist (a novelist, in this case), and one that Atwood reviewed favorably. This novel revises *The Tempest* in its focus on female experience and its vision of alliance between outsiders by sex, race, and class; yet when its main character celebrates the vision she finds in such passages as Prospero's epilogue, there is no hint of critical distance: "That incredibly moving statement, 'What strength I have's mine own, which is most faint—' If only he can hang onto that knowledge, that would be true strength."[71] Atwood's contrasting treatment of Shakespeare, in the novel where she engages with him most, probably results in part from the fact that more of Atwood's self-construction as a writer than Laurence's has been involved with the feminist movement as well as from the further development of feminist Shakespeare criticism between 1974 and 1989.[72]

Shakespeare most often appears in Atwood's collected essays as one of many British writers preoccupied with class. There is, however, one passage in her 1980 essay "An End to Audience," in which there appears a vestige of the tradition of emphasizing Shakespeare's selflessness. Here, however, he appears as an example of the paradoxical change-ability and identity of the self shared by each writer. "The person who wrote the poem I seem to remember composing yesterday no longer exists, and it's merely out of courtesy to librarians that we put everything with the word Shakespeare on the title page into the card file together. Or it would be merely out of courtesy, were it not for the fact that each piece of writing changes the writer. . . . Shakespeare, whoever he was, was also the only creature who went through the experience of writing those plays, one after another after another."[73]

Like Drabble, Atwood grew up learning that novel writing was an achievement possible for women and is much more interested in some nineteenth-century women novelists than in Shakespeare. She refers more often to George Eliot in her collected essays than to anyone else; in "Writing the Male Character" (1982) she says of *Middlemarch,* "the greatest single English novel of the nineteenth century," "The wonder of this book is that George Eliot can make us understand not only how awful it is to be married to Mr. Casaubon, but how awful it is to *be* Mr. Casaubon. This seems to me a worthy model to emulate."[74] What she praises in George Eliot here is close to what Eliot herself wrote of aiming at in her novels, and the last words of the last essay in her volume sound like an attempt, however qualified, to bring Eliot's theory of literature into the present. "If writing novels—and reading them—have any redeeming social value, it's probably that they force you to imagine what it's like to be somebody else. Which, increasingly, is something we all need to know."[75] The idea that writing can help readers understand the suffering of characters who are unattractive and very different from themselves repeats the idea of writing as extending sympathy, and some of the language Atwood uses evokes some of the images of the writer's "negative capability" that so many of the figures treated in this book have used. "In writing, your attention is focused not on the self but on the thing being made, the thing being seen. . . . It is bringing the dead to life and giving voices to those who lack them so that they may speak for themselves. . . . It is opening yourself, discarding your *self,* so that the language and the world may be evoked through you."[76] Nevertheless, Atwood is the first of these writers to explain that the ability to arouse a reader's sympathy through literature has nothing to do with one's sympathy in everyday life. "Writers, both male and female, have to be selfish just to get the time to write, but women are not trained to be selfish."[77]

Atwood's view here is a kind of mediation between the nineteenth-century view associating art with sympathy and the dominant modernist view of the artist. In this context, the image of the novelist as promoting understanding of other people that she, Drabble, Woolf, Cather, and Murdoch all maintain, and the association that three of them make between this image and the image of the sympathetic Shakespeare, afford an interesting contrast to the image of the artist and of Shakespeare that we find in the work of James Joyce, whose engagement with Shakespeare probably surpasses that of any other well-known Anglophone male modernist novelist. In *Ulysses,* his Stephen Dedalus hypothesizes a Shakespeare alienated from his wife, in conflict with his father, writing partly to take revenge on his brothers. In the Nighttown section, as Bloom and Stephen watch sex between Molly Bloom and Blazes Boylan, Shakespeare's face appears in a mirror, and incoherent words identify him as primarily a vengeful cuckold. "Iagogo! How my Oldfellow chokit his Thursdaymomun. Iagogo! . . . Weda seca whokilla farst."[78] (Unlike Keats's Shakespeare, this one has much more delight in conceiving an Iago than an Imogen.) The earlier Stephen of *Portrait of the Artist as a Young Man* imagines the artist as "within or behind or beyond or above his handiwork, invisible, refined out of existence, indifferent, paring his fingernails." Bloom's vision is, of course, identified as a nightmare, but the image of Shakespeare's troubled marriage persists: compare *Nothing like the Sun,* a 1970 fiction about Shakespeare's life by Anthony Burgess, who has written about Joyce, among many other topics. Neither Stephen's artist nor his Shakespeare sounds sympathetic, and even if we argue that Joyce undercuts Stephen's views with various kinds of irony, Stephen's are the views of the artist and of Shakespeare that have been particularly influential in male modernism. Similarly, in "Everything and Nothing," an essay written close in time to Iris Murdoch's and using some of the same imagery derived from Hazlitt and Keats, Borges imagines Shakespeare as not sympathetic or loving but frigid and empty: "There was no one in him; behind his face (which even through the bad paintings of those times resembles no other) and his words, which were copious, fantastic and stormy, there was only a bit of coldness, a dream dreamt by no one."[79]

On the other hand, several other female modernists write about Shakespeare in ways much like those discussed in this chapter. H.D.'s *By Avon River,* as Susan Stanford Friedman has shown, rewrites Claribel, a marginal character in *The Tempest,* as the speaker and the quester and gives her a mystical epiphany of love at Avon. Both in the poetic section, and in the scholarly section that emphasizes Shakespeare's gentleness and his love for his daughter Judith, *By Avon River* reimagines Shakespeare to empower women writers.[80] A similar move occurs in Sylvia Townsend Warner's essay "Women as Writers" (1959), where, emphasizing women's lack of academic training, as did Aphra Behn to the same purpose, she writes, "Women, entering literature, entered it on the same footing as William Shakespeare."[81] She attributes to both Shakespeare and women writers an appreciation of active female characters: "Lady Macbeth, and Beatrice, and Helena in *All's Well,* could almost be taken for women writers' heroines, they are so free and uninhibited, and ready to jump over stiles and appear in the drawing-room with muddy stockings, like Lizzie Bennet." And she finds in both Shakespeare and women writers a "kind of workaday democracy, an ease and appreciativeness in low company."

Townsend Warner and H.D. wrote poetry and experimental fiction. For them, while Shakespeare was the ancestor who could be reclaimed for empowerment, George Eliot was the dull, too recent past; Townsend Warner, in fact, finds her the rare woman writer who lacks immediacy, who uses too much "the lecturer's little wand." Similarly, for male modernists such as Ford Madox Ford, E. M. Forster, T. S. Eliot, and even, at times, Henry James, George Eliot was, as Karen Chase writes, "the bearer of an obsolete sensibility that needed to be swept from their path."[82] For Atwood and Drabble, in contrast, affiliating themselves both with the nineteenth-century tradition of women novelists and the late twentieth-century feminist movement, George Eliot seems to have taken Shakespeare's place as a model, and their emphasis on promoting the understanding of other people's inner lives sounds like a twentieth-century rewriting of her aesthetic.[83] But Atwood's greater skepticism about the image of the sympathetic writer correlates, perhaps, with her formal moves away from nineteenth-century realism.[84]

As Elaine Showalter has demonstrated, many recent women writers such as Joyce Carol Oates, Gail Godwin, and Susan Cheever find George Eliot of continuing interest, though recent male writers tend not to.[85] In a 1990 *New Yorker* story, Cynthia Ozick's fictional alter ego Puttermesser tries to communicate her fascination with Eliot to Rubino, a man who "re-enacts" famous paintings, hoping that he will be her George Lewes and they will have a "marriage of true minds" (appropriating Shakespeare's sonnet somewhat as did Eliot).[86] Like some of the male writers discussed by Showalter, he knows Eliot only from a high school reading of *Silas Marner;* though he joins Puttermesser in reading aloud Eliot's novels and biography, he becomes more interested in the men in Eliot's life. Puttermesser and Rubino marry, but immediately afterward Rubino reenacts John Cross's mysterious jump out of a window on his honeymoon with Eliot and unlike Cross leaves his wife. Rubino says of his visual "re-enactments," "You think I care about what some dead painter feels? Or what anyone with a brush in his hand thought about a couple of hundred years ago?" The ending reveals his apparent interest in Puttermesser and Eliot to be inseparable from hostility to them. Although Rubino is a harsh picture of a post-modernist artist, Ozick's choice of Eliot as the novelist at issue is not an arbitrary one. With most of the writers to be discussed in the next chapter, either their greater concern with race or their more experimental, postmodernist style means that George Eliot becomes less important as a model. Yet their engagement with Shakespeare continues, and it is neither as sentimental as Puttermesser's identification with Eliot nor as hostile and shallow as Rubino's use of her.

Chapter Eight

Shakespeare in the Cultural Hybridity of Contemporary Women Novelists

FIVE NOVELS by women published in the 1980s and '90s engage with Shakespeare at the same time as they engage with other literary traditions very different from those of Shakespeare or of British women novelists. For these novelists Shakespeare is not primarily the image of the sympathetic artist, nor does George Eliot take his place in that role. Shakespeare is present instead more as a representative of a past tradition, and accordingly, these novelists engage particularly, though not exclusively, with *King Lear* and *The Tempest,* with their father-daughter emphasis. Angela Carter's *Wise Children* combines Shakespearean pastiche with a celebration of other kinds of show business such as vaudeville. Gloria Naylor's *Mama Day* and Nadine Gordimer's *My Son's Story* rewrite Shakespearean plots and also play with the complexity of a central character's interest in Shakespeare that crosses racial boundaries; they combine Shakespeare with black culture. Jane Smiley's *A Thousand Acres* transforms the plot of *King Lear* against the setting of conflicting farming cultures of the American Midwest. Smiley's and Gordimer's novels are the first works by their authors to engage with Shakespeare, but Carter's and Naylor's follow earlier works that also use his image, characters, and themes for their own purposes, if less intensely. Margaret Drabble's novel *The Gates of Ivory* uses Shakespearean references—more than ever before in her novels—to deal with Southeast Asian history and international politics in a global culture.

The context of all these novels includes the important explosion of postcolonial rewritings of Shakespeare from Africa, Asia, and the Caribbean, from Ngugi wa Thiong'o's novel *A Grain of Wheat* (1967) and Aimé Césaire's play *Une Tempête* (1969) through Salman Rushdie's epic novel *The Satanic Verses* (1988), which of course rewrites many other kinds of earlier literature and tradition as well. Thiong'o and Césaire rewrite *The Tempest* to criticize Prospero and give Caliban more voice. Rushdie, like James Joyce, is especially interested in male jealousy, and writes a version of *Othello* in which both Othello and Iago are Indians (Gibreel and Saladin), with problematic relationships to white women and to British culture.[1] The women novelists I will discuss in this chapter generally pay more attention to expanding the stories of the female figures in Shakespeare's plots or to telling the story of the black female figures mostly absent from Shakespeare's plots or subordinated in those of the male postcolonial writers.[2]

Some links between several of these writers emblematize their participation in an international literary world. Rushdie memorialized Angela Carter in the *New York Times Book Review* upon her death in 1992; Gordimer is quoted on the jacket of Rushdie's *Satanic Verses*. Their shared use of Shakespeare is, among other things, a sign of their shared interest in an Anglophone literature that is international, as they reinvent it for a postcolonial age. The writings of Rushdie and Carter, in particular, have been considered postmodernist with reference to the fantastic and parodic elements of their many allusions to earlier literatures, but while Naylor uses fantasy in a different way, and Gordimer's *My Son's Story* and Smiley's *A Thousand Acres* are realist or modernist in style, all of these novels engage with Shakespeare in a way that questions dominant cultural tradition's use of him more starkly than almost all the works discussed in the previous chapter.

Angela Carter

Angela Carter, only a year younger than Atwood and Drabble, has been even closer to the feminist movement, and her attitude makes a more explicit break with many of the attitudes held by earlier writers. More clearly than Atwood, she breaks the link between art and sympathy maintained by most of the writers discussed in the previous chapter. "Writing . . . certainly doesn't make better people, nor do writers lead happier lives. . . . most of the great male geniuses of Western European culture have been either depraved egomaniacs or people who led the most distressing lives. . . . the actual satisfactions of artistic production are peculiarly lonely and solipsistic ones."[3] In a 1983 essay, "Notes from the Front Line," she discusses her location as a woman writer, and the question that plagued Virginia Woolf in *A Room of One's Own* is raised in these terms: "One last thing. So there hasn't been a female Shakespeare. Three possible answers: (a) So what. (This is the simplest and best.) (b) There hasn't been a *male* Shakespeare since Shakespeare, dammit. (c) Somewhere, Franz Fanon opines that one cannot, in reason, ask a shoeless peasant in the Upper Volta to write songs like Schubert's; the opportunity to do so has never existed. The concept is meaningless" ("Notes" 75–76). The multiplicity of answers here suggests a tension— enjoyment of Shakespeare (that "dammit") versus consciousness of his associations with male, European, and class privilege—similar to tensions revealed in, for example, Woolf, but resolved with a very different balance.

Carter frequently alludes to Shakespeare but with a strongly revisionary motive. In "Notes," she writes, "I/we are not the slaves of the history that enslaved our ancestors, to quote Franz Fanon (although he meant specifically chattel slavery). So I feel free to loot and rummage in an official past, specifically a literary past. . . . This past, for me, has important decorative, ornamental functions; further, it is a vast repository of outmoded lies, where you can check out what lies used to be a la mode and find the old lies on which new lies have been based" (74). Perhaps considering her uses of Shakespeare as well as other writers, she feels "much . . . in common with certain Third World writers, both female and male, who are transforming actual fictional forms to both reflect and to precipitate changes in the way people feel about themselves—putting new wine in old bottles and, in some cases, old wine in new bottles" (76).

In some of her writing, Carter appropriates from Shakespeare's comedies the potentially subversive theme of cross-dressing and uses it with reference to contemporary culture. In a 1967 essay, she draws from *As You Like It* an example of the freedom gained from disguise parallel to 1960s style. "Rosalind in disguise in the Forest of Arden could pretend to be a boy pretending to be a seductress, satisfying innumerable atavistic desires in the audience of the play."[4] In her 1977 novel, *The Passion of New Eve,* she critiques her culture's gender roles in a plot involving a much more violent version of transsexualism than Woolf's *Orlando,* but like Woolf evokes the Shakespearean cross-dressing that provided a kind of hint for her exploration. The narrator, having been forcibly castrated and transsexualized, is dressed in male evening clothes, and thinks, "Under the mask of maleness I wore another mask of femaleness but a mask that now I never would be able to remove, no matter how hard I tried, although I was a boy disguised as a girl and now disguised as a boy again, like Viola [*sic*] in the Forest of Arden."[5]

In her later fantasy, *Nights at the Circus,* however, Carter evokes Shakespearean comedy to point out that her novel is going to refuse the conventions of female subordination in marriage as closure. One character predicts that the novel will end like "the customary endings of the old comedies of separated lovers. . . . Orlando takes his Rosalind. She says: 'To you I give myself, for I am yours.' And that . . . goes for a girl's bank account, too." In response, the heroine Fevvers says, "But it is not possible that I should give myself. . . . My being, my me-ness, is unique and indivisible. . . . Surely he'll have the decency to give himself to me, when we meet again, not expect the vice versa!"[6] Fevvers, like Rosalind, has had more power than other women in some respects, but that power results largely from her mysterious wings, and unlike Rosalind, she speaks of the possibilities that social change will give such power to other women: "And once the old world has turned on its axle so that the new day can dawn, then, ah, then! all the women will have wings, the same as I" (285). The novel ends not with a marriage ceremony but with Fevvers's cataclysmic laugh at having discovered, in conversation with her lover, that she has deceived him about her virginity. She laughs away all attempts to restrict and classify women's sexuality.

Carter's last novel, or more accurately romance, *Wise Children,* appropriates Shakespearean themes throughout, most explicitly evoking them by making its narrator, Dora, a daughter of Sir Melchior Hazard, a famous Shakespearean actor.[7] In a critique of patriarchal ideology, she is his illegitimate daughter and he resists many opportunities to acknowledge her. This grieves her but does not leave her isolated; unlike the daughters of Shakespeare's romances, she has a strong, loving, and independent adoptive mother, a companionable twin sister, a generous, if frequently absent, surrogate father (her father's twin), many other quasi-familial relations and some lovers, and a career—mostly in the *illegitimate* theater. On his hundredth birthday and their seventy-fifth, in a parody of Shakespeare's many father-daughter reunions, Sir Melchior finally acknowledges his illegitimate daughters (after discovering that the daughters he thought his were begotten by his brother). There are gestures of both reconciliation and demystification with Melchior as Dora sees that he has had problems with his own father, and her sister wonders "if we haven't been making him up all along" (230). But the narrative goes even further beyond the bounds of Shakespeare's plots when the seventy-five-year-old Dora makes love with her one-hundred-year-old uncle, who a few minutes later literally produces out of his pockets three-month-old twins—more illegitimate branches on the family tree—eagerly adopted by her seventy-five-year-old twin Nora, with the expectation of Dora's help. Dora is comparatively realistic about problems this may entail; she says, "if you choose to stop the story there, at such a pause, and refuse to take it any further, then you can call it a happy ending" (227). But the real end is a description of the sisters doing a song and dance act for their babies, which Dora concludes by writing, "What a joy it is to dance and sing!" (232). The book is a playful parable about fictions of parenthood and about how women can enjoy surviving as outsiders, or perhaps more accurately as outsider/insiders, as marginal, as hybrids. Carter's embrace of hybridity, analogous to that of the novelists I will discuss next, is underlined not only by Dora's involvement with musical comedy and other popular cultural forms but also by the fact that the infant twins adopted at the end are "brown as a quail," children of Dora's family's Jesuit half brother and someone he met working in South America.[8] In an essay published close in time to this novel, Carter tells one of its jokes, with the punchline *"He's* not your father," and continues, *"father* is a social and legal fiction. . . . the term *mother* can also be a fiction, a social construction."[9] Deflating the myth of a unified fatherhood, biological, legal, social, and emotional, Carter imagines hybrid families with multiple parents as she grafts Shakespeare, the music hall, musical comedies, and other sources together in her literary family tree.

Gloria Naylor and Nadine Gordimer

The twentieth-century novels by women discussed thus far rewrite Shakespeare mostly with regard to gender, but for Gloria Naylor and Nadine Gordimer race is important as well. In the two most recent novels by these women, they respond to Shakespeare in a particularly complex way by giving a race-crossing interest in him to one of their characters. While this theme occurs in Naylor's earlier works, it is new in Gordimer's.

Gloria Naylor, born in 1950, is the only writer I discuss originally from a black, poor family and also the only one who has a degree in Afro-American Studies.[10] The genealogy of her responses to Shakespeare includes not only the white women novelists and black male novelists I have discussed but also the other black writers, male and female, for whom claiming Shakespeare was an important way of claiming a place in an American culture that had previously made him its own—W. E. B. Du Bois, Anna Julia Cooper, Zora Neale Hurston, Maya Angelou.[11]

In Naylor's first two books, the image of the "black Shakespeare" has a mythic importance comparable to that of Woolf's Judith Shakespeare. In *The Women of Brewster Place,* seeing a black performance of *Midsummer Night's Dream* motivates Cora Lee to more care and hope for her children (giving a meaning to the word "dream" that resonates with its use by Langston Hughes—in the book's epigraph—and Martin Luther King). When one of her children asks, "Shakespeare's black?" "Not yet," is her answer, spoken softly, for "she had beaten him for writing the rhymes on her bathroom walls."[12] In other words, she starts to think of graffiti not as vandalism but as a sign of a potential writer who ought to be encouraged. The book does not actually show Cora Lee behaving differently after this day; in Mattie's dream at the end, she is pregnant again, repeating problematic behavior, but participates in the collective, liberating tearing down of the wall. Peter Erickson has noted that the absence of clear change in Cora Lee questions any confidence that she would improve by "moving up from the low culture of white-produced TV soaps to the high culture of black-produced Shakespeare."[13] Yet the allusions to dreams in Shakespeare, to Shakespearean comedy as a dream, and to the dreams of achievement provoked by Shakespeare can be seen as preparation for Mattie's final, symbolically revolutionary dream.

In *Linden Hills,* Lester, complaining about how much he's been working, says, "And yet people wonder why black folks ain't produced a Shakespeare," and his friend Willie, also a poet, says of their upwardly mobile suburb, "You'd think of all the places in the world, this neighborhood had a chance of giving us at least one black Shakespeare."[14] "But Linden Hills ain't about that," says Lester, and in this context this is part of its condemnation as a place of soul-denying materialism.

"The use of Shakespeare by both Canadian and American writers has built-in contradictions that impede its revolutionary power," writes Elaine Showalter, citing Henry Gates's warning against "description of the works of women and the works of persons of color as . . . shadowy fragments of a Master Text that we, somehow, have been unable to imitate precisely."[15] This critique may hold against Naylor's work in this novel; perhaps these conversations, like the Dantean architecture, reveal Naylor's too imitative attitude toward European literary tradition. On the other hand, one could argue that they are appropriate in a novel dealing with modes of assimilation into the dominant culture and that the image of "the black Shakespeare" is associated with the characters more than with the novelist's voice.[16] If that image does not have revolutionary power, *Linden Hills* is not a novel of revolution, although perhaps one could appropriate to it Adrienne Rich's line about poetry and say that it "isn't revolution but a way of knowing why it must come."[17]

In *Mama Day,* Naylor more clearly provides a complex interplay among different responses to Shakespeare, some of them attributed to her characters and associated with other aspects of their location. George, an assimilated black urban professional brought up in a male-run orphanage, loves reading Shakespeare. While this taste correlates with his assimilation, its psychology is more complex. The center of his interest is his identification with Edmund, a Shakespearean outsider who shares his rage at an abandoning father, if not his color. He has gone through *Lear* "uncountable times. It had a special poignancy for me, reading about the rage of a bastard son, my own father having disappeared long before I was born."[18] Cocoa, who contrasts with George in her upbringing in female-dominated, black-dominated Southern tradition, has rejected her given Shakespearean name, Ophelia. She makes fun of wishes to claim black Shakespearean characters—"Shakespeare didn't have a bit of soul. I don't care if he did write about Othello, Cleopatra, and some slave on a Caribbean island" (62).

Much of the novel is structured around the interplay and intermingling of perspectives of Cocoa and George, in a narrative told alternatingly by each of them as if talking to the other. He shows her New York and lends her *Lear;* when he comes to her apartment ostensibly to talk about it—"the games people play"—she too has begun to identify with Shakespearean characters on the grounds of family situation. He remembers, "It seemed that although your parents were married, your father had taken off before you were born, too" (106). Cocoa's identification with Edmund crosses barriers of both race and sex, and she even seems, like some of the women writers discussed in the first chapter of this book, to claim Shakespeare as a protofeminist who, she says, "tried to convey that men had the same feelings as women." Cocoa may be referring to the fact that both male and female characters are rejected by fathers in *Lear,* but she may also be thinking of the fact that Lear associates his tears, "women's weapons" (2.4.277), and his madness— "Oh, how this mother swells up toward my heart!" (2.4.55)—with women.[19] From Cocoa's viewpoint, an androgynous Shakespeare becomes the mediator who helps provide a situation in which she "opened up" (George's significant words) in an emotional closeness that helped prepare her for their first lovemaking. Meanwhile, George is "touched by your sharing that part of your life with me—more than I had been willing to do" (he doesn't tell her about his identification with Edmund) but he is now thinking, like Cocoa earlier, about Shakespeare's limitations: "Along with *The Taming of the Shrew,* this had to be Shakespeare's most sexist treatment of women—but far be it from me to contradict anything you had to say; I didn't want to waste any more time than necessary for you to work yourself up to untying the strings on that red halter."

The juxtaposition of literature and sexuality in this scene is not accidental but emphasized by imagery. Cocoa was "glad I'd turned you on" to *Lear;* just before narrating this conversation, George says to women in general, "How can there be anything personal about you to turn me on? At this stage of the game, it's my own hormones." Are Cocoa and George turned on to Shakespeare just because of the literary equivalent of hormones, an undiscriminating, promiscuous search for literary characters to get into? Indeed, Cocoa and George are not sophisticated literary critics (possibly there is irony that works against George when he tries to talk like a critic, commenting on Shakespeare's sexism, given that readers might well find as much sexism in his previous commentary on women). But just as the novel presents their relationship as more than hormonal attraction, it presents their shared, if discontinuous, interest in Shakespeare as more than a sharing in the cultural interests associated with upward mobility. For Cocoa, who has initially seen practically everyone in terms of some stereotype imaged by a food, it is a significant moment when she can literally open up across lines of gender and race to Edmund in his dispossession, and the novel may hint that she and George have created, out of their interest in Edmund, a community of father-abandoned children. Of course, as Erickson points out, "Edmund is defeated by Edgar in the end," but this defeat does not mean that the text must be read as just a monolithic condemnation of Edmund.[20] His protest against legitimacy, primogeniture, and his father's lack of love can as plausibly be valorized in rereadings as Caliban's protest against colonialism.

But being father-abandoned children together is not enough basis for a relationship, whether or not—to use an image that Naylor does not use—Cocoa and George adopt Shakespeare as a substitute father. George's reminders of Shakespeare's limitations and of his own limitations keep this scene from being a sentimental one. The possibilities of appropriating characters and of judging dramatic structures as too confining are put in play with each other, as Naylor puns on the sexual/

dramatic possibilities of the word. "Didn't I want to get into the play now? Yes, that's exactly what I wanted to do, but instead we opened our copies of *King Lear*."

From Naylor's textual play with Shakespeare in the rest of the novel, more radical literary re-vision occurs. Prospero's island in *The Tempest* is transformed into the black-dominated, female-dominated island of Willow Springs, presided over by Cocoa's great-aunt, who has changed her name from Miranda to Mama Day. She has magical powers analogous to Prospero's, but unlike him she knows their limitations and works along with nature more than in opposition to it. Unlike him, too, she cannot finally maintain a marriage against its elements of strain. Cultural differences between female and male, south and north, urban and rural, create conflict between George and Cocoa and ultimately lead to George's death. But Cocoa survives—Mama Day persuades her to go on living—and at the end of the novel she describes George, for her son by her second husband, as "a man who looked just like love." While the marriage it portrays has been fragile, the novel creates a permanent conversation among the viewpoints of George, Cocoa, and Mama Day, which includes a conversation among the different modes of reading Shakespeare associated with George and Cocoa and the drastic rewriting of him associated with Mama Day herself.[21]

Unlike Naylor, Nadine Gordimer has not shown much interest in Shakespeare in her novels, but in her recent *My Son's Story* the main character, Sonny, names his son Will "for Shakespeare, whose works, in a cheap complete edition bound in fake leather, stood in the glass-fronted bookcase in the small sitting-room and were no mere ornamental pretensions to culture."[22] Sonny is a "coloured" schoolteacher, in his family "the first to complete the full years of schooling"; as with George, his love of Shakespeare accompanies his social mobility and is associated with improvements of other kinds of taste—"with an understanding of Shakespeare there comes a release from the gullibility that makes you prey to the great shopkeeper who runs the world, and would sell you cheap to illusion" (11). For an explanation of the context of his life, he turns to Kafka rather than to Shakespeare, but for some time, while blacks are organizing, learning seems to him a better alternative than political action. "He was set on sitting up a night studying for a higher qualification, maybe even getting a university degree; that was how he would better himself, not by going to meetings or getting arrested on the march. Equality; he went to Shakespeare for a definition with more authority than those given on makeshift platforms in the veld" (23). Antiapartheid activity wins him over, however; he discovers ability as a speaker, becomes a leader, and goes to jail, and while in prison he is visited by a woman from a human rights organization who unknowingly connects with his love of Shakespeare by saying to him, "Well, I suppose you find sermons in stones" (49), an allusion to the speech in which the Duke of *As You Like It,* talking about the use he makes of his unjust exile, says he finds "sermons in stones and good in every thing" (2.1.17).

This meeting is the beginning of one way in which the novel rewrites Shakespeare in addition to characterizing Sonny by his Shakespearean interest, for it precipitates an interracial love affair that alludes to and transforms the plot of *Othello.* Gordimer makes the "coloured" man and the white woman lovers rather than a married couple, shows their relationship as doomed even without murderous jealousy, and adds the story, missing from *Othello* (and almost completely missing from *The Satanic Verses*), of *women* of color. The novel does not tell that story from the women's point of view, however, but shows how the men of the novel, father and son, underestimate and alienate themselves from Aila (Sonny's wife) and Baby (their daughter), as well as from each other, partly because of their fascination with white women. At the end of the novel the father-son relationship is reconstituted—a conclusion hinted at by the title and the epigraph from Sonnet 13, "You had a Father, let your son say so." But Sonny and Will are separated from Hannah (the white woman), Aila, and Baby, who are all living abroad because of political danger and commitment.

Shakespearean quotations play the largest role in the novel when Sonny realizes that some of his political comrades are beginning to doubt him. "*Not all the perfumes of Arabia*" (188), he thinks, mixing the beginning of Iago's line observing Othello's initial suspicion of Desdemona, "Not poppy, nor mandragora" (3.3.335), with Lady Macbeth's guilty "All the perfumes of Arabia" (5.1.49–50), a slip revealing his own guilt, which will later become conscious. He repeats part of Shakespeare's Sonnet 121, "*Better to be vile than vile esteemed, when not to be receives reproach of being*" (190). When his wife is in prison, and he blames his love for Hannah for blinding him to Aila's developing political commitment, he thinks of Othello's words to Desdemona, "*Oh thou weed: who art so lovely faire, and smell'st so sweet that the sense aches at thee, Would thou had'st never been born*" (224). These lines are all expressions of regret and bitterness. Sonny had earlier realized that Shakespeare did not explain his political situation; now he finds that remembering Shakespeare does not help him feel any transcendence in personal situations rather like those evoked in the plays. "He hated to have coming up at him these tags from an old habit of pedantry; useless, useless to him. In a schoolteacher's safe small life, aphorisms summed up so pleasingly dangers that were never going to have to be lived. There is no elegance in the actuality—the distress of calumny and self-betrayal, difficult to disentangle" (190). Yet this, unlike ignorance of the woman of color, works more against Sonny's previous, safe reading of Shakespeare than against the plays themselves. The narrator makes a similar point when Sonny identifies himself with Lear in his loss both of his daughter and his beloved Hannah: "Sonny had Lear-like lost his, his Baby—*Best thou had's not been born, than not t'have pleas'd me better*. . . . Oh schoolmaster taunted by the tags of passion he didn't understand when he read them in the little son-of-sorrow house. Oh Hannah. *Beat at this gate that let thy folly in*" (252). Yet given the absence of the black woman's perspective in *Othello,* of an extended look at Cordelia's perspective in *Lear,* would understanding the passions in the plays better have been any help?[23]

The final twist of the Shakespearean themes of the novel comes at the end when Will reveals that he has been the narrator of the whole book as well as of the sections told from his point of view, in which he generally seems disgusted with his father. All the sympathetic exploration of Sonny's consciousness, we now see, has been Will's work in spite of his own past hostility; Will even takes over, or rather reveals as his own, his father's habit of remembering Shakespearean tags, as he thinks, quoting Hamlet, "*I have that within that passeth show*" (276).[24] But Will is explicit about being a writer of a different sort than Shakespeare: the last poetry in the novel is one of his own poems, "not Shakespeare," and he announces his literary program: "I'm going to be the one to record, someday, . . . what it really was like to live a life determined by the struggle to be free." In his writing, as he speaks in this final chapter about this novel as his own work, the view of the artist as sympathetic merges with the view of the artist as politically committed.

Like Naylor, Gordimer decenters Shakespeare in a novel that treats issues of race with much more complexity than his works ever do. But also like Naylor, she envisions an engagement with Shakespeare that need not be repudiated. Will's final attitude to him can be aligned, perhaps, with Gordimer's as expressed in a 1982 interview. "Blacks in South Africa are writing mainly in English: what forms are they using? They are writing plays, short stories, novels, and poems. These forms come from Europe. Blacks have a rich oral tradition, but they did not have a written literature. It came with conquest. . . . Each country and nationality has borrowed from another. There is a commonwealth of literature and it belongs to all of us. A Shakespeare sonnet belongs as much to a black man writing poetry as it does to you or me."[25]

In a collection of interviews with Nadine Gordimer and a collection of her essays from 1963 to 1985, there are only two other references to Shakespeare beside this quotation.[26] Gordimer's interviews show more interest in writers such as Conrad, Forster, Hemingway, Lessing, Woolf, Proust, Lawrence, James, and Faulkner than in Shakespeare.[27] Sonny's literary interests are clearly more focused on Shakespeare than Gordimer's have been, partly to make a point about his accessibility; one of her other references to Shakespeare is as a writer still available even under South African censorship.[28] His work is more important in South African schools that someone like Sonny could have attended than are these novelists, even if they are not censored. One might also speculate about whether Gordimer's interest in *Othello* was provoked partly by Janet Suzman's South African production of *Othello* as an explicitly antiapartheid play, in a version that is now circulating internationally on film. In any event, making Shakespeare the site of Sonny's literary interests enables both the novel's suggestions of conflicts between his aesthetic and political sides—which fit with a still often prevalent interpretation of Shakespeare as universal and therefore above politics—and the final synthesis of aesthetics and politics in Will's commitment.

My Son's Story is explicitly concerned with the issue of universality and its relation to particularity. The last, crucial section begins, "It's an old story—ours. My father's and mine. Love, love/hate are the most common and universal of experiences. But no two are alike, each is a fingerprint of life" (275). Perhaps it is partly to facilitate the theme of how colonized characters claim a share in literature and experience considered universal that Gordimer makes Sonny and Will not black but "coloured." Sonny is a hybrid; his interest in Shakespeare came earlier in his life than his identification with the "real" blacks in the antiapartheid movement. Sonny and Will can claim to be the heirs of both white and black culture in a metaphorical as well as a biological sense. Their hybrid culture is one to which Gordimer herself lays claim. In the continuation of the interview quoted above, for example, Gordimer says, "We were never told that this wonderful drumming was part of being born in Africa. I had a right to regard this as my musical heritage, but it was never given me. Whites are beginning to think this way now. There are many who want to strike down roots into a new culture, a third culture" (214). Her position here and in the novel breaks down claims for cultural purity and exclusive ownership of any culture, black or white. Expressing similar views, the African-American Cornel West writes of "the thoroughly hybrid culture of almost every culture we have ever discovered. . . . To talk about hybrid culture means you give up all quests for pure traditions and pristine heritages. . . . Europe has always been multicultural. Shakespeare borrowed from Italian narratives and pre-European narratives."[29]

The role of Shakespeare reading for Sonny and George makes significant contrasts with the role of Shakespeare reading in novels discussed earlier, for example *Daniel Deronda*. In this novel, as in many of Eliot's, Shakespeare is such a common cultural property that the ability to quote him is shared by many of the characters, while in recent novels it is generally a distinguishing trait of one character, which he (the usual gender of the primary Shakespeare reader) may pass on to one other. Daniel, like George, has a special interest in Shakespeare's presentation of illegitimacy, but unlike George he is not interested in "the rage of a bastard son." Unlike George, too, as we have seen, he finally finds his mother, discovers that he is not actually illegitimate, and identifies himself with his biological heritage of Jewishness. Though it requires leaving England, genealogical knowledge is possible for him as it is not for George, and this possibility parallels the fact that there is a greater gap between George and Shakespeare than between Daniel and Shakespeare. It is hard to imagine Daniel criticizing any play by Shakespeare for prejudice against women (though, long before, Eliot seems to have made such a comment about *Two Gentlemen of Verona*), and during a political argument he seems to present *The Tempest* as facilitating an enlightened view on race: "Deronda said he had always felt a little with Caliban, who naturally had his own point of view and could sing a good song."[30]

Gordimer's use of Sonny's memories of Shakespeare lines that he can apply to his situation also has a different effect from Gwendolen's memories of Shakespeare in *Daniel Deronda*. The irony is always against Gwendolen, who makes her Shakespeare allusions in the early part of the novel while unaware of the disasters to follow from her choices. She doesn't know how very different her life is going to be from Rosalind's, and not just because Grandcourt does not carve her name on trees. Eliot leaves open the possibility that for a serious reader like Daniel, Shakespeare may prepare for life, within limits, even if it does not help Gwendolen. Gordimer suggests that such reading helps Sonny up to a point, but then shows its help breaking down. Gordimer makes this a more painful perception by treating Sonny's early Shakespeare reading as much more thoughtful than Gwendolen's, involving quests for equality and understanding rather than for conversational ornament and parts in which to be a spectacle. Sonny's pain at remembering Shakespearean speeches about regret may suggest, among other things, pain at the failure of the humanist ideal that literature can teach and console; but the novel may also suggest omissions that in the humanist institutionalization of Shakespeare have blended with other cultural prejudices. Not only does *Othello*, like Sonny's own consciousness, ignore the woman of color, but also, among Shakespeare's plays, it far overshadows *Antony and Cleopatra* in canonical status.

When Will reveals himself as the narrator of *My Son's Story*, and when he includes one final Shakespeare line in his own voice, so to speak—Hamlet's words "I have that within that passeth show" (276)—

arguably the synthesis of aesthetics and politics reclaims the relevance of Shakespeare. The next sentence after Hamlet's line is "I've imagined, out of their deception, the frustration of my absence, the pain of knowing them too well, what others would be doing, saying and feeling in the gaps between my witness." Will's simultaneous identification with Hamlet and with the sympathy of the ideal writer is amazingly close to George Eliot's association of Daniel with both Hamlet and sympathy, which I discussed in the sixth chapter. Yet the novel's treatment of interracial complexity emphasizes much more than Eliot's how different its culture is than his.

Neither Gordimer nor Naylor gives a female character an interest in Shakespeare comparable to that of Sonny or George, though Gordimer makes recognizing an allusion an important bond between Sonny and Hannah and Naylor voices both extremely rejecting and extremely accepting attitudes through Cocoa. It is interesting to compare this gendering with that of Charlotte Brontë in *Shirley* and Virginia Woolf in *Night and Day,* where the interest in Shakespeare belongs to a woman. Caroline's reading of *Coriolanus* has authority and would provide a useful warning to Robert if he would listen. While Mrs. Hilbery often seems rather silly, she facilitates (by her trip to Shakespeare's grave and her return) an ending in which the right couples get matched, against the force of convention and propriety. Thus, Carol Thomas Neely has suggested, she appropriates Shakespeare on behalf of women's power.[31] Arguably the move to give Shakespeare reading to male rather than to female characters, even in novels by women, is another symptom of a cultural shift. It shows greater self-consciousness about the gendercrossing involved in appropriating him and its parallel to the gendercrossing they do in creating male characters.[32]

Jane Smiley

Unlike this series of recent novels in which characters read and allude to Shakespeare, Jane Smiley's *A Thousand Acres* returns to the mode in which fiction repeats a Shakespearean plot without any explicit verbal allusion, the mode of *Silas Marner* and of portions of *Adam Bede.*[33] Indeed, the word "repeats" is more appropriate here than usual, since the novel begins with a father's offer to retire and turn over his large farm to his three daughters, shows the family conflicts that this plan precipitates, and ends soon after his death. The jacket copy explicitly suggests that the novel is a translation of Shakespeare's play to an American farm—"The forces that bound Lear and his daughters reverberate beneath the surface"—and that it is, but it is also a devastating critique of the Lear figure, the patriarchy that maintains his domination, and other aspects of the power structure in the contemporary United States. The novel's connections between *Lear* and U.S. policy in Vietnam most obviously link it with the others considered in this chapter, but with the conversion of Shakespeare's tragic hero into Larry Cook, a secretly incestuous child beater, Smiley attacks the dominant assumptions in Anglo-American cultural tradition as drastically as does any postcolonial writer.

Smiley's narrator is Ginny, the oldest daughter, who welcomes receiving the farm and has always spoken carefully to her father, "as a daughter, not as a woman," she puts it. Alliteration as well as initial response to Larry's offer indicates to a large extent which of Smiley's characters is playing which *Lear* character's part; thus her most drastic decentering of the original story is to retell it not from Cordelia's point of view but from Goneril's and to imagine that the resentment the two oldest daughters have toward their father is motivated partly by his history of cruelty to them, cruelty that includes sexual abuse. As in Shakespeare's play, the family crisis is connected to crises in the whole society's well-being and ideology, but the visions of these connections are articulated by the daughters, not by the father. Rose, the second sister, says of her community, "They all accept beating as a way of life." Ginny questions her husband's assumptions of "progress" and "grand history," which he uses to justify his continued investment to expand the farm, and which she formerly shared, and says,

> I see taking what you want because you want it, then making something up that justifies what you did. . . . Do I think Daddy came up with beating and fucking us on his own? . . . No, I think he had lessons, and those lessons were part of the package, along with the land and the lust to run things exactly the way he wanted to no matter what,

poisoning the water and destroying the topsoil and buying bigger and better machinery, and then feeling certain than all of it was "right," as you say. (342–43)

The novel's connection between familial, national, and ecological issues is clinched by the rewriting of Edmund as Jess, who has just returned from Canada, where he had gone to escape being sent to Vietnam, and who brings to the dialogue an educated knowledge of organic farming and chemical poisoning. The original Lear had cursed Goneril with infertility; Ginny has had five miscarriages, and Jess explains to her that they probably result from the fertilizer runoff into their well water.

Caroline, the only daughter who went to college, resists her father's plan to give away the farm and eventually helps him sue the other daughters to get it back. The one most likely to have read the play, she sees the family story in a way close to the conventional reading of *Lear:* "He knew he'd treated me unfairly, but that we really felt love for each other. He made amends. We got really close at the end" (362). She says to Ginny, "You have a thing against Daddy. It's just greed or something. . . . I realize that some people are just evil" (363). The novel shows this view to be inadequate.

Ginny's viewpoint, however, does not maintain itself in a self-righteous insistence that, on the contrary, she is all good and her father is all evil. Without being disabled by it, she remembers the evil she herself has done—in another rewriting of Goneril's behavior, she has, rather circuitously, tried to poison Rose, largely out of resentment at her affair with Jess. Unlike Goneril's attempt, hers fails, and as Rose is dying of cancer, she confesses. Rose's response is anticlimactic but thematically apt—"you didn't have to bother. All that well water we drank did the trick instead" (355). But Ginny uses her memory of this attempted crime for greater understanding, emphasized in the novel's final paragraph. "I can't say that I forgive my father, but now I can imagine what he probably chose never to remember—the goad of an unthinkable urge, pricking him, pressing him, wrapping him in an impenetrable fog of self" (370–71).[34]

The novel has a number of rough paraphrases of *Lear,* including such dialogue as "I gave you everything, and I get nothing in return, just some orders about doing this and being that and seeing points of view"

(182); "I curse you! You'll never have children, Ginny, you haven't got a hope" (183). "Threw a man off his own farm, on a night when you'd a let a rabid dog into the barn" (218). But no one consciously quotes Shakespeare or says anything like, "I saw a play once where something like this happened." In this respect, the novel is partly seeking verisimilitude with regard to the cultural resources of midwestern farmers in 1979; they read such magazines as *Reader's Digest, Creative Farming,* and *Good Housekeeping,* and Rose's daughter, who is in high school, finds *David Copperfield* too difficult because of the old-fashioned language. But it is also clear that reading *Lear* wouldn't have helped anyone in the novel, since they, like most more literary people, would either have read it the way Caroline reads the story of her family or would have dismissed it as totally irrelevant. Like most of the novels I have been discussing, *A Thousand Acres* is concerned with heritage, but it is less self-consciously concerned with literary heritage and more with a heritage of ideologies and material practices as well as with literal familial heritage. The novel is less about Shakespeare's cultural place than about beliefs in patriarchy evident in traditional Shakespeare readings as well as elsewhere in our society.

Nevertheless, it could be argued that this novel is also concerned with cultural hybridity. The jacket guides readers to recognize that the novel has translated *Lear* into a completely different world. In this world, a conservative midwestern American tradition of farming, family, and war clashes with a more critical political consciousness aware of ecological, psychological, and international damage. Furthermore, the jacket of this novel, in its initial hardback edition, by its red stripes suggests its concern with American national identity; it is a detail from a quilt, suggesting also the patchwork quilt that, as Elaine Showalter has written, has long been identified with women's culture and now, in its suggestion of diversity united, is "the central metaphor of American cultural identity."[35]

Margaret Drabble

Margaret Drabble's return to an interest in Shakespeare is perhaps the most surprising of my recent examples. In 1991, after *A Natural Curiosity,* with few Shakespeare allusions, she published *The Gates of Ivory,* about half of it set in Southeast Asia, where Stephen Cox goes to understand Cambodia and Pol Pot and where Liz Headland goes to find him.[36] "Alas, poor Yorick!" is a repeated phrase and Yorick's skull a central symbol. The novel refers to a poem by a Vietnamese, Che Lan Vien, called "Hamlet in Vietnam," which "looks back to the days of innocent history when one man could interrogate one skull. Nixon, the poet says, has no liking for the philosophic skull, which smiles back. He prefers the seven-ton bomb which destroys the lot" (215–16, 225). But the Vietnamese woman who recommended the poem says, "It is also about Cambodia." Several central characters in the novel are trying to come to terms with the fact that it is not just First World colonialist powers that inflict mass violence. Aaron, Liz's son, directs *Coriolanus* as "a vision of a world of arbitrary, bloody power, of power for its own sake, of power beyond ideology or justification . . . , the rule of the old men. . . . We are ruled by the handful who set the diamonds in the sockets, who then retire behind the screen" (179–80). The vision of war the novel conveys is very similar.

Two of Drabble's main uses of Shakespeare in this novel—allusions to *Coriolanus* and to Hamlet's "Alas, poor Yorick"—in some ways resemble the two main uses of Shakespeare in Charlotte Brontë's *Shirley* but with significant differences. While Brontë opposed a determined individual, modeled on Coriolanus, to the ideal of sympathy with a larger community, Drabble opposes the violent mob, taken from the Roman and Volscian citizens of that play at their worst, to an individual expression of sympathy made powerless by the fact that its object is dead and distanced because it is expressed by a cliché. Coriolanus's heroism is an illusion, for Aaron, and probably for Drabble; he too was manipulated along with the rest. Coriolanus instead has become the missing soldier Mitra Akrun, who "does not care whether his mother lives or dies. He marches on. He is multitudes" (462). Individual acts of kindness are still important in this novel, but the characters whose minds we follow have given up hope that they can establish a just society—evoked partly in terms from Lear's visionary call to the rich: Agencies such as Oxfam and UNICEF "had been founded . . . to shake down the superflux and to spread around the good things of the earth. . . . But it had appeared that they had all been misguided. . . . For there was, it had turned out, no superflux. There was no limit to man's greed" (124).

Stephen, a novelist who sometimes experiences moments when "he as observer dissolves and flows away into the daily life of others" (205; like Stephen Dedalus's artist), can also be seen as a rewriting of Hamlet, comparable to Eliot's rewriting in Daniel Deronda, who also has moments of "half-speculative, half-involuntary identification of himself with the objects he was looking at."[37] We are told that Stephen wanted to find out what was happening in Cambodia, having a view "that there were more than two sides to every story" (17)—like Daniel's many-sided sympathy. Before he leaves, he thinks that "he has nothing to lose. Except his life, except his life, except his life," echoing Hamlet's lines to Claudius. But while Daniel finds a political movement that seems to flow from his rediscovered identity, and the book ends with hope for his epic accomplishments, Stephen finds a political movement that leads to a world recalling *Macbeth*. His notebook, mailed back to Liz after his death, has "quite a few *Macbeth* quotes dotted about. . . . Bleed, bleed, poor country. Blood will have blood, they say" (50). Sometimes Stephen himself seems to be identified with Macbeth: the narrator says, "like Macbeth he has no children" (136), and he "wants to sup full of horrors."

There are comic uses of Shakespeare in this novel—the versions of Cleopatra in Miss Porntip, the international entrepreneur from Bangkok, and in Hattie Osborne, the forty-year-old literary agent and former B-movie performer, who says she is haunted by the lines "And from the blown rose, many stop their nose / That kneeled unto the bud" (50), decides she wants a child, and, at the end of the novel, has one by Aaron, who is attracted to her because of his buried memory of one of those movies. But even after the renewing post-Memorial party at the end, some ominous words from *Macbeth*, "Fail not our Feast" (19), written in red in Stephen's notebooks, echo in Liz's mind when she thinks about absent guests: "Why had they failed her feast?" (461). Like George Eliot, Drabble plays Shakespearean genres off against each other, but the comic elements in the resolution are pitted against a vision of a victimized country, partly evoked through *Macbeth*, unprecedented in the works of earlier women novelists discussed here.

Even more than most of the other authors I have discussed in this chapter, Drabble has written a consciously international novel, and has engaged with Shakespeare as an international author. It is part of the context of her novel, not only that Che Lan Vien could write a poem contrasting Yorick's skull with those created by modern mass killing, but also that in the 1980s the French-Russian-English Ariane Mnouchkine used Eastern theatrical techniques to produce *Richard II* and *Henry IV, Part I* at her Paris Théâtre du Soleil, and that Hélène Cixous then wrote, for the same theater, a play on Cambodian history called *The Terrible but Unfinished History of Norodim Sihanouk, King of Cambodia* that used techniques from Shakespeare's histories.[38] It is also part of its context that *Macbeth* and *Hamlet* have frequently been produced, especially in continental Europe, as protests against tyranny.

When theater directors give plays post-seventeenth-century settings and costumes, they still often justify the practice by speaking of Shakespeare's universality.[39] Even when Ariane Mnouchkine says, "Shakespeare is not our contemporary and must not be treated as such," she goes on to say, "he is distant from us, as distant as our own profoundest depths."[40] When the women novelists I discuss imagine versions of Shakespearean characters and plots in different settings, however, the point is usually to emphasize how they would be different—to qualify the idea of Shakespeare's universality. Angela Carter uses for one of her epigrams Ellen Terry's complaint, "How many times Shakespeare draws fathers and daughters, never mothers and daughters," and structures the families in *Wise Children* differently. Jane Smiley draws her epigram from Meridel LeSueur, which begins, "The body repeats the landscape," to emphasize that she will write a plot like Shakespeare's *Lear* but with a consciousness that is feminist, socialist, and ecologically minded as well as rooted in the Midwest, like that of LeSueur.[41]

But in *The Gates of Ivory* Drabble suggests a different approach to the question of Shakespeare's universality. Unlike Smiley, Carter, or Gordimer, she is not organizing her novel centrally on a revision of one of his plots. Instead, when Stephen uses lines from *Macbeth* to write about Cambodia, it represents, ambiguously, the possibility of literary response to mass killing. The response is inadequate, and may seem old-fashioned, "humanistic," but Stephen—and Drabble—make it anyway. This recontextualizing of Shakespeare, giving his words a new meaning, could easily be interpreted as confirming his universality, although other uses of Shakespeare in the same novel deny it. The novel puts these views of Shakespeare in tension, as it puts different genres in tension. Indeed, the narrator is self-consciously explicit about its tension: "Perhaps, for this subject matter, one should seek the most disjunctive, the most disruptive, the most uneasy and incompetent of forms, a form that offers not a grain of comfort or repose" (138). *The Gates of Ivory* engages with Shakespeare, but it also engages with Joyce, Conrad, Rimbaud, Gide, and Malraux, with Graham Greene, John Buchan, and travel writing, and, as the appended bibliography emphasizes, with other books on topics ranging from refugees, war, and Bangkok masseuses to Southeast Asian religion. Close to the end of his journey, Stephen meets a Japanese journalist, Akira, who describes himself in a way that echoes, oddly, Keats's description of Shakespeare ("every thing and no thing"; see Chapter 1) but with a very different tone. "I am pulled . . . like the man on the rack. Because I am all things and nothing. No nation, no place, all places. No thing. All things crammed into me, all contradictions of history. . . . I am not *viable.* I am sacrifice. I am explosion, implosion" (232). Akira is an emblem for what the ideal of universality or inclusiveness means in the contemporary world as seen through the postmodern novel.

Changes in Re-Visions of Shakespeare

The continuum of attitudes toward Shakespeare shown by the novelists I discuss in chapters 7 and 8 is not strictly chronological: Cather is more of a bardolater than Eliot; Murdoch more than Woolf in some ways. (Perhaps North American women writers have often found Shakespeare more malleable for appropriation according to their desires than English writers, who are more conscious of the ways his works have been interpreted by the dominant culture.) All of the novels can be read as ambivalent to some degree, but overall women's use of Shakespeare as a model of the sympathetic writer drastically declines from the 1960s onward. Some women writers have expanding their readers' understanding of other people as a goal, others do not; neither kind evokes a cultural image of Shakespeare as a model as strongly as did Woolf, Murdoch, Cather, Eliot, and Brontë, though there is a hint of this usage in Gordimer, Naylor, and Drabble.[42]

This decline is not surprising. Many women writers are critical of the tradition that associates writing with sympathy, or ambivalent about it. For example, Gordimer, like Atwood, stresses the need for writers to be ruthless in order to find time to write, while she believes that writers "can enter other people's lives."[43] Those who still make use of this tradition have many more possible models in established women writers; they no longer need to choose for model a man they can create in their own image. And they may well be aware of the many readings—materialist, feminist, postcolonial—that deny Shakespeare's universality and show his limitations.

Yet many of them are still rewriting Shakespeare in other ways, for other reasons. When I began looking for twentieth-century women novelists' rewritings of Shakespeare, around 1983, the only relevant post–1960 examples seemed to be *The Diviners, Realms of Gold,* and several novels by Iris Murdoch. Since then, Murdoch seems to have become less interested in Shakespeare, but Carter, Atwood, Naylor, Gordimer, Smiley, and, circuitously, Drabble, have become more so— not at all in adulatory ways but in self-conscious explorations of the relation of contemporary cultures to traditions.[44] Clearly the spread of postcolonial criticism and rewritings has added dimensions to women writers' interest in examining their relations to Shakespeare. Not only *The Tempest* but also *King Lear*—both plays of fathers and daughters, thus making it possible to criticize heritage in relation to gender as well as to colonialism—have been much more prominent in recent appropriations than they were in the nineteenth century. Contrary to the views of Elaine Showalter, I would argue that the recent appropriations I have discussed are not self-defeating and obsolete strategies of legitimation.[45] Rather, they appear in novels that meditate on the links of the present to a past that includes cultural fathers as well as cultural mothers, not necessarily for legitimation (note the importance of illegitimacy in *Mama Day* and *Wise Children*), but often for the sake of understanding a condition of hybridity.

While in nineteenth-century Anglo-America many well-known

white male novelists, such as Scott, Dickens, Thackeray, and Melville, engaged with Shakespeare, it seems that in the twentieth century most of the well-known novelistic rewriters in English have been either female or males with some kind of minority identity, from the Irish Joyce onward.[46] On the other hand, there are far more revisions of Shakespeare by well-known white male playwrights and film directors. Some of them, such as Edward Bond's *Bingo* and *Lear,* Arnold Wesker's *The Merchant,* and Gus Van Sant's *My Own Private Idaho,* can also be seen as oppositional responses, from perspectives based on class, ethnicity, or sexuality. Others, such as Peter Greenaway's *Prospero's Books,* seem more simply celebratory.

The few Shakespeare-engaged plays by women that have reached the stage deal with many of the same issues that are addressed by the women novelists I have discussed: to my knowledge, most of them focus on rewriting the plots of Shakespeare's tragedies. Anne-Marie Mac-Donald's *Goodnight Desdemona (Good Morning Juliet),* winner of Canada's Governor General's Award for Drama in 1990, shows a female Shakespearean scholar who magically travels into *Othello* and *Romeo and Juliet,* changing their worlds from tragic into comic at the same time that she learns to express her own love and anger, cross-dresses, and eventually comes to see herself as an author. In Alison Lyssa's *Pinball,* a child custody trial scene has clear references to *The Merchant of Venice* in the use of cross-dressing and several other ways but also questions the authority of a Lear-like father.[47] A feminist theater collective called Hormone Imbalance imagines Ophelia running away with a maidservant, and the Women's Theatre Group's *Lear's Daughters* shows a multiracial father-absent family (with a nanny) competing for a crown.[48] The relatively few cases of women's plays or films rewriting Shakespeare, in contrast to women's novels rewriting him or men's plays or films rewriting him, can largely be attributed, I believe, to women's greater difficulty in getting plays or films produced in the first place. On the other hand, the novel has been a form relatively accessible to women from its beginning.

Yet I want to return to the point that in twentieth-century Anglophone literature, more women than men, and particularly more women than white men, have written novels engaging with Shakespeare. Per-

haps this contrast occurs partly because a difference in perspective beyond the obvious difference of three hundred years provides a greater
opportunity for an interesting novel. Yet when women (and some men)
differentiate their visions from Shakespeare's by their writing, that differentiation is often combined with affection. The most startling example of this is Carter's *Wise Children,* because her criticism is so emphatic about the revisionary purpose of her use of the "outmoded lies"
of past literature, and yet this fantasy is full of detailed loving parody.

Many contemporary women novelists, of course, never allude to
Shakespeare, or do so only briefly and critically. This fact, combined
with the analyses in this chapter, helps make it plain that engaging
with him does not mean submitting to an imposed monolithic figure of
authority. It is a choice that involves many other choices and coexists
with many other engagements. In the revisionary family metaphors of
Wise Children, for Carter and for many others, Shakespeare is less like
the monumental and rejecting Melchior, the begetter of Nora and Dora,
than like their generous, if often disappearing, uncle Peregrine. He is
both elusive and surprisingly useful as a resource. Even writers chal-
lenging a father's moral authority and legal and physical power may
find that the words of Shakespearean characters who are also protesting
against their fathers make a good beginning for a late twentieth-century
protest, though it is only a beginning. On the other hand, *The Gates
of Ivory,* which of all these recent novels seems to express the greatest
nostalgia for Shakespeare as a moral touchstone, engages mostly with
Macbeth, Hamlet, and Coriolanus, two childless men and one who is
seen much more in relation to his mother than to his son. Shakespeare,
in *The Gates of Ivory,* is not associated with fatherhood but rather dis-
persed into a multiplicity of plots, lines, and characters; the novel seems
to mourn him rather than to criticize him.[49]

George Eliot's uses of Shakespeare combined with her uses of
Sophocles, Milton, Goethe, Strauss, Schlegel, Feuerbach, Wordsworth,
Rousseau, Wollstonecraft, Austen, and Brontë, to name a few. This list
is diverse, and yet the writers are all from Europe; many of the later
writers knew much of the earlier writers' work. Though voices of her
characters from different classes, genders, and points of view contrast,
the tone of Eliot's novels, and her narrative voice, encourage reading

them as unified—as what she called "wholes composed of parts more & more multiplied & highly differenced, yet more & more absolutely bound together by various conditions of common likeness or mutual dependence."[50]

In more recent novels, the engagement may be not only with Shakespeare but also with literature from Africa, Asia, Native America, or African America. The novelist may reconstruct Shakespeare's "popular voice," as Annabel Patterson has called it,[51] by linking him with music hall traditions, or his "green" vision, as in Smiley's rewriting of Edmund's nature speeches into the language of contemporary environmentalists and of Lear into a farmer who colludes in the destruction of nature. But there is more apt to be a sense of surprise, of bridging gaps, of cross-breeding, in their uses of Shakespeare. Often several sharply differentiated narrative voices appear in the same novel, and more different forms of discourse are incorporated without being assimilated. The reader meets heterogeneous materials with incomplete mediation, in a way more analogous to the experience of reading a play than to the experience of reading a novel with one central guiding narrator. Eliot was, in her own time, bridging some gaps in extending tragic language to such characters as Maggie Tulliver, in using scientific language in her novels, and in combining Shakespearean rewriting with analysis of Victorian Anglo-Jewish life in *Daniel Deronda*. But to the late twentieth-century reader, these combinations have lost most of their earlier daring.

Early critics associated Shakespeare with nature, and nineteenth-century women novelists could use him as a kind of mediating figure suggesting the possibility of bringing more nature into the realm of culture, as Eliot had associated his women, in contrast to Scott's, with frank passion. For contemporary women novelists, his writings are human constructions. Yet, although now often without the privileged place in English departments they once had, Shakespeare's plays are more likely to be known to readers than are any other pre-twentieth-century works. Women novelists may rewrite them to attack the problems of our dominant cultural tradition or evoke them to suggest hopeful possibilities or at least productive contradictions within it. But in our condition of cultural hybridity, a novelist's engagement with Shakespeare appears as part of a complex, discontinuous genealogy that includes many voices in dialogue.[52]

I have frequently used the term "appropriation" for women novelists' use of Shakespeare; this choice should not suggest, however, that they are trying to make him their private property, unavailable to any group of readers. Rather, their revisions serve more to combat exclusionary uses of Shakespeare fostered by the belief that the white male critic has a privileged perspective. Thus the novels I discuss in this chapter, like most of those I discuss in this book, are political as well as literary. Few, if any, of them claim that Shakespeare is universal, but they do claim the importance of women's voices in the public conversation about what to celebrate in his works, what to criticize, and, in general, what to juxtapose with today's world. In Virginia Woolf's words, "Literature is no one's private ground; literature is common ground."[53]

Notes

Introduction

1. Myra Jehlen, "Archimedes and the Paradox of Feminist Criticism," *Signs* 6, 4 (Summer 1981):582.
2. Michael Bristol, *Shakespeare's America, America's Shakespeare* (New York: Routledge, 1990), 5.
3. For some studies of male authors' uses of Shakespeare, see G. B. Evans, ed., *Shakespeare: Aspects of Influence* (Cambridge, Mass.: Harvard University Press, 1976), and Ruby Cohn, *Modern Shakespeare Offshoots* (Princeton: Princeton University Press, 1976); Cohn discusses works by two women, Barbara Garson and Alethea Hayter, and eighty-three men. More recently, *The Appropriation of Shakespeare: Post-Renaissance Reconstructions of the Works and the Myth,* ed. Jean Marsden (New York: St. Martin's, 1992), includes discussion of rewritings by Mrs. Humphrey Ward and Louisa May Alcott in John Glavin's "Caught in the Act; or, The Prosing of Juliet" (93–110), and by Angela Carter in Marjorie Garber's "The Transvestite's Progress: Rosalind the Yeshiva Boy" (145–62), but does not explore a tradition of women novelists' uses of Shakespeare as I do. Peter Erickson's *Rewriting Shakespeare, Rewriting Ourselves* (Berkeley: University of California Press, 1991), discusses post–1960 American women writers, only one of whom, Gloria Naylor, is a novelist. My anthologies *Women's Re-Visions of Shakespeare* (Urbana: University of Illinois Press, 1990) and *Cross-Cultural Performances: Differences in Women's Re-Visions of Shakespeare* (Urbana: University of Illinois Press, 1993) include essays on several women novelists (Eliot, Charlotte Brontë, Woolf, Margaret Laurence, Sarah Murphy, Toni Morrison, and Naylor), among essays on poets, playwrights, actresses, directors, and critics, rather than focusing on the novel.
4. See U. C. Knoepflmacher, *"Daniel Deronda* and William Shakespeare," *Victorian Newsletter* 19 (1961):27–28.
5. M. M. Bakhtin, "Discourse in the Novel," in *The Dialogic Imagination* (Austin: University of Texas Press, 1981), 259–422, esp. 324.
6. I am here using the term as does Susan Stanford Friedman, in "Weav-

ings: Intertextuality and the (Re)Birth of the Author," in *Influence and Intertextuality in Literary History,* ed. Jay Clayton and Eric Rothstein (Madison: University of Wisconsin Press, 1991), 146–80, esp. 157, maintaining the concept of the writer's subjectivity but also including unconscious rewritings. But see the discussion of influence and intertextuality as contrasted in "Figures in the Corpus: Theories of Influence and Intertextuality," by Jay Clayton and Eric Rothstein, in the same volume, pp. 3–36.

7. See, for example, Gary Taylor, *Reinventing Shakespeare* (New York: Weidenfeld & Nicholson, 1989), 167.

8. My approach is similar to the use of Bakhtin by Patricia Yaeger in *Honey-Mad Women* (New York: Columbia University Press, 1988); see esp. 165–66, 180–206, in particular her argument that "the novel is an emancipatory form which permits the woman novelist to refuse and revise other literary genres" (186).

9. I have particularly benefited from analogous work by Nina Auerbach in *Woman and the Demon* (Cambridge, Mass.: Harvard University Press, 1982) and Margaret Homans in *Bearing the Word* (Chicago: University of Chicago Press, 1986).

10. For analyses of such experiences of reading in women who are *not* novelists or poets, see Joan Hutton Landis, " 'Another Penelope': Margaret Hutton Reading William Shakespeare," in Novy, *Women's Re-Visions,* 196–211; Carol Thomas Neely, "Epilogue: Remembering Shakespeare, Revising Ourselves," in the same volume, pp. 242–52; and Paula Bennett, "Gender as Performance: Shakespearean Ambiguity and the Lesbian Reader," in *Sexual Practice, Textual Theory: Lesbian Cultural Criticism,* ed. Julia Penelope and Susan J. Wolfe (Boston: Blackwell, 1993).

11. For a recent discussion of this second mode dealing with male writers other than Shakespeare, see Laura Claridge and Elizabeth Langland, "Introduction," in *Out of Bounds: Male Writers and Gender(ed) Criticism,* ed. Claridge and Langland (Amherst: University of Massachusetts Press, 1990), 3–21.

12. Jay Clayton, in "The Alphabet of Suffering: Effie Deans, Tess Durbeyfield, Martha Ray, and Hetty Sorrel," in Clayton and Rothstein, *Influence and Intertextuality,* 37–60, studies the network of associations in works by Scott, Hardy, Wordsworth, and George Eliot along with the history of infanticide as well as listing as other possible sources "traditional ballads, folklore, other works of fiction and drama, newspaper accounts of infanticide, broadsides of criminals' confessions, court records, historical archives, scientific works, popular science articles, religious tracts, scholarly works of history and social theory, philosophy, personal reminiscences, advice from friends, letters from informants, firsthand obser-

vations, and more" (45). A similar list could be made for the works I
discuss.

Chapter 1. Women Novelists' Engagements with Shakespeare:
Prehistory, Early Tradition, and Critical Contexts

1. Sandra Gilbert and Susan Gubar, *The Madwoman in the Attic* (New Haven:
   Yale University Press, 1979), 187–212.
2. Gilbert and Gubar, *Madwoman,* 29–30, 48.
3. Lady Macbeth is associated with women's anxieties about authorship on
   pp. 35 and 66, Goneril and Regan are mentioned on pp. 30, 34, 266, 241,
   and 285, Ophelia is mentioned on pp. 68, 285, and 618, Cordelia on pp.
   266 and 285. The importance of these characters is not supported with
   direct quotations from the authors discussed except insofar as the echoes
   that Gilbert and Gubar hear, for example those of Lear's daughters in
   Wuthering Heights, are convincing.
4. Mary Wollstonecraft, *A Vindication of the Rights of Woman,* ed. Carol H.
   Poston, rev. ed. (New York: Norton, 1988), 19; *The Female Reader,* ed.
   Moira Ferguson (1789; facs. rpt., Delmar, New York: Scholars' Facsimiles and Reprints, 1980), contains two passages from Milton. In
   Feminist Milton (Ithaca: Cornell University Press, 1987), Joseph Wittreich tries to show that "an early female readership found comfort and
   support in Milton's poetry," p. xiii, and he may be right about some of
   the eighteenth-century women he discusses, but his reading of *Vindication* on pp. 414–42 is less convincing than the interpretation in Gilbert
   and Gubar, *Madwoman,* p. 204. "The first of the masculinists" comes
   from Woolf's *A Writer's Diary* (New York: Harcourt, Brace, 1954), 6,
   quoted in Gilbert and Gubar, *Madwoman,* 190. Woolf describes Shakespeare as androgynous in *A Room of One's Own* (New York: Harcourt
   Brace Jovanovich, 1929), 102, 107, and contrasts him with Milton, whose
   poetry is impeded by grudges (58) and who has "a dash too much of the
   male" (107).
5. But see Diana Postlethwaite, "When George Eliot Reads Milton: The
   Muse in a Different Voice," *ELH* 57 (1990):197–222, for a much more
   positive picture of Eliot's relation to Milton.
6. George Eliot, *A Writer's Notebook, 1854–1879, and Uncollected Writings,* ed.
   Joseph Wiesenfarth (Charlottesville: University Press of Virginia, 1981),
   255. See discussion in my chapter 3.
7. Several feminist critics have related appropriative creativity among
   women writers to Nancy Chodorow's theories about cultural patterns of
   women's development in *The Reproduction of Mothering* (Berkeley: University of California Press, 1978); see Judith Kegan Gardiner, "On Female

Identity and Writing by Women," *Critical Inquiry* 8 (1981): 347–62; Mary
Poovey, *The Proper Lady and the Woman Writer* (Chicago: University of
Chicago Press, 1984), esp. 44, 254n; and Michael Awkward, *Inspiriting
Influences: Tradition, Revision, and Afro-American Women's Novels* (New
York: Columbia University Press, 1989). Jonathan Bate, *Shakespearean
Constitutions* (Oxford: Clarendon Press, 1989), 2–5, discusses the term
"appropriation" and its uses by Hans Robert Jauss, Robert Weimann,
and Walter Benjamin.

8. Judith Fetterley, *The Resisting Reader* (Bloomington: Indiana University
Press, 1978), xx.

9. Ann Rosalind Jones, *The Currency of Eros: Women's Love Lyric in Europe,
1540–1620* (Bloomington: Indiana University Press, 1990), 4. Jones is
building on the work of Stuart Hall in "Encoding/Decoding," *Culture,
Media, Language,* ed. Stuart Hall et al. (London: Hutchinson, 1980), 128–
38. Gilbert and Gubar have themselves recently argued that the woman
writer of the twentieth century can ease the "anxiety of influence" by
"looking *for*—seeking out, choosing, and thus achieving a kind of power
over—precursors"; see their *No Man's Land,* Vol. 1, *The War of the Words*
(New Haven: Yale University Press, 1988), 199. They apply this possibility of choice only to female precursors, however. Perhaps I should
distinguish my use of "negotiations" from that of Stephen Greenblatt,
who in *Shakespearean Negotiations* (Berkeley: University of California
Press, 1988), is concerned with works' relations to "social energy" in
their culture rather than with their relation to literary tradition.

10. For the view that the characters are ambiguous, so that either assertion
or subordination (or a combination) may be emphasized, see my *Love's
Argument* (Chapel Hill: University of North Carolina Press, 1984). For
the related view that many plays provide a temporary space for women's
freedom, see Carol Neely, *Broken Nuptials in Shakespeare's Plays* (New
Haven: Yale University Press, 1985). On containment, see especially
Peter Erickson, *Patriarchal Structures in Shakespeare's Drama* (Berkeley:
University of California Press, 1985).

11. Feminist criticism of Milton has flourished since the exchange between
Marcia Landy, "Kinship and the Role of Women in *Paradise Lost,*" *Milton
Studies IV,* ed. James D. Simmonds (Pittsburgh: University of Pittsburgh
Press, 1972), 3–18, and Barbara Lewalski, "Milton on Women—Yet Once
More," *Milton Studies VI,* ed. James D. Simmonds (Pittsburgh: University
of Pittsburgh, 1974), 3–20, with more recent books by Diane McCol-
ley, *Milton's Eve* (Urbana: University of Illinois Press, 1986), Catherine
Belsey, *John Milton* (Oxford: Blackwell, 1988), Wittreich, *Feminist Milton,*
Julia Walker's anthology *Milton and the Idea of Woman* (Urbana: Univer-

sity of Illinois Press, 1989), and some articles in Margaret Ferguson's and Mary Nyquist's *Re-Membering Milton* (New York: Methuen, 1989).

12. The Proteus image was used of Burbage by Richard Flecknoe in his *Short Discourse of the English Stage* (1664), quoted in John Russell Brown, "On the Acting of Shakespeare's Plays," in *The Seventeenth Century Stage,* ed. Gerard Eades Bentley (Chicago: University of Chicago Press, 1968), 49. The connection between Shakespeare the actor and Shakespeare the artist of sympathy has been noted by Jonathan Bate, *Shakespeare and the English Romantic Imagination* (Oxford: Clarendon Press, 1986), 165. Bate discusses the growth of Shakespeare criticism as it relates to the eighteenth- and nineteenth-century development of theories of creative imagination on pp. 6–20. See also Earl R. Wasserman, "The Sympathetic Imagination in Eighteenth Century English Theories of Acting," *JEGP* 46 (1947): 264–72, and Meredith Skura's *Shakespeare the Actor* (Chicago: University of Chicago Press, 1993), on his plays in relation to actors' psychology. In the following discussion I draw in part on Marianne Novy, "Women's Re-Visions of Shakespeare, 1664–1988," in Novy, *Women's Re-Visions of Shakespeare,* 2–7.

13. Robert Greene, *Groatesworth of Witte* (1592), ed. G. B. Harrison (1922; rpt., New York: Barnes & Noble, 1966), 45. Susan Wolfson has noted that this is an image of cross-dressing; it suggests the cross-class dressing that most Elizabethan actors did on stage in every performance and, if "beautified" is taken as feminine (but I'm not sure it was so understood in 1592), the cross-gender dressing of the boy actor.

14. Jonas Barish, *The Antitheatrical Prejudice* (Berkeley: University of California Press, 1981), 89–106; Jean Howard, "Renaissance Antitheatricality and the Politics of Gender and Rank in *Much Ado About Nothing,*" in *Shakespeare Reproduced,* ed. Jean Howard and Marion O'Connor (New York: Methuen, 1987), 166–69. Modern psychologists' descriptions of actors—see, for example, Philip Weissman, *Creativity in the Theater* (New York: Basic Books, 1965), 12—are similar to descriptions of women in Chodorow's *The Reproduction of Mothering.* See my *Love's Argument,* 83–98, which also discusses other aspects of the woman/actor connection.

15. C. L. Barber and Richard Wheeler, *The Whole Journey: Shakespeare's Power of Development* (Berkeley: University of California Press, 1986), 61.

16. See Brian Vickers, ed., *Shakespeare: The Critical Heritage, 1623–1801,* 6 vols. (London: Routledge, 1974–81); R. D. Stock, *Samuel Johnson and Neoclassical Dramatic Theory* (London: University of Nebraska Press, 1983). One female critic, Charlotte Lennox, criticized Shakespeare for lack of decorum in her *Shakespeare Illustrated* (London: A. Millar, 1754), a study of his relation to his sources.

17. Aphra Behn, "Preface to *The Dutch Lover,*" in *Works,* 6 vols., ed. Montague Summers (1915; rpt., New York: Phaeton, 1967), 1:224. See the discussion of this passage as well as of Behn's other uses of Shakespeare in Margaret Ferguson, "Transmuting Othello: Aphra Behn's *Oronooko,*" in my anthology, *Cross-Cultural Performances.* Ferguson notes that the condition of being an outsider is relative and that Behn herself was privileged in comparison with nonliterate and nonwhite women.

18. See Taylor, *Reinventing Shakespeare,* 27–28, which also documents the greater stage success of Beaumont and Fletcher at this time.

19. Margaret Cavendish, "General Prologue," in *Playes* (London: A. Warren, for John Martyn et al., 1662). I learned of this source from "'Yet Full Well He Writ': The Duchess of Newcastle's View of Shakespeare," an essay by Brenda Ameter, department of British literature, Troy State University, Dothan, Alabama.

20. Margaret Cavendish, *CCXI Sociable Letters* (1664; rpt., Menston: Scolar Press, 1969), 245–46.

21. John Dryden, "An Essay of Dramatic Poesy," in *Literary Criticism: Plato to Dryden,* ed. Allan Gilbert (Detroit: Wayne State University Press, 1962), 637, 640.

22. Mary Pix, quoted in Constance Clark, *Three Augustan Women Playwrights* (New York: Peter Lang, 1986), 262.

23. Fidelis Morgan, *The Female Wits: Women Playwrights on the London Stage, 1660–1720* (London: Virago, 1981), blames, among other causes, the increasing control of actor-managers. She also notes the twentieth-century persistence of theater's inaccessibility to women playwrights: "in all London's theatres during the sixty years from 1920 to 1980, . . . fewer plays by women writers have been performed than were played by the two London companies which held the dramatic monopoly from 1660 to 1720" (xi).

24. See Joseph Donohue, *Theatre in the Age of Kean* (Totowa, N.J.: Rowman & Littlefield, 1975), 161, on the growth of the habit of reading plays, and its development as an alternative to theatergoing; see also Taylor, *Reinventing Shakespeare,* esp. 92–93, on early women readers of Shakespeare such as the "Shakespeare Ladies Club."

25. See, for example, George Levine, *The Realistic Imagination* (Chicago: University of Chicago Press, 1981), 72, and Harry Levin, *The Gates of Horn* (New York: Oxford University Press, 1963), 47.

26. Sarah Fielding and Jane Collier, *The Cry* (Delmar, N.Y.: Scholars' Facsimiles and Reprints, 1986), 2:241. I owe this reference and the next to Lissette Carpenter, who has also pointed out how in Fielding's novel Portia's knowledge of logic develops the learning of Shakespeare's Portia. Carpenter notes that Fielding's Portia stays more in control of the

conditions of her marriage and is critical of flattery such as that which Shakespeare's Portia accepts from Bassanio.

27. Sarah Fielding, *The Lives of Cleopatra and Octavia,* ed. R. Brimley Johnson (London: Scholartis Press, 1928), xliii.

28. Sarah Fielding, *The History of the Countess of Delwyn* (1759; rpt., New York: Garland, 1974), 2:15–16, quoted and discussed in Susan Lanser, *Fictions of Authority* (Ithaca: Cornell University Press, 1992), 50.

29. Sarah Fielding, *The History of Ophelia* (New York: Garland, 1974), 161.

30. Frances Burney, *Camilla* (New York: Oxford University Press, 1972), 323.

31. Margaret Doody, *Frances Burney* (New Brunswick, N.J.: Rutgers University Press, 1988), 224–25. She also recalls the comparison made between Desdemona and Burney herself in her marriage with d'Arblay, a foreign general. She observes that the cruelty of Sedley's imagined "pleasure of seeing him stop up those distressing nostrils of the gentle Desdemona" (322) "points out in the process some elements of real cruelty in the dramatist's treatment of Desdemona" (258).

32. See also Burney's *Cecilia* (1782), in which the basic situation—a woman can inherit money only if her husband takes on her surname—is compared by Doody (111) to that of Portia in *The Merchant of Venice*. Deborah Ross, in *The Excellence of Falsehood: Romance, Realism, and Women's Contribution to the Novel* (Lexington: University Press of Kentucky, 1991), 154–59, finds much rewriting of *Romeo and Juliet* in *Cecilia* and in Ann Radcliffe's *The Italian* (1797), which was one of the first novels to use chapter epigraphs from Shakespeare. According to J. M. S. Tompkins, *The Popular Novel in England, 1770–1800* (London: Constable, 1932), 146, Mrs. Peach in the anonymous *The Correspondents* (1775), wrote of Shakespeare, "he is the only poet (that I know of) who has delineated to perfection the character of a *female friend,*" especially in Celia; Tompkins also notes Lady Mary Walker's interest in Rosalind and Celia in her *Letters from the Duchess de Crui* (1776).

33. Henry Fielding, "The Preface," in Sarah Fielding, *The Adventures of David Simple* (New York: Oxford University Press, 1969), 5, 7.

34. Janet Todd, *The Sign of Angellica: Women, Writing, and Fiction, 1660–1800* (London: Virago, 1989), 121–22; see also Poovey, *The Proper Lady,* 3–47, and, on the regulation of the female voice, Lanser, *Fictions of Authority,* 25–49.

35. Edward Burnaby Greene, *Critical Essays* (1770), 226, quoted in Taylor, *Reinventing Shakespeare,* 137.

36. Anonymous, *The Critical Review,* ser. 2, II (August 1794), in *Novel and Romance, 1700–1800,* ed. Ioan Williams (New York: Barnes & Noble, 1970), 389. According to Tompkins, *The Popular Novel,* 248, 252, Nathan

Drake, *Literary Hours* (1798), called her the "Shakespeare of Romance-writers" because of her mingling of beauty and terror.

37. Todd, *Sign of Angellica,* 127.

38. Burke, *Philosophical Enquiry,* ed. J. B. Boulton (Notre Dame: University of Notre Dame Press, 1968), 44.

39. Adam Smith, *The Theory of Moral Sentiments* (New Rochelle, N.Y.: Arlington House, 1969), 5, 4.

40. David Marshall, *The Figure of Theater: Shaftesbury, Defoe, Adam Smith, and George Eliot* (New York: Columbia University Press, 1986), 181, 184.

41. This passage is discussed by Poovey on p. 19. Compare a condescending treatment of women in connection with the related concept of pity in David Hume, *A Treatise of Human Nature* (Oxford: Clarendon Press, 1896): "Women and children are most subject to pity, as being most guided by that faculty [imagination]. The same infirmity, which makes them faint at the sight of a naked sword, tho' in the hands of their best friend, makes them pity extremely those, whom they find in any grief or affliction" (370).

42. Heinz Kohut, *How Does Analysis Cure?* (Chicago: University of Chicago Press, 1984), 174–75, quoted by Judith Kegan Gardiner in *Rhys, Stead, Lessing, and the Politics of Empathy* (Bloomington: Indiana University Press, 1990), 2. "Empathy," according to the *Oxford English Dictionary,* first appeared in English in 1912, in the translation of "Einfühlung" in the aesthetic theory of Theodor Lipps. Probably intended to sound more scientific than "sympathy," it has taken on some of the same range of meaning. Gardiner emphasizes with respect to empathy, in her second definition, as I would do for both definitions and for sympathy, that "it is not an intuitive natural capacity but one formed through experience and capable of training and development, a training currently [and in the eighteenth and nineteenth centuries] more common among women than men" (2–3). In *The Lifted Veil* (written 1859), George Eliot's narrator has an involuntary and totally loveless knowledge of other people's unspoken feelings (a parody of the detached form of sympathy), and it fuels his disgust for them; see chapter 3.

43. Elizabeth Montagu, *An Essay on the Writings and Genius of Shakespear* (1769; rpt., New York: Augustus M. Kelly, 1970), 36, 201.

44. Montagu, *An Essay,* 37.

45. Elizabeth Montagu, to Lord Lyttelton, September 10, 1760, in *Letters of Mrs. Elizabeth Montagu,* 4 vols. (1813; rpt., New York: AMS Press, 1974), 4:299. For calling my attention to this letter, in which Montagu originally developed the Dervish comparison, I am indebted to the late Sylvia Myers.

46. Montagu's importance is stressed by Stock, *Samuel Johnson,* 45, and by

Robert Babcock, *The Genesis of Shakespeare Idolatry, 1766–1799* (1931; rpt., New York: Russell & Russell, 1964), 109.

47. Montagu, *An Essay*, 17–18.

48. Coleridge, *Biographia Literaria*, chap. 15, in R. A. Foakes, ed., *Coleridge's Criticism of Shakespeare* (Detroit: Wayne State University Press, 1989), 30. Jonathan Bate, *Romantic Imagination*, 14–15, notes antecedents of Coleridge's Proteus image in Montagu, Edward Capell, William Richardson, and A. W. Schlegel; Richardson had read Montagu, and Schlegel, Bate notes, was influenced by the English preromantics.

49. See John Barrell, *Poetry, Language, and Politics* (Manchester: Manchester University Press, 1988), 65–77. On p. 16, Bate, *Romantic Imagination*, notes the qualification "yet forever remaining himself" in the notebook Coleridge used for his 1811–12 Shakespeare lectures. He quotes *The Notebooks of Samuel Taylor Coleridge*, ed. Kathleen Coburn, 3 vols. (Princeton: Princeton University Press, 1957–), 3:4115, and argues, on p. 15, that this combination of sympathy and detachment influenced Hazlitt. See also Foakes, *Coleridge's Criticism*, 23–24.

50. William Hazlitt, "On Shakespeare and Milton," in *Complete Works*, ed. P. P. Howe, 21 vols. (1930; rpt., New York: AMS Press, 1967), 5:47, 48; *Characters of Shakespear's Plays*, in *Complete Works*, 4:346–47.

51. John Keats, *Letters*, 2 vols., ed. Hyder Rollins (Cambridge, Mass.: Harvard University Press, 1958), 1:386–87. I owe the last point to Susan Wolfson. For Hazlitt's influence on Keats, see Bate, *Romantic Imagination*, 15, 157–74, and David Bromwich, *Hazlitt* (New York: Oxford University Press, 1983), 362–75.

52. Isobel Armstrong, *Victorian Scrutinies: Reviews of Poetry, 1830–1870* (London: Athlone Press, 1972), 38–39.

53. Hazlitt, *Characters*, in *Complete Works*, 4:347.

54. Hazlitt, "A Letter to William Gifford, Esq.," in *Complete Works*, 9:24n. This passage is quoted by Bate, *Shakespearean Constitutions*, 159. On anger, see Bromwich, *Hazlitt*, 5, and G. F. Parker, *Johnson's Shakespeare* (Oxford: Clarendon Press, 1989), who notes that Hazlitt twice quotes "The thing of courage, / As rowz'd with rage, with rage doth sympathize" (*Troilus and Cressida*, 1.3.51–52) to describe Shakespeare's effect on the reader. Sympathy can still be political. In Pennsylvania in 1993, "understanding others" was deleted from the list of goals for "Outcome-Based Education" because of right-wing fear that this would promote homosexuality.

55. William Hazlitt, *Characters*, in *Complete Works*, 4:180.

56. Samuel Taylor Coleridge, *Table Talk*, September 26, 1830; *Shakespearean Criticism*, ed. Thomas Middleton Raysor, 2 vols. (New York: Dutton, 1960), 1:119.

57. Samuel Taylor Coleridge, *Biographia Literaria*, ed. James Engell and W. Jackson Bate, 2 vols. (Princeton: Princeton University Press, 1983), 225. Christine Battersby, *Gender and Genius* (Bloomington: Indiana University Press, 1989), 7, discusses this passage as typical of the exclusion of women from the category of genius even when by writers who describe genius in feminine imagery.

58. Hazlitt, "On the Living Poets," in *Complete Works*, 5:148. I owe this reference to Barbara Schroeder.

59. Nina Auerbach, *Woman and the Demon* (Cambridge, Mass.: Harvard University Press, 1982), 207–17. See also Susan Wolfson's essay on Mary Lamb and Christy Desmet's on Anna Jameson in my *Women's Re-Visions of Shakespeare*.

60. Anna Jameson, *Shakespeare's Heroines: Characteristics of Women: Moral, Political, and Historical*, new ed. (London: George Bell, 1889), 33–34; Elizabeth Barrett Browning, *Aurora Leigh*, introd. Cora Kaplan (London: Women's Press, 1978), 285 (7:224–27). Some analogous female interpretive communities existed in the many study groups in which women discussed Shakespeare. See Theodora Penny Martin, *The Sound of Our Own Voices: Women's Study Clubs, 1860–1910* (Boston: Beacon Press, 1987). It is also worth noting, as Gary Taylor has reminded us, that in the late nineteenth century more women than men studied English, and therefore Shakespeare, at Cambridge and Oxford; see *Reinventing Shakespeare*, 205. For the concept of female interpretive communities, I am indebted to Annette Kolodny, "Dancing Through the Minefield: Some Observations on the Theory, Practice, and Politics of a Feminist Literary Criticism," *Feminist Studies* 6 (1980):1–25, and Patrocinio Schweickart, "Reading Ourselves: Toward a Feminist Theory of Reading," in *Gender and Reading*, ed. Elizabeth A. Flynn and Patrocinio P. Schweickart (Baltimore: Johns Hopkins University Press, 1986), 31–62.

61. Bristol, *Shakespeare's America*, 5.

62. Jameson, *Characteristics of Women*, 5.

63. Catherine Belsey, "Disrupting Sexual Difference: Meaning and Gender in the Comedies," in *Alternative Shakespeares*, ed. John Drakakis (New York: Methuen, 1985:166–90); Jameson, *Characteristics of Women*, 19.

64. George Eliot, *A Writer's Notebook and Uncollected Writings*, ed. Joseph Wiesenfarth (Charlottesville: University Press of Virginia, 1981), 255.

65. On the influence of Wordsworth, see esp. Levine, *Realistic Imagination*, 20; Janice Carlisle, *The Sense of an Audience* (Athens: University of Georgia Press, 1981), 3; see also Donald Stone, *The Romantic Impulse in Victorian Fiction* (Cambridge, Mass.: Harvard University Press, 1980).

66. George Eliot, *Middlemarch*, ed. David Carroll (Oxford: Clarendon Press, 1986), 183 (chap. 19). The immediate reference is to his art criticism, not his literary criticism, but clearly she knew both well.

67. Jameson's book, first published in 1832, had ten editions before her death in 1860, including two German editions; see Clara Thomas, *Love and Work Enough* (London: Macdonald, 1967), 72. Early editions have the title *Characteristics of Women*, which is the title in the running heads of the edition I cite. Geoffrey Ashton, *Shakespeare's Heroines in the Nineteenth Century* (Buxton: Derbyshire Museum Service, 1980), 37, claims that hers was the most widely read Shakespeare criticism in the nineteenth century. Bate makes the same claim for Hazlitt in *Shakespearean Constitutions*, 200. See also John Kinnaird, *William Hazlitt* (New York: Columbia University Press, 1978), 364–65. Wiesenfarth's introduction to *A Writer's Notebook*, xxiii–xxv, discusses Eliot's use of Jameson's *Sacred and Legendary Art* (1848).

68. George Eliot, *The Mill on the Floss*, ed. Gordon S. Haight (Oxford: Clarendon Press, 1980), 314. In *Darwin's Plots* (London: Routledge, 1983), 165–70, Gillian Beer discusses other Victorian uses of web imagery; none includes the word "mingled."

69. Stuart Tave, *The Amiable Humorist* (Chicago: University of Chicago Press, 1960), 212. Bate, *Romantic Imagination*, 261n, gives seven uses in Hazlitt and also notes Keats's use of it in *Letters* (1:169), after he had read Hazlitt's *Round Table*.

70. Carol Gilligan, *In a Different Voice* (Cambridge, Mass.: Harvard University Press, 1982), 48, 62. Gilligan discusses *Mill on the Floss* on pp. 69, 130–31, 143, and 148–49, where she quotes the *Mill* narrator on the need for sympathy in making moral judgments. N. Katherine Hayles, "Anger in Different Voices: Carol Gilligan and *The Mill on the Floss*," *Signs* 12 (Autumn 1986):23–39, argues that Gilligan misses the novel's analysis of Maggie's difficulty in dealing with her anger. Gilligan's book also includes a brief discussion of *The Merchant of Venice* that emphasizes Portia's speaking for mercy and ignores problems with the ending. Gilligan is now working with Kristin Linklater in The Company of Women, an acting company in which women use Shakespeare to gain access to their own voices.

71. Bate, *Shakespearean Constitutions*, 7. Compare also Annabel Patterson's use of both Renaissance history and later references to Shakespeare to argue against the antipopular Shakespeare in *Shakespeare and the Popular Voice* (Cambridge: Blackwell, 1989). I note Peter Erickson's caution, however, with regard to Bate's sentence just quoted, that we should "recognize the dimensions of the change in our conception of liberty" from Hazlitt's and value new literature "that opposes and eludes the Shakespearean mold"; see "The Two Renaissances and Shakespeare's Canonical Position," *Kenyon Review*, n.s., 14 (Spring 1992): 62.

72. Similar points have been made by Auerbach in *Woman and the Demon* and by many of the contributors in Novy, *Women's Re-Visions of Shakespeare*.

73. Natalie Zemon Davis, *Society and Culture in Early Modern France* (Stanford: Stanford University Press, 1975), 143.
74. George Eliot, *A Writer's Notebook*, 255.

Chapter 2. Jane Austen and Charlotte Brontë

1. Jane Austen, *Mansfield Park* (Boston: Houghton Mifflin, 1965), 256. This passage is discussed by Frank Bradbrook, *Jane Austen and Her Predecessors* (Cambridge: Cambridge University Press, 1967), 71, and more recently by Jonathan Bate, *Shakespearean Constitutions.*
2. Edward Bulwer Lytton, "On Art in Fiction," in *Victorian Criticism of the Novel*, ed. Edwin M. Eigner and George J. Worth (Cambridge: Cambridge University Press, 1985), 23–38.
3. George Moir, "Modern Romance and Novel," in Eigner and Worth, *Victorian Criticism*, 40–41, 55. On the identification between Shakespeare and Scott, which tended to be nationalistic and conservative, see Nicola Watson, "Kemble, Scott, and the Mantle of the Bard," in Marsden, *The Appropriation of Shakespeare*, 83–85. See also James Fitzjames Stephen, "The Relation of Novels to Life" (1855), in Eigner and Worth, *Victorian Criticism*, 99, and David Masson, "Pendennis and Copperfield: Thackeray and Dickens," *North British Review* (1851), in *Victorian Fiction: A Collection of Essays from the Period*, ed. Ira Bruce Nadel (New York: Garland, 1986), 75, 76.
4. Archbishop Whateley, review of *Northanger Abbey* and *Persuasion*, *Quarterly Review* 24 (January 1821): 352–76, reprinted in *Jane Austen: The Critical Heritage*, ed. B. C. Southam, rev. ed. (London: Routledge, 1986), 98.
5. One isolated comparison between Charlotte Brontë and Shakespeare, relating to their power of characterization, is Swinburne, "A Note on Charlotte Brontë" (1877), in *The Brontës: The Critical Heritage*, ed. Miriam Allott (Boston: Routledge, 1974), 407. Swinburne was here making a point of praising Brontë over Eliot, whose work he disliked. Emily Brontë is compared to Shakespeare more often: see G. W. Peck (1848) on her dramatic power (241); Sydney Dobell (1850) on her ability at psychological and medical case study (281); Angus Mackay (1898) on imagination (446–47), all in Allott, *The Brontës*. I do not discuss Emily Brontë because I believe Gilbert and Gubar, *Madwoman*, 248–97, makes a good case for her response to Shakespeare (*King Lear*, in particular) in *Wuthering Heights* and because Austen and Charlotte Brontë had more influence on George Eliot and on the later novelists I discuss.
6. Poovey, *The Proper Lady;* Nancy Armstrong, *Desire and Domestic Fiction* (New York: Oxford University Press, 1987); Homans, *Bearing the Word.*
7. For Dallas, see Elaine Showalter, *A Literature of Their Own* (Princeton:

Princeton University Press, 1977), 79; for Ludlow, see Showalter, 71 and 83.

8. Battersby, *Gender and Genius,* 7 and passim.

9. Gilbert and Gubar, *Madwoman,* 3–4.

10. G. H. Lewes, "The Lady Novelists," *Westminster Review* (1852), excerpted in Elizabeth Helsinger et al., *The Woman Question: Society and Literature in Britain and America, 1837–1883,* 3 vols. (Chicago: University of Chicago Press, 1989), 3:56–57. In his 1850 review of *Shirley* (*Edinburgh Review*), however, we can see the repressive language to which his insistence that women should "speak sincerely and energetically as woman" could take him: "Currer Bell! if under your heart had ever stirred a child . . . , never could you have imagined such a falsehood as that!" is his way of dealing with a mother's hatred of her infant. Excerpted in Allott, *The Brontës,* 162, 167.

11. Lewes, review of "Recent Novels: French and English," *Fraser's Magazine* 36 (December 1847), 687, reprinted in Southam, *Jane Austen,* 125.

12. Woolf, *Room,* 102, specifically referred to Coleridge's idea of the androgynous Shakespeare (while aware that the image did not involve specific partiality to women); it could also be related to Keats's contrast between the "camelion poet" and the "wordsworthian or egotistical sublime," discussed in my chapter 1. But Lewes was much more interested in women writers than was Coleridge or Keats.

13. Lewes, review of *The Fair Carew, The Leader* (November 22, 1857), 115, reprinted in Southam, *Jane Austen,* 130.

14. G. H. Lewes, "The Novels of Jane Austen," *Blackwood's Edinburgh Magazine* 86 (July 1859):102, 104, 105. In his essay he quotes an earlier passage by Whateley claiming that by her writings "a sympathy is induced which, if extended to daily life and the world at large, would make the reader a more amiable person," 103, as well as one of Eliot's addresses to the reader about sympathy in *Scenes of Clerical Life.*

15. Jane Austen, *Northanger Abbey* (New York: Penguin, 1972), 39. The quotations are from *Othello* 3.3.327–29, *Measure for Measure* 3.1.77–79, and *Twelfth Night* 2.4.114–15. Even earlier, when she was about sixteen, Austen made fun of Shakespeare's cultural authority in "The History of England from the reign of Henry the 4th to the death of Charles the 1st": "the King made a long speech, for which I must refer the Reader to Shakespear's Plays, & the Prince made a still longer." *Minor Works,* ed. R. W. Chapman, rev. B. C. Southam, *The Works of Jane Austen,* vol. 6 (Oxford: Oxford University Press, 1969), 139.

16. Jameson, *Characteristics of Women,* 151.

17. C. L. Barber, *Shakespeare's Festive Comedies* (Cleveland: World Publishing, 1963), 247.

18. Richard Simpson, review of *Memoir of Jane Austen, North British Review* 52 (April 1870):129–52, reprinted in Southam, *Jane Austen,* 242.

19. On "indeterminacy of meaning" in Austen as "a consequence of her more or less conscious collaboration with an indefinite number of earlier texts," see Alistair M. Duckworth, "Jane Austen and the Conflict of Interpretations," in *Jane Austen: New Perspectives,* ed. Janet Todd, Women and Literature, n.s., vol. 3 (New York: Holmes & Meier, 1983), 39–52, quotation from 42. On Shakespeare's endings, see my *Love's Argument* (Chapel Hill: University of North Carolina Press, 1984).

20. Jane Austen, *Emma,* ed. Lionel Trilling (Boston: Houghton Mifflin, 1957), 57.

21. Jane Austen, *Pride and Prejudice* (New York: Penguin, 1972), 90.

22. Review of *Pride and Prejudice, Critical Review* 4th ser., no. 3 (March 1813) in Southam, *Jane Austen,* 45. See also Simpson, "Her Beatrices and Benedicks only discover their mutual attraction by their failure to love elsewhere," review of *Memoir* in Southam, *Jane Austen,* 263.

23. Sylvia Townsend Warner, "Women as Writers," in *The Gender of Modernism,* ed. Bonnie Kime Scott (Bloomington: Indiana University Press, 1990), 544.

24. Thus Jean Howard has argued that the marriage of Beatrice and Benedick results from the authority that rank gives Don Pedro to stage deception rather than from their psychology; see "Renaissance Antitheatricality," in Howard and O'Connor, *Shakespeare Reproduced.*

25. See Margaret Kirkham, *Jane Austen: Feminism and Fiction* (New York: Barnes & Noble, 1983).

26. Simpson in Southam, *Jane Austen,* 256; Bradbrook, *Jane Austen,* 73; Jocelyn Harris, "Anne Elliott, the Wife of Bath, and Other Friends," in Todd, *Jane Austen,* 290–91; Nina Auerbach, *Romantic Imprisonment* (New York: Columbia University Press, 1985), 51; this essay was first published in 1972.

27. Williams's most thorough explanation of his contrast among dominant, emergent, and residual ideologies is in *Marxism and Literature* (Oxford: Oxford University Press, 1977). In "Historical Differences: Misogyny and *Othello,*" in her anthology *The Matter of Difference* (Ithaca: Cornell University Press, 1991), 153–79, Valerie Wayne helpfully uses Williams's categories to differentiate various coexisting Renaissance ideologies; she may be right that misogyny was already residual in Shakespeare's day.

28. Jane Austen, *Persuasion* (New York: Penguin, 1965), 237.

29. T. J. Wise and J. A. Symington, ed., *The Brontës: Their Lives, Friendships, and Correspondence,* 4 vols. (Oxford: Blackwell, 1932) 3:159 (September 18, 1850).

30. See Michael Wheeler, *The Art of Allusion* (New York: Barnes & Noble,

1979), 34–36. A study of Brontë's many allusions to Milton would show that her attitude to him is more complicated than simple hostility.

31. Christine Alexander, *The Early Writings of Charlotte Brontë* (Buffalo: Prometheus Books, 1983), 22.

32. Charlotte Brontë to Ellen Nussey (July 4, 1834), in Wise and Symington, *The Brontës*, 1:22.

33. See, for example, Helsinger et al., *The Woman Question*, 1:xv.

34. Charlotte Brontë, *Shirley* (New York: Penguin, 1974), 115. Further citations from this work will be noted parenthetically in the text.

35. Montagu, in *An Essay*, writes of "our Shakespeare," and the opposition between England and France is a recurring theme in her essay; for example, comparing Shakespeare's *Julius Caesar* and Corneille's *Cinna*, she says, "our countryman has been far more judicious in his choice of the story" (245). When Caroline says, "You are not going to be sceptical and French," she is using the language of the Montagu/Voltaire debate. John Barrell discusses Coleridge's nationalistic uses of his universally sympathetic Shakespeare in *Poetry, Language, and Politics*, 65–77, and Derek Longhurst, " 'Not for all time, but for an Age': An Approach to Shakespeare Studies," in *Re-reading English*, ed. Peter Widdowson (New York: Methuen, 1982), 151, 155, discusses twentieth-century English nationalism in educational uses of Shakespeare.

36. The narrator says, "A hybrid in nature, it is probable he had a hybrid's feeling on many points—patriotism for one; it is likely that he was unapt to attach himself to parties, to sects, even to climes and customs; it is not impossible that he had a tendency to isolate his individual person from any community amidst which his lot might temporarily happen to be thrown" (60). The role of hybridity here may be contrasted with its role in the novels discussed in this book's final chapter. See also Robert Martin, *The Accents of Persuasion: Charlotte Brontë's Novels* (London: Faber & Faber, 1966), 137.

37. Armstrong, *Desire and Domestic Fiction*, 215–19; Annabel Patterson, *Shakespeare and the Popular Voice*, 147–48.

38. See Linda C. Hunt, *A Woman's Portion* (New York: Garland, 1988), esp. 73–75. Hunt notes that Robert and Louis Moore eventually show some sympathy for other people.

39. William Hazlitt, "A Letter to William Gifford, Esq.," in *Complete Works*, 9:24n.

40. William Hazlitt, *Characters*, in *Complete Works*, 4:216. Bate, *Shakespearean Constitutions*, 200, believes that Brontë was influenced by this essay, and given her father's interest in political journalism, it seems quite likely, but the novel suggests that she didn't find the dramatic moral of *Coriolanus* quite as clear.

41. Keats, *Letters,* 1:386–87.
42. Jameson, *Characteristics of Women,* 37–38. Jameson and Brontë were both influenced by romantic associations of women and Shakespeare with nature and were both interested in women's socioeconomic situation. Chapter 1 discusses Jameson's book and its influence.
43. Margaret Arnold, "Coriolanus Transformed: Charlotte Brontë's Use of Shakespeare in *Shirley,*" in Novy, *Women's Re-Visions of Shakespeare,* 76–88.
44. Deirdre David, *Fictions of Resolution* (New York: Columbia University Press, 1981).
45. I am indebted here to Margaret Arnold's "Coriolanus Transformed" and to discussions with her.
46. See Carol Ohmann, "Charlotte Brontë: The Limits of Her Feminism," *Female Studies* 6 (1972):160–64. John Kucich, however, stresses the reversibility of power in Brontë's novels; see *Repression in Victorian Fiction* (Berkeley: University of California Press, 1987), 102–5. The echo of Coriolanus's name that can be heard in Caroline's could hint that she has a hidden identification with his pride or could simply be irony. "Caroline" is etymologically related to "Charlotte" as a feminine form of "Charles."
47. See Elizabeth Gaskell, *The Life of Charlotte Brontë* (New York: Penguin, 1975), 258. Brontë's comparison of Wellington and Coriolanus was not idiosyncratic. A radical journalist wrote, "The modern English Tories have made him [Coriolanus] all their own, and have been accustomed to liken their leader to him. . . . His Grace of Wellington has occasionally figured in the print shops in a Roman garb making scorn of sundry plebeian leaders, attired as 'unwashed artisans' "; see William Bridges Adams, writing as Junius Redivivus, "Coriolanus No Aristocrat," *Monthly Repository* 8 (1834):142. Adams then argues that Coriolanus himself is much more humane than Wellington. Adams addresses the reader directly, in a style often associated with Brontë, in words such as "Reader, are you a radical?" (129) and "Reader, did you ever mingle in the din of battle?" (137). I will discuss this article further in chapter 4.
48. See Stone, *Romantic Impulse,* 122.
49. Hazlitt, *Characters,* in *Complete Works,* 4:214.
50. Charlotte Brontë, *Jane Eyre,* ed. Margaret Smith (Oxford: Oxford University Press, 1981), 138. The echo is not so much of Hamlet's exact words as of the thought of his first speech to the ghost: "Be thou a spirit of health, or goblin damn'd, / Bring with thee airs from heaven, or blasts from hell" (1.4.40–41). The passage appears shortly after Rochester's denial of being a villain, or "any such bad eminence"—recalling Milton's Satan only to deny the similarity. The novel's imagery here may conflate

Shakespearean and Milton echoes, as Susan Wolfson has suggested, and may offer us the choice of reading Rochester's situation as having either the moral ambiguity of Hamlet's or the masked evil of Satan's.

51. Margaret Smith, "Introduction," in *Jane Eyre*, ix. This association is presumably intended to suggest that Bertha's mental disturbance has been brought on partly by guilt as well as to recall Rochester's picture of her as a temptress. Feminist views of Bertha after Gayatri Spivak's "Three Women's Texts and a Critique of Imperialism," *Critical Inquiry* 12, 1 (1985):243–61, and Jean Rhys's *Wide Sargasso Sea* are very different.

52. Robert Martin, *Accents of Persuasion,* makes some of these connections on p. 80. See also Karen Rowe, "'Fairy-born and human-bred': Jane Eyre's Education in Romance," in *The Voyage In,* ed. Elizabeth Abel et al. (Hanover, N.H.: New England Universities Press, 1983), 82, 87.

53. The contrast between Jane's naturalness and honesty (which Rochester praises when she won't compliment his appearance) and Blanche's artificiality is another version of the contrast between Cordelia, also associated with nature, and her sisters.

54. See Meredith Skura's discussion of how Jane's relationship to Rochester has elements of the infantile symbiosis of child and mother, in *The Literary Use of the Psychoanalytic Process* (New Haven: Yale University Press, 1981), 92; see also Gilbert and Gubar, *Madwoman,* 352–55.

55. Oliver is the name of Orlando's older brother in *As You Like It.* Rosamond eventually becomes the daughter-in-law of a Sir Frederic; Rosalind's uncle is named Duke Frederick. Also relevant is Samuel Daniel's Rosamund, discussed in chapter 5.

56. She wrote this to Lewes, who had encouraged her after reading *Jane Eyre;* this letter responds to the 1847 review in which he praised *Jane Eyre* and compared Austen to Shakespeare. See Gaskell, *The Life of Charlotte Brontë,* 337, and Allott, *The Brontës,* 83.

57. See Ellen Moers, *Literary Women* (Garden City: Anchor/Doubleday, 1977), 72–78. In *GEL* 1:355, June 20, 1851, writing to John Chapman, she objects to asking "Miss Bronty" to write the article on Modern Novelists because "she would have to leave out Currer Bell, who is perhaps the best of them all."

58. See *GEL* 2:358, and GHL's journal in the Beinecke Library, Yale University. J. W. Cross, ed., *George Eliot's Life as Related in her Letters and Journals,* 3 vols. ([c. 1885]; rpt., Grosse Pointe, Mich.: Scholarly Press, 1968), 1:282–83, lists her Shakespeare readings in Weimar and Berlin with Lewes in 1855 as *Merchant of Venice, Romeo and Juliet, Julius Caesar, Antony and Cleopatra, Henry IV, Othello, As You Like It, Lear, Taming of the Shrew, Coriolanus, Twelfth Night, Measure for Measure, Midsummer Night's Dream, Winter's Tale, Richard III,* and *Hamlet.*

Chapter 3. George Eliot: Early Works

1. I will almost always use the name George Eliot, although my discussion includes works written before the adoption of this pseudonym, and letters signed, for example, Marian Lewes, as well as the novels. The persistence of her pseudonym, as distinguished, for example, from Charlotte Brontë's, seems in part a sign of the "created" nature of her identity; see Ruby Redinger, *George Eliot: The Emergent Self* (New York: Knopf, 1975). I am not assuming that everything she wrote and did was consistent. On the other hand, it seems too simple to suggest, as Dorothea Barrett does in *Vocation and Desire* (New York: Routledge, 1991), 175, that George Eliot, the novelist, was a feminist, while Marian Lewes, the letter writer, was not.

2. Gilbert and Gubar, *Madwoman,* 48.

3. Gordon Haight, *George Eliot* (New York: Oxford University Press, 1968), 468.

4. Cross, 2:71.

5. Mary Sibree Cash as quoted in Cross, 1:373. Did Marianne Moore read Cross before defining poetry as "imaginary gardens with real toads"? Neither Moore's *Collected Prose* nor recent books about her suggest interest in George Eliot. "No other book than Shakespeare" is close to a passage in Keats's letters: "I am very near Agreeing with Hazlit that Shakespeare is enough for us" (1.43), quoted in Jonathan Bate, *Romantic Imagination,* 161. She may have read Hazlitt by this time.

6. *Essays,* ed. Thomas Pinney (New York: Columbia University Press, 1963), 261. In *Complete Works,* 6:348, Hazlitt similarly compares Shakespeare and Sophocles with architectural masterpieces of different kinds.

7. The nine volumes include eighteen references to *As You Like It,* and she frequently includes it in short informal lists of Shakespeare's works, for example in 6:113. *As You Like It* 1.3.12 is the source of what she calls "my favorite little epithet: 'this working day world'" (1:44), a phrase that appears frequently in her essays and novels; see her *Essays,* 302n. For example, visiting Goethe's birthplace, this woman who grew up near Stratford wrote of the value of the birthplace shrine to remind us "that the being who has bequeathed to us immortal thoughts or immortal deeds, had to endure the daily struggle with the petty details, perhaps with the sordid cares, of this working-day world" (*Essays,* 92).

8. Lillian Faderman, *Surpassing the Love of Men* (New York: Morrow, 1981). See the discussion of other such letters in Bonnie Zimmerman, "'The Dark Eye Beaming': Female Friendship in George Eliot's Fictions," in *Lesbian Texts and Contexts,* ed. Karla Jay and Joanne Glasgow (New York: New York University Press, 1990), 126–32.

9. Eliot, *A Writer's Notebook,* 255. Lewes had left the editorship of the journal the previous year when he and "Eliot"—a name she first used in 1857—made their relationship public by going to Germany together. (Thornton Hunt, Lewes's wife's lover, was the other cofounder.) Of course, the review, like most journalism then, was published anonymously. For an earlier violation of propriety similar to those she notes in Shakespeare's women, see her passionate letter to Herbert Spencer (*GEL* 8:56–57).

10. William Hazlitt, *Characters, Works,* 4:180.

11. See Watson, "Kemble, Scott," in Marsden, *The Appropriation of Shakespeare,* 83–85. Watson quotes much such praise of Scott and dissent by Hazlitt.

12. See Anne Russell, "Rosalind, Viola, and Early Nineteenth Century Gender Ideologies" (Ph.D. diss., York University, 1987). Auerbach, *Woman and the Demon,* 207–15, discusses Victorian celebrations of Shakespeare's women.

13. Russell Jackson, " 'Perfect Types of Womanhood': Rosalind, Beatrice, and Viola in Victorian Criticism and Performance," in *Shakespeare Survey* 32, ed. Kenneth Muir (Cambridge: Cambridge University Press, 1979), 16. Jackson shows such unease even in Mary Cowden Clarke and Anna Jameson, two of Auerbach's major examples of the Victorian celebration of the individuality of Shakespeare's women. The mythic female power Auerbach finds in such Victorian Shakespeare criticism, as elsewhere in Victorian culture, must be distinguished from Eliot's interest here, social assertiveness.

14. Eliot, *Writer's Notebook,* 11.

15. Cross, 1:287–88. Others had criticized this scene, but some Victorians liked it: Holman Hunt painted *Valentine Saving Sylvia from Proteus.*

16. Elizabeth D. Ermarth, *George Eliot* (Boston: Twayne, 1985), 14.

17. Gilbert and Gubar, *Madwoman,* 66.

18. Eliot's interest in the theme of sympathy in Sophocles and Wordsworth has been discussed by David Moldstad, "*The Mill on the Floss* and *Antigone,*" *PMLA* 85 (1970):527–31; Stone, *Romantic Impulse;* and Homans, *Bearing the Word,* among others. See Suzanne Graver, *George Eliot and Community* (Berkeley: University of California Press, 1984), esp. 263–73, and Carlisle, *The Sense of an Audience,* esp. 1–63, 166–219, for more context of her "aesthetic of sympathy." On pp. 190–93, Carlisle shows how Eliot's treatment of Hetty Sorrel echoes Wordsworth's "Thorn" but with less sentimentality about maternal instinct.

19. On her first trip to Germany with Lewes, she records with pleasure meeting Dessoir, an actor who said, "Shakespeare ist mein Gott" (Haight, *George Eliot,* 171). But they were not uncritical bardolaters. In

1851, early in their acquaintance, when they attended a performance of
Merry Wives of Windsor, she wrote that Lewes "helped to carry off the
dolorousness of the play by such remarks as 'There's the swan preening,'
'The swan comes out now and then'" (1:37).

20. G. H. Lewes, "Shakespeare," in *Literary Criticism of George Henry Lewes,*
ed. Alice Kaminsky (Lincoln: University of Nebraska Press, 1964), 139.
This article first appeared in 1849. Compare his emphasis on sympathy
in Austen, Shakespeare, and Eliot, discussed in chapter 2.

21. William Hazlitt, "On Shakespeare and Milton," in *Complete Works,* 5:50.

22. Many examples are enumerated in U. C. Knoepflmacher, "*Daniel
Deronda,*" 27, one of the starting points for my book.

23. Some of her accommodations of this conflict are discussed in Alison
Booth, *Greatness Engendered: George Eliot and Virginia Woolf* (Ithaca: Cornell University Press, 1992). Anxiety about whether the vocation of
writer was too selfish was, as Elaine Showalter shows, generated by
the nineteenth-century construction of women's role; see *A Literature
of Their Own.* Homans, *Bearing the Word,* 161–88, shows the attempts of
Eliot, Charlotte Brontë, and Elizabeth Gaskell to deal with the culturally
constructed opposition "between selfish writing and a woman's selfless
duties" (173). See also Stone, *The Romantic Impulse,* 136. Eliot's letters
mention anxiety about egotism even more than those of Brontë and
Gaskell.

24. Redinger, *George Eliot,* 42.

25. Erik Erikson, *Young Man Luther* (New York: Norton, 1958). Erikson
connects Luther's anxiety with sociohistorical changes and finds similar anxiety in twentieth-century students related to their own time.
Although Erikson's comments on women have rightly been criticized by
feminists, his analyses of identity crises may still be useful.

26. Chodorow, *The Reproduction of Mothering.* Critics whose use of Chodorow
in discussing women's writing are relevant here include Judith Kegan
Gardiner, "On Female Identity," 347–62, and *Rhys, Stead, Lessing,* and
Poovey, *The Proper Lady,* esp. 44, 254n, as well as Homans, *Bearing the
Word,* esp. 11–17, 21–29. On pp. 177–78 Homans discusses how Eliot's
work as a translator comes to accommodate "the claims both of self and
of selflessness." The recollection of Erikson may serve to add to Chodorow's theories an emphasis about how specific religious contexts can, for
example, heighten the pressure on women to be self-sacrificing.

27. Deirdre David has discussed how this essay reveals "her strong ideological bond to patriarchal culture and to certain conservative modes
of thought," in *Intellectual Women and Victorian Patriarchy* (Ithaca: Cornell University Press, 1987), 185; yet Nancy Paxton shows that Eliot's
view of women writers is even here less biologically based than many

other views in her time: see *George Eliot and Herbert Spencer* (Princeton: Princeton University Press, 1991), 24.

28. The conclusion, which oddly anticipates imagery of multiculturalism in the United States in the 1990s, also echoes the imagery in the marriage masque in *The Tempest,* which includes Iris, goddess of the rainbow, addressed as "many-colored messenger," Ceres, goddess of natural generativity, who wishes Ferdinand and Miranda "Spring come to you at the farthest / In the very end of harvest" (4.1.114–15), and Juno, goddess of marriage.

29. "Evangelical Teaching: Dr. Cumming" (October 1855), "Worldliness and Other-Worldliness: The Poet Young" (January 1857), "Silly Novels by Lady Novelists" (October 1856), and "Three Novels" (October 1856) all appear in her *Essays.* Janet Todd discusses Young's sentimentalism in *Sensibility* (New York: Methuen, 1986), 51–52.

30. See Gillian Beer, *George Eliot* (Bloomington: Indiana University Press, 1986), 41–51, on her responses to Austen, Charlotte Brontë, George Sand, Bremer, and Geraldine Jewsbury. Margaret Anne Doody, in "George Eliot and the Eighteenth Century Novel," *Nineteenth Century Fiction* 35, 3 (1980):260–91, discusses her debt to eighteenth-century novelists, particularly women, in terms of the development of the style *indirect libre* as a way of conveying sympathy for a range of characters.

31. Haight, *George Eliot,* 59. This biography also contains many references to her interest in Shakespeare performances and Shakespeare readings at many stages of her life.

32. Keats's letters, edited by Richard Monkton Milnes, were published in 1848: see Armstrong, *Victorian Scrutinies,* 39. On Eliot's "chameleon" nature and her ambivalence about it, see Auerbach, *Romantic Imprisonment,* 257. She had written of her "chameleon-like spirits" earlier, on December 21, 1840 (*GEL* 1:76).

33. Notice that in one letter she wants letters because she has too much identity, and in the other she wants letters because she has too little identity. Kucich, *Repression in Victorian Fiction,* 184, notes that the two fears expressed in her early letters, of being too egotistical and of being too dependent on others, may seem opposite but are actually closely linked. Erikson's adolescents in identity crises frequently experienced both opposite fears.

34. For discussions of Feuerbach's ideas and their influence on Eliot, see, for example, Bernard Paris, *Experiments in Life* (Detroit: Wayne State University Press, 1965); Valerie Dodd, *George Eliot: An Intellectual Life* (New York: St. Martin's Press, 1990), 181–90; and Elizabeth Ermarth, "George Eliot's Conception of Sympathy," *Nineteenth Century Fiction* 40 (1985):23–42.

35. Hazlitt, *Complete Works,* 4:346–47. Jonathan Bate, *Shakespearean Constitutions,* 158, stresses the importance of this passage. In his *Life of Goethe* (I refer to the 2d ed., London: Smith, Elder, 1864), 190, in progress at this time, Lewes discusses Goethe's organization of a Shakespeare celebration at Frankfort in 1771 and his speech there about the sense of freedom that reading Shakespeare's plays had given him.
36. Armstrong, *Victorian Scrutinies,* 40.
37. See discussions by Patterson, *Shakespeare and the Popular Voice,* and Bate, *Shakespearean Constitutions,* who associate this combination especially with Coleridge. *Coriolanus* criticism is particularly relevant here, as consideration of *Shirley* in chapter 2 may suggest, and I will return to it, and to the conservative elements in Eliot's class attitudes, in discussing *Felix Holt.*
38. *Samuel Johnson on Shakespeare,* ed. W. K. Wimsatt, Jr. (New York: Hill & Wang, 1960), 23. This aspect of Shakespeare is related to Eliot's novels by G. F. Parker, *Johnson's Shakespeare* (Oxford: Clarendon Press, 1989), 43.
39. *Scenes of Clerical Life,* ed. Thomas A. Noble (Oxford: Clarendon Press, 1985), 110. Caterina's other talent is singing, and she has a musical education, if not a scientific one. While the paragraph ends with a joke about the irrelevance of astronomy to love, its concern with the lack of scientific knowledge shared by epic and tragic heroines and most nineteenth-century women of all classes anticipates the concern with women's education in Eliot's later work. Other literary echoes, such as those of *Wuthering Heights,* are mentioned by U. C. Knoepflmacher in *George Eliot's Early Novels* (Berkeley: University of California Press, 1966), 65–66.
40. Madame de Staël, *Corinne; or, Italy,* trans. Isabel Hill (New York: W. I. Pooley, 1870), 124.
41. *Writer's Notebook,* 255.
42. See Elaine Showalter, "Representing Ophelia: Women, Madness, and the Responsibilities of Feminist Criticism," in *Shakespeare and the Question of Theory,* ed. Patricia Parker and Geoffrey Hartman (New York: Methuen, 1985), 80–94, on how common the visual image of the drowning Ophelia was in Victorian culture. Ophelia's clothes caught on a branch, and she was always pictured wearing white.
43. "But the delicate plant had been too deeply bruised, and in the struggle to put forth a blossom it died" (185). There is no mention of the birth, death, or survival of a child.
44. Beer, *George Eliot,* 70.
45. These Shakespeare allusions coexist with the allusions to Milton and Wordsworth found by Knoepflmacher, *Early Novels,* 93–126. For the

novel's possible relations to Wordsworth and Scott, see Carlisle, *The Sense of an Audience,* 188–213; for these elements and its relation also to Hardy, to the literary conventionality of the abandoned woman's story, and to the history of child murder, see Jay Clayton, "The Alphabet of Suffering," in Clayton and Rothstein, *Influence and Intertextuality,* 37–60. The rewriting of Milton is further developed by Paxton, *Eliot and Spencer,* 44–68.

46. George Eliot, *Adam Bede,* ed. John Paterson (Boston: Houghton Mifflin, 1968), 314. All further citations of this work in the text refer to this edition.

47. Elaine Showalter, "Representing Ophelia," 83–87.

48. In *Fictions of Authority,* 92, Susan Lanser suggests that the models for these narrators were George Sand's male eyewitness narrators.

49. The novel's critique of notions of "maternal instinct" is discussed by Paxton, *Eliot and Spencer,* 60.

50. The imagery of mother-child merger here can be seen in psychoanalytic terms as pre-Oedipal. Yet the end of the sentence also associates Hetty with a sexually tempting Eve. On fluctuations of gender in the narrator's stance in *Adam Bede,* see Robyn Warhol, *Gendered Interventions* (New Brunswick: Rutgers University Press, 1989), 115–33.

51. Lanser makes this observation in *Fictions of Authority,* 93, drawing on linguistic theories of Robin Lakoff and, especially, Julia Penelope Stanley, "The Stylistics of Belief," in *Teaching about Doublespeak,* ed. D. J. Dietrich (Urbana: National Council of Teachers of English, 1976). She gives examples particularly of qualifying tags attached to generalizations, such as the "religious history" phrase, which she quotes from *Adam Bede* (Harmondsworth: Penguin, 1980), 81.

52. George Eliot, *Mill on the Floss,* 172. Further citations of this Clarendon Press edition will be indicated parenthetically in the text.

53. Knoepflmacher, *Early Novels,* compares *Mill*'s structure to that of *Antony and Cleopatra* and notes that "the only quotation from *Antony and Cleopatra* in all of GE's letters occurs while she was writing *The Mill*" (*GEL* 3:53). In the same chapter he also discusses the influence on Eliot of Gruppe's ideas about classical and Shakespearean drama (171–73). He makes a number of other comparisons between figures in *Mill* and in *Lear, As You Like It,* and other Shakespearean plays, but claims a "factual basis" only for the association with *Antony and Cleopatra* (194) and the "carefully implanted parallels with figures like the drowning Ophelia" (220).

54. On associations of Hamlet with women, see Chapter 6 and also Lawrence Danson, "Gazing at Hamlet, or the Danish Cabaret," *Shakespeare Survey* 45 (1993):37–51. Maggie has also been compared to Hamlet by

A. G. van den Broek, in "Reading George Eliot Reading Shakespeare" (Ph.D. diss., Dalhousie University, 1990) and by Daniel W. Ross.

55. The implicit criticism of some varieties of sympathy in Philip becomes magnified in the characterization of the narrator of *The Lifted Veil,* written in 1859 while Eliot was at work on *Mill* though not published as part of her work until much later. (It was first published anonymously in the same issue of *Blackwood's*—July 1859—in which Lewes quoted a passage from *Scenes of Clerical Life* about sympathy in discussing Jane Austen.) His "abnormal sensibility" creates what he calls "the obtrusion on my mind of the mental process going forward in first one person, and then another, with whom I happened to be in contact." See *Lifted Veil* (1878; rpt., London: Virago, 1985), 18–19. He has "the poet's sensibility without his voice" (8) and knowledge of others' thoughts without any affection, which leads to more alienation from them.

56. See Knoepflmacher, *Early Novels,* 229, 231, 236, 242, for detailed discussion of similarities such as the fact that Eppie is associated with gold, as is Perdita in *The Winter's Tale.* See also Beer, *George Eliot,* 108–46, for more discussion of Eliot's use of the theme of foster parents and genetic parents in fiction about this time.

57. Romola's devotion to her father also recalls the later Cordelia's to Lear, and one of Bardo's speeches echoes Lear: "your man in scarlet and furred robe who sits in judgment on thieves, is himself a thief of the thoughts and the fame that belong to his fellows," *Romola* (New York: Penguin, 1980), 102; compare *Lear* 4.6.153, 165: "which is the justice, which is the thief? . . . Robes and furr'd gowns hide all."

58. Bate, *Romantic Imagination,* 47, says, speaking of these plays, "In 1797–8 both Coleridge and Wordsworth attempted to imitate Shakespeare. They both failed, but then went on to write their best and most distinctive poetry—poetry that was responsive to Shakespeare without being in thrall to him." Eliot's relation to the nineteenth-century theater, which she and Lewes considered to be in decline, was also part of her difficulty. She wrote in April 1864, a few months before she began *Spanish Gypsy,* of Helen Faucit as "a flash of real acting in the evening twilight of the stage" (*GEL,* 4:143).

59. See Barbara Hardy, *The Novels of George Eliot* (London: Athlone Press, 1959), 215.

60. Wheeler, *Art of Allusion,* 23–24.

61. Lanser, *Fictions of Authority,* 99. Lanser argues that epigraphs were especially common among women novelists in England and America and cites Susanna Rowson's *Charlotte* (1791), Mary Brunton's *Discipline* (1815), Susan Ferrier's *Marriage* (1818), Susan Warner's *The Wide, Wide World* (1851), Elizabeth Gaskell's *North and South,* and Harriet Wilson's

Our Nig (1859). She argues that Eliot's epigraphs are more diverse in language and less diverse in gender of quoted author than those of these other women; she calls on "a pan-European canon of learned men" (98) and cites only one woman, Elizabeth Barrett Browning. Lanser also notes the irony of Eliot's professed distrust of quotation.

62. Quoted in Harold Orel, *Victorian Literary Critics* (New York: St. Martin's, 1984), 19.

63. See, for example, William A. Wilson, "The Magic Circle of Genius: Dickens' Translations of Shakespearian Drama in *Great Expectations,*" *Nineteenth Century Fiction* 40 (1985):154–74; Alexander Welsh, *From Copyright to Copperfield: The Identity of Dickens* (Cambridge, Mass.: Harvard University Press, 1987), and other examples in Evans, *Shakespeare*; Cohn, *Modern Shakespeare Offshoots;* and Douglas Brooks-Davies, *Fielding, Dickens, Gosse, Iris Murdoch, and Oedipal Hamlet* (New York: St. Martin's Press, 1989).

64. This is Judith Fetterley's term for a process by which women, reading a male author, are taught to identify with a male point of view and a male system of values: see *The Resisting Reader,* xx.

65. See Susan Morgan, *Sisters in Time* (New York: Oxford University Press, 1989), 127–29, for a discussion of these two trends in Eliot criticism and a concluding argument for seeing nineteenth-century fiction as integrated rather than divided into traditions separated by sex.

66. Elaine Showalter, "Feminist Criticism in the Wilderness," in *The New Feminist Criticism,* ed. Showalter (New York: Pantheon, 1985), 265.

67. Beer, *George Eliot,* suggests that George refers to both Lewes and Sand and on pp. 43–44 demonstrates that Eliot admired Sand in the 1850s. Sand, who often dressed in men's clothes, was even more interested in *As You Like It* than was Eliot: she wrote a French adaptation of it entitled *Comme Vous Plaira.* See Adeline Tintner, *"As You Like It* as George Sand Liked It," *Revue de Littérature Comparée* 3 (1986):337–44. Eliot discusses her admiration for Sand in the same early letter, just quoted, in which she discusses Rousseau.

68. Judith Butler, *Gender Trouble* (New York: Routledge, 1990), 126.

Chapter 4. Felix Holt

1. Walter Bagehot, "Shakespeare—The Individual," *Prospective Review* (July 1853), quoted in Aron Y. Stavisky, *Shakespeare and the Victorians* (Norman: University of Oklahoma Press, 1969), 75. See also the discussion of the Tory, nationalist Shakespeare in Watson, "Kemble, Scott," in Marsden, *The Appropriation of Shakespeare,* 73–92.

2. Jeremy Crump, "Shakespeare in Nineteenth-Century Leicester," in

Shakespeare and the Victorian Stage, ed. Richard Foulkes (Cambridge: Cambridge University Press, 1986), 274. E. P. Thompson writes, "not only Hazlitt, but also Wooler, Bamford, Cooper, and a score of self-taught Radical and Chartist journalism were wont to cap their arguments with Shakespearian quotations"; see *The Making of the English Working Classes* (New York: Penguin, 1980), 809. See also Richard D. Altick, *The English Common Reader* (Chicago: University of Chicago Press, 1983), 207, 243–44.

3. Crump, "Shakespeare," 276.

4. George Eliot, *Felix Holt,* ed. Fred Thomson (Oxford: Clarendon Press, 1980), 64. Further citations will appear in the text. According to Redinger, *George Eliot,* 458, Mrs. Oliphant, in declining to review *Felix Holt,* compared it to " 'Hamlet' played by six sets of gravediggers."

5. Adams [Junius Redivivus], "Coriolanus No Aristocrat," 41–54, 129–39, 190–207, 292–99. Further citations will appear in the text. I owe this reference to Isobel Armstrong, "Thatcher's Shakespeare?" *Textual Practice* 3 (Spring 1989):14. Thanks to Curt Breight, who told me of Armstrong's article.

6. Artisans were the largest number of participants in the workers' organizations studied by E. P. Thompson; in at least one division of the London Constitutional Society of the 1790s, which he studies in depth, watchmakers were the largest single group, and he includes them also in "the very heart of the artisan culture and political movements" of the 1820s. See *English Working Classes,* 170, 264. Furthermore, he describes popular Radicalism of the 1820s and later as "an intellectual culture" (781) that would motivate a shoemaker to read Thomas Paine and "a schoolmaster, whose education had taken him little further than worthy religious homilies," to "attempt Voltaire, Gibbon, Ricardo" (782).

7. Compare the discussion of the two novels' use of *Coriolanus* in Sally Shuttleworth, *George Eliot and Nineteenth Century Science* (Cambridge: Cambridge University Press, 1984), 132–33, and in Patterson, *Shakespeare and the Popular Voice,* 146–53. I agree, however, with Jennifer Uglow, *George Eliot* (New York: Pantheon, 1987), 184, and Beer, *George Eliot,* 145, that he is not always idealized. It is his antifeminist Hamlet mode, discussed further on in this article, that is most criticized.

8. Catherine Gallagher, *The Industrial Reformation of English Fiction: Social Discourse and Narrative Form, 1832–1867* (Chicago: University of Chicago Press, 1985), 241, shows how the details in the descriptions of Felix here and elsewhere "always stand for the same qualities, qualities that can be summed up in the word 'culture.' "

9. Elizabeth Barrett Browning, *Aurora Leigh,* introd. Cora Kaplan (London: Women's Press, 1978), 179 (4:752, 754–55). And see, more recently,

Annabel Patterson's "radical Hamlet, the Hamlet who spoke the language of popular sports and inversion rituals," in *Shakespeare and the Popular Voice*, 103.

10. The same year the *Repository* published a review, "Macready's *Coriolanus*," and Adams briefly refers to the 1832 production in his essay; but to judge from titles, only one or two other essays in its pages were devoted to a specific Shakespearean (or other) play. See Francis Mineka, *The Dissidence of Dissent: The Monthly Repository, 1806–1838* (Chapel Hill: University of North Carolina Press, 1944). In the *Repository* of the previous year, Adams published "On the Conduct of the Police at the Late Meeting," 7 (May 23, 1833), 426–37, about brutal crowd control at an incident analogous to the uprising with which Felix becomes involved. On the Brays and the Hennells, see Haight, *George Eliot,* esp. 36–39, 44–49, and, on their shared interest in Shakespeare, 57, 59.

11. William Hazlitt, *Characters,* in *Complete Works,* 4:214.

12. George Odell, *Shakespeare from Betterton to Irving,* 2 vols. (1920; rpt., New York: Dover, 1966), 2:212–13, quoting *John Bull,* March 19, 1838. See also Bate, *Shakespearean Constitutions,* esp. 102–3 on Cruikshank's caricature *Coriolanus Addressing the Plebeians.*

13. Peter Coveney, "Introduction," in *Felix Holt,* ed. Peter Coveney (New York: Penguin, 1972), 28–30, 65. The quotation is from George Eliot, *Essays,* ed. Pinney, 272. Deirdre David connects Eliot's interest in Riehl, reviewed in that essay, particularly with Eliot's "subversive" portrayal of Mrs. Transome, in *Intellectual Women,* 197–99.

14. Linda Bamber neatly says that Eliot "could have wished for a way of giving the working man his slice of the pie without putting the knife in his hands," in "Self-Defeating Politics in George Eliot's *Felix Holt,*" *Victorian Studies* 18 (June 1975):430. Compare Raymond Williams's analysis of the disturbances in Eliot's attitude toward the communities in her novels in *The Country and the City* (New York: Oxford University Press, 1973), 166–81.

15. Compare Patterson, " 'Speak, speak': The Popular Voice and the Jacobean State," in her *Shakespeare and the Popular Voice,* 120–53, esp. 130, 134. The chapter is full of fascinating documentation on the reception of the politics of this play.

16. Mineka, *Dissidence,* 201–2. Eliot had known Fox at least since the 1843 wedding of Rufa Brabant and Charles Hennell, at which he officiated and she was a bridesmaid. In 1852 he wrote the first article of the new series of *Westminster Review,* under her editorship. Lewes had, earlier, given a series of lectures at Fox's Chapel. See Haight, *George Eliot,* 49, 96, 129. Eliot would have been interested in the fact that Fox had led the *Repository* to champion modern German theology, and Lewes, work-

ing on his Goethe biography, might have consulted the 1832–33 issues, which contained "the first systematic survey of Goethe's work to appear in English." In the 1832 *Repository* Fox had also championed the poetry of the poor, exemplified especially by Ebenezer Elliott, perhaps another, at least subliminal, source for the choice of Eliot as a pseudonym. See Mineka, *Dissidence,* 209, 318, 305. One of Elliot's poems began "Bread-tax'd weaver, all can see / What that tax hath done for thee"; see Thompson, *English Working Classes,* 336. From 1819 on, weavers "were among [the] staunchest and most extreme adherents" of reform, according to Thompson, *English Working Classes,* 710.

17. On Felix's emphasis on rationality, see esp. Shuttleworth, *George Eliot,* 119–20.

18. Mineka, *Dissidence,* 173, 201. If his echo of Fox's name and similar views made any readers think of Fox, the association might also have had relevance to Felix's reluctance to marry, since Fox's incompatibility with his wife had led to a notorious separation (in 1834) and expulsion from the association of Unitarian ministers. He then established a household and not a marriage with a longtime female friend—another reason Eliot and Lewes might have felt a special affinity with him (Mineka, *Dissidence,* 188–97).

19. Simon Dentith, *George Eliot,* Harvester New Readings (Atlantic Highlands, N.J.: Humanities Press International, 1986), 65. See also Shuttleworth's comparison, in *George Eliot,* 122, of Felix's emphasis on education with that of, for example, an English Chartist circular of 1861. She argues that the novel's popularity benefited from the fact that "radicals and conservatives alike adhered to the doctrine of self-culture," a doctrine that "led to radicalism being coopted by the system" (122). Altick, *The English Common Reader,* 242, claims that the novel draws on the career of Gerald Massey, a former silk mill worker who became "a versifying propagandist for Chartism and Christian Socialism, and later . . . a student of psychic phenomena, Egyptology, and the hidden meaning of Shakespeare's sonnets."

20. On pp. 259–60 of *Dissidence,* Mineka discusses the radicalism of the *Repository;* on 261, he summarizes the Radical program of 1832.

21. Poovey, *The Proper Lady;* Susan Wolfson, "Explaining to Her Sisters: Mary Lamb's *Tales from Shakespear,*" in Novy, *Women's Re-Visions of Shakespeare,* 17.

22. G. H. Lewes observed Hamlet's antifeminism; the copy of Charles Knight's edition of Shakespeare, which he and Eliot shared, included Coleridge's claim, "Surely it ought to be considered a very exalted compliment to women that all the sarcasms on them in Shakespeare are put in the mouths of villains," and Lewes wrote in the margin, "This is not

quite true. Hamlet for instance." See volume 8, notes on *Othello* 2.1, in the Folger Shakespeare Library, Washington, D.C.

23. Wollstonecraft, *Vindication*, 10.

24. On contrasting attitudes to surfaces in Esther and Felix, see Gallagher, *Industrial Reformation*, 237–40.

25. In the combination of her essays, letters, and novels, these are the two characters that she alludes to or quotes most often. Allusions to Rosalind are most numerous in her early letters (see previous chapter) but remain important in *Middlemarch* and *Daniel Deronda*; *Hamlet* is quoted fairly steadily throughout the letters.

26. In the frequent allusions to history plays, this novel recalls Scott's novel *Woodstock* (1826), which is mentioned by one of *Felix Holt*'s minor characters: Watson, "Kemble, Scott," discusses the function of Scott's appropriations from *Richard II, Henry VIII, Henry IV, Richard II,* and *King John* in term of royalist ideology (80–83).

27. George Eliot's copy of *Vindication* (the third edition, printed for J. Johnson in 1796, now in Dr. Williams' Library in London), has a marginal line alongside this passage, on p. 341.

28. Cf. Wollstonecraft's association of female subordination with the seraglio, in the passage quoted from *Vindication*, 10. This orientalism was frequent in "progressive" English discourse. Adams, "On the Condition of Women in England," quoted in Mineka, *Dissidence*, 294, writes, "The rich man [seeks] an agreeable well-taught harem slave."

29. Ironically, Margaret is ambitious. The triangle Margaret-Henry-Suffolk has affinities with the triangle between the Transomes and Jermyn. Very similar words are spoken by Demetrius in *Titus Andronicus* (2.1.82–83).

30. Like Henry IV, Harold has a son named after himself and called Harry, whose mother is hardly ever mentioned. On p. 20, he says of Jermyn's bad management, "That will not last under *my* reign." Mrs. Transome is "queenly" on p. 102, and Esther is Queen Esther on p. 160. Mrs. Transome's maid, Denner, the one person who loves her, also felt "sorry for the poor French queen" (487). The reference is to Marie Antoinette, important as a symbol in Wollstonecraft. Two epigraphs drawn from history plays are appropriated to apply to Esther's relation with her father, but both suggest a different world from Realpolitik. The epigraph to chapter 13, "Give sorrow leave awhile, to tutor me / To this submission," implicitly compares Rufus's grief about losing Esther to Richard's grief about losing his kingdom—note that neither of them plot to maintain their position as Henry and Harold do. The epigraph to chapter 26 applies lines about Prince Hal's reform and reconciliation with his father (*Henry V*, 1.1.28–31) to Esther, changing the gender of the pronoun. "Consideration like an angel came / And whipped the offending Adam

out of her; Leaving her body as a paradise / To envelop and contain celestial spirits." It has been suggested that the gender change turns the epigraph into a pregnancy image, but this potentiality will not be actualized for Esther until the last sentence of the novel. Her attitude toward Rufus, when she discovers that he is not her biological father, redefines fatherhood in the same way that Eppie does in *Silas Marner*.

31. See David, *Intellectual Women,* 200–201, on how Mrs. Transome's adultery "demolishes a male world of political action . . . and fractures the linear order of inheritance." See also Phyllis Rackin, *Stages of History* (Ithaca: Cornell University Press, 1990), 160.

32. See Susan Stanford Friedman, "Creativity and the Childbirth Metaphor," *Feminist Studies* 13, 1 (1987):49–84.

33. Jameson, *Characteristics of Women,* 324. Jameson's insistence, on pp. 317–23, that Constance is not just motherly can be compared to the insistence in *Felix Holt,* 198, that mothers "have a self larger than their maternity." See Christy Desmet, " 'Intercepting the Dew-Drop': Female Readers and Readings in Anna Jameson's Shakespearean Criticism," in Novy, *Women's Re-Visions of Shakespeare.*

34. See Watson, "Kemble, Scott," 76, and Altick, *English Common Reader,* 210. Watson says that when a *Woodstock* character cites a discussion of illegitimacy in *King John,* it emphasizes "the importance of maintaining the closest links between legitimacy and the monarchy" (80).

35. Sonnet 23 actually reads "belongs to love's fine wit."

36. *Daniel Deronda* will also give visions to Daniel and to Gwendolen.

37. Jameson, *Characteristics of Women,* 77.

38. Jameson, *Characteristics of Women,* 161.

39. G. H. Lewes, "First Impressions of Salvini, 1875," in *On Actors and the Art of Acting* (1875; rpt., New York: Greenwood, 1968), 231. Although this was written later than *Felix Holt,* the "angry pedagogue" description referred to productions he had seen earlier; he might have described them so orally at the time.

40. My view of his limited area of development is close to that of Shuttleworth, *George Eliot,* 127. Gallagher, *Industrial Reformation,* 244, and Bamber, "Self-Defeating Politics," 432, are even more emphatic about his lack of development, while Beer, *George Eliot,* 145, Uglow, *George Eliot,* 184, and Elizabeth Ermarth, "Eliot's Sympathy," 23–42, emphasize his development more.

41. Esther's plot has also been compared to that of *Shrew* by Barrett, *Vocation and Desire,* 113.

42. See my chapter on *Shrew* in *Love's Argument* for discussion of how significant stress on play can make the male dominance/female submission pattern appear a pretense. Esther, at the beginning, is presented as more

playful than Felix, while Petruchio, at the beginning, can be read as playful more easily than can Kate.

43. The phrase, used in the title of *Relative Creatures: Victorian Women in Society and the Novel,* by Françoise Basch (New York: Schocken, 1974), is derived from Rousseau. On p. 79, Wollstonecraft quotes these passages from his *Emile* as examples of views she criticizes: "The men depend on the women only on account of their desires; the women on the men both on account of their desires and their necessities. . . . For this reason, the education of the women should always be relative to the men." Eliot does not agree with Rousseau here (Esther does not depend on Felix for her necessities).

44. Jameson, *Characteristics of Women,* 327.

45. Adams echoes Wollstonecraft's language here, saying that Volumnia perceives that woman in relationship to man "is at best not a sympathizing friend, but an amusing toy" (51).

46. See Bonnie Zimmerman, "*Felix Holt* and the True Power of Womanhood," *ELH* 46 (1979):446–47.

47. Dorothy Thompson, "Women and Nineteenth Century Radical Politics: A Lost Dimension," in *The Rights and Wrongs of Women,* ed. Juliet Mitchell and Ann Oakley (New York: Penguin, 1976), 15–16; Haight, *George Eliot,* 381. In the *Monthly Repository* of 1832, Fox strongly championed women's right to vote: see Mineka, *Dissidence,* 262, 286. In spite of the use of "man"—and perhaps partly because of it—these lines were appropriated across barriers of gender and race by Anna Julia Cooper as an epigraph to the second half of her book *A Voice from the South* (1892; rpt., New York: Oxford University Press, 1988), 147. Cooper's use of Shakespeare and Eliot is discussed in Chapter 6.

48. See Zimmerman, "*Felix Holt,*" 434; Beer, *George Eliot,* 155–59, 168–70, 181–83.

49. Shuttleworth, *George Eliot,* 128–32; Zimmerman, "*Felix Holt.*"

50. This passage is on p. 426 of the 1796 edition. Emphasis is Eliot's.

51. Beer, *George Eliot,* 143.

52. Cf. Uglow, "It makes the Victorian ideology of feminine submissiveness a basis for a genderless ideal of a harmonious society" (*George Eliot,* 187); this is a positive view of the same process that Zimmerman, "*Felix Holt,*" and Bamber, "Self-Defeating Politics," especially, criticize.

53. Bessie Rayner Parkes, *Essays on Women's Work* (London, 1865), 216, quoted in Helsinger et al., *The Woman Question,* 2:113–14.

54. Florence Nightingale, *Cassandra,* quoted in Helsinger et al., *The Woman Question,* 2:144–45.

Chapter 5. Middlemarch

1. *Bearing the Word,* 138. Homans's chapter emphasizes the Wordsworth rewritings. Rewritings of Milton are emphasized by Gilbert and Gubar, *Madwoman,* 217–18, and, in a contrasting tone, by Diana Postlethwaite, in "Eliot Reads Milton."

2. Other discussions of Shakespeare allusions in *Middlemarch* occur in van den Broek, "Reading George Eliot Reading Shakespeare," and also in Otice C. Sircy, " 'The Fashion of Sentiment': Allusive Technique and the Sonnets of *Middlemarch,*" *SP* 84 (1987):219–43.

3. Cross, 3:75.

4. David Carroll, "Introduction," in George Eliot, *Middlemarch,* ed. David Carroll (Oxford: Clarendon Press, 1986), xvii. I quote only this edition of the novel.

5. See John Clark Pratt and Victor A. Neufeldt, "Introduction," in *George Eliot's Middlemarch Notebooks: A Transcription,* ed. Pratt and Neufeldt (Berkeley: University of California Press, 1979), xxiii–xxiv. This volume includes the Folger Notebook and the Berg Notebook: the notes on the sonnets on which I focus are almost all in the Berg.

6. *Notebooks,* 211. The numbers Eliot gives the sonnets are all off by one from the usual system, which refers to these sonnets as 58 and 57; Clark and Pratt believe that she used Charles Knight's second edition of Shakespeare's *Works,* but this edition does not use her numbering. (I have inspected the copy that she shared with Lewes, which is in the Folger.)

7. This aspect of the sonnets has been well discussed by Barber and Wheeler, *The Whole Journey,* esp. xviii, 158–97. For an analogous ambivalence expressed about women's love of unworthy men, described as both "dog-like attachment" and "human pity," see *GEL* 5:132–33, written in January 1871, during work on *Middlemarch.* She criticizes "dog-like attachment" with an adaptation of a line from Shakespeare: "Their sex as well as I, may chide them for it" (See *A Midsummer Night's Dream* 3.2.218). In this same play, Helena compares her devotion to the rejecting Demetrius to that of a spaniel (2.1.203).

8. Thomas Pinney, in his edition of Eliot's *Essays,* 302n, has noted the importance of the phrase "working day" for George Eliot's conception of realism.

9. Cf. Homans's observation that "many readers have found it difficult to share Eliot's interest in and sympathy for Fred, but Fred's value in the story is his lack of admirable qualities" (143).

10. Eliot's novels and Shakespearean tragedy are compared on this point in general terms by Jeannette King, *Tragedy in the Victorian Novel* (Cambridge: Cambridge University Press, 1970), 27, among others.

11. Jameson, *Characteristics of Women,* 28. Jameson also links Imogen and Juliet as conveying "extreme simplicity in the midst of the most wonderful complexity" on p. 215, and Eliot discusses Imogen as a character Dorothea might play on p. 424.

12. Jerome Beaty, *Middlemarch from Notebook to Novel,* Illinois Studies in Language and Literature, vol. 47 (Urbana: University of Illinois Press, 1960), 24.

13. Eliot has Lydgate quote from Daniel's "Musophilus"—"What good is like to this / To do worthy the writing, and to write / Worthy the reading and the world's delight?" Roy Lamson and Hallett Smith, the editors of *The Golden Hind,* rev. ed. (New York: Norton, 1956), my source for Daniel, date "Rosamund" to 1592 and put it in the "falls of princes" tradition, in which the fifteenth-century Lydgate wrote. Daniel, like Eliot, frequently plays on the heroine's name with flower imagery. The poem treats Rosamund as an emblem of women's temporary power; she says, "What cannot women do who know their power?"

14. Dorothea's visit to Rosamond, conquering her jealousy, implicitly contrasts with this murderous visit.

15. Brontë, *Jane Eyre,* 380. See chapter 2.

16. Jameson, *Characteristics of Women,* 90, 91.

17. Recent feminist critics rarely discuss Rosalind as sympathetic, but nineteenth-century women did: see, for example, Helena Faucit, Lady Martin, *On Some of Shakespeare's Female Characters,* 5th ed. (1893; rpt., New York: AMS Press, 1970), 270: "There is in her a vein of tenderness which would make it impossible for her to inflict pain deliberately." Eliot knew Faucit, praised her acting (she played Rosalind, among other characters), and thought of writing a play for her. See also Jameson, *Characteristics of Women,* 90.

18. Rosamond has been horseback riding with his glamorous cousin, whom she now seems to admire more than her husband. This passage faintly echoes the transfer of love between brothers that provoked Hamlet to say of Gertrude, "Frailty, thy name is woman" (1.2.146).

19. Neely, *Broken Nuptials,* 110. Many previous critics have found comic elements in this play. One of the quotations Eliot copied into her *Middlemarch Notebooks* for possible use comes from Othello's speech when he is reunited with Desdemona on Cyprus: "Not another comfort like to this / Succeeds in unknown fate" (2.1.192–93); see *Middlemarch Notebooks,* 84.

20. Jameson, *Characteristics of Women,* 77; see Gillian Beer, *Darwin's Plots* (London: Routledge, 1983), 176–77, for Eliot's use of Jameson's *Sacred and Legendary Art,* particularly for Dorothea's name.

21. Isabella shows "the selfishness of selflessness," according to Skura, *The Psychoanalytic Process,* 248; some of her analysis fits Dorothea as well.

22. This is no longer true in the time period summarized in the "Finale," however, when Dorothea "had now a life filled also with a beneficent activity which she had not the doubtful pains of discovering and marking out for herself" (894).

23. Cf. Linda Bamber, *Comic Women, Tragic Men* (Stanford: Stanford University Press, 1982), 37–38.

24. Cf. Nancy Armstrong, "The Rise of Feminine Authority in the Novel," *Novel* 15 (1981–82):128; this article has now been expanded in her book, *Desire and Domestic Fiction*. See also Judith Lowder Newton, *Women, Power, and Subversion* (Athens: University of Georgia Press, 1980), 1–21.

25. See my *Love's Argument*, esp. chap. 2, where the passage in *As You Like It* is discussed.

26. Compare the discussion of the complicated relation between the theater and sympathy in *Daniel Deronda* in Marshall, *The Figure of Theater*, 193–232. Marshall also connects Eliot's interest in this theme with Shakespeare's.

27. *Middlemarch Notebooks*, 212. On 78, in the same volume's transcription of the Folger Notebook, she writes, "'We acknowledge great power, but we experience great weariness,' says Landor of reading Shakespeare's sonnets." For a recent treatment of how nineteenth-century emphasis on the conventional element in the sonnets was often related to homophobia, see Bruce Smith, *Homosexual Desire in Shakespeare's England* (Chicago: University of Chicago Press, 1991), 230.

28. There is a sensitive discussion of this chapter in Barbara Hardy, "*Middlemarch* and the Passions," in *This Particular Web*, ed. Ian Adam (Toronto: University of Toronto Press, 1975), 12–21.

29. John Kucich notes that Dorothea's mental state here is one of internal conflict, not "homogeneous sympathy," in *Repression in Victorian Fiction*, 369; his sense of such limits in the sympathies of Eliot's characters could be related to Marshall's view that *Deronda* explores the limits of sympathy. My point is not that Dorothea achieves perfect sympathy but that sympathy is part of her motivation.

30. Compare Barber and Wheeler's observation that "the friend in the sonnets . . . is never characterized fully; for the poet to do that would limit the 'all' which he requires of the friend" (169). The description of Dorothea's changing attitude toward Casaubon echoes imagery from the sonnets at one point: "her wifely relation . . . was gradually changing with the secret motion of a watch-hand from what it had been in her maiden dream" (189); cf. "yet doth beauty, like a dial hand, / Steal from his figure" (Sonnet 104). Eliot's list of "fine" sonnets, *Middlemarch Notebooks*, 213, includes this one.

31. This point has been emphasized by Elizabeth Ermarth, most recently

in "Teaching *Middlemarch* as Narrative," in *Approaches to Teaching Eliot's "Middlemarch,"* ed. Kathleen Blake (New York: Modern Language Association, 1990), 35–37.

32. Bonnie Zimmerman, " 'The Mother's History' in George Eliot's Life, Literature, and Political Ideology," in *The Lost Tradition,* ed. Cathy Davidson and E. M. Broner (New York: Ungar, 1980), 85–86, observes this year of preoccupation with motherliness and notes a contrast to the lack of motherhood imagery in Eliot's earlier letters, especially those before 1856. Also studying the letters, Homans, *Bearing the Word,* 179–80, emphasizes the extent to which she took on the role of mother to Lewes's sons, especially from 1860 on.

33. Mary Garth forgives Fred because she feels "something like what a mother feels at the imagined sobs or cries of her naughty truant child, which may lose itself and get harm" (249); Dorothea's suffering over her disillusionment with Will is compared to the pain of "a mother who seems to see her child divided by the sword" (775).

34. Homans discusses Celia's maternal egotism on 185–86; this is part of her analysis of Eliot's difficulties in defining writing as maternal (*Bearing the Word,* 179–88).

35. *Middlemarch Notebooks,* 212. The sonnet (23, although she calls it 22) actually speaks of "love's fine wit." Eliot's other uses of this line, and her association of it with Guido Aretino's emphasis on "hearing with the eye," are discussed by A. G. van dan Broek, in "Additional Notes to Shakespearean Entries in the Pfortzheimer Holographs," *George Eliot/ George Henry Lewes Newsletter* 12–13 (1988):6–11. The language of the novel's first description of Mrs. Vincy recalls the sonnets, though by negation: in her face "forty-five years had delved neither angles nor parallels" (96), recalling "Time . . . delves the parallels in beauty's brow" (Sonnet 60). For an overview of nineteenth-century discourse on the sonnets, which Eliot employs, for example, when she uses "fine" and "exquisite" as words of praise and "tedious" as a word of criticism, see Kenneth Muir, *Shakespeare's Sonnets* (London: Allen & Unwin, 1979), 140–41.

36. On the importance of the sickroom scene in Eliot's fiction, and its ideological significance, see Daniel Cottom, *Social Figures* (Minneapolis: University of Minnesota Press, 1987), 141–60.

37. Homans, *Bearing the Word,* 311; for caution on the motherhood/writing comparison, see Auerbach, *Romantic Imprisonment,* 171–83. See also Paxton, *Eliot and Spencer,* 186, noting that Eliot "detaches maternal sentiments from the biological facts of maternity" and from maternal instinct.

38. Barber and Wheeler, *The Whole Journey,* 182–83.

39. *Middlemarch Notebooks,* 209–10. She calls them Sonnets 70, 89, and 92.

(She refers to them by their first line as well as by number.) Others that she includes, to which I have given the usual number, not hers, are 22, 23, 29, 30, 33, 54, 64, 66, 68, 73, 76, 91, 94, 97, 98, 102, 104, 106, 107, 109, and 116.

40. Cf. Judith Kegan Gardiner, "The Marriage of Male Minds in Shakespeare's Sonnets," *JEGP* 84 (1985):328–47.
41. See, for example, the biographical picture in Phyllis Rose, *Parallel Lives: Five Victorian Marriages* (New York: Vintage, 1984), 193–237.
42. Cross, 3:234.
43. "Confidence in his poetic immortality . . . on the other hand in S. 31 [32] he depreciates his own verse": *Middlemarch Notebooks,* 209–10. On 211, this notebook also shows Eliot depreciating some of the verse and comparing Shakespeare to a woman (surely Elizabeth I in the original context) at the same time: "Here is what might serve as a motto for the blind laudations given to his own writings: S.95 [96] 'As on the finger of a thronèd queen / The basest jewel will be well esteemed, / So are those errors that in thee are seen, / To truths translated & for true things deemed.'"
44. *Middlemarch Notebooks,* 213.
45. Maya Angelou, "Journey to the Heartland" address delivered at the National Association of Local Arts Agencies convention, Cedar Rapids, Iowa, June 12, 1985, 4–5. Lynne Cheney's appropriation of these words in *Humanities in America* (Washington, D.C.: National Endowment for the Humanities, 1988), 14–15, is discussed by Erickson, *Rewriting Shakespeare,* 111–23. Erickson places Angelou in the context of other black women's responses to Shakespeare, as does my introduction to Novy, *Cross-Cultural Performances.*
46. Chodorow, *The Reproduction of Mothering*; Gilligan, *In a Different Voice.*
47. Postlethwaite makes the application of Gilligan to Dorothea's development. For a more complex view of the novel and of feminist theory, see Suzanne Graver, "'Incarnate History': The Feminisms of *Middlemarch,*" in Blake, *Approaches to Teaching Eliot's Middlemarch.*
48. Jameson, *Characteristics of Women,* 5.

Chapter 6. Daniel Deronda

1. Knoepflmacher, *"Daniel Deronda,"* 27.
2. Knoepflmacher, *"Daniel Deronda,"* 28.
3. Compare Deirdre David's view that the Deronda plot becomes an epic and the Gwendolen plot is social realism; see *Fictions of Resolution,* 133–206.
4. G. H. Lewes, *Life of Goethe,* 2d ed (London: Smith, Elder, 1864), 54.
5. Cross, 3:344–45.

6. On identification of Hamlet and Shakespeare, see Bate, *Romantic Imagination*, 19. The review, which misses the extent to which the narrator discusses Daniel's ambiguous parentage as a grievance (151–60), is "Daniel Deronda," *Edinburgh Review* 144 (1876), 468, quoted by Edgar Rosenberg, *From Shylock to Svengali* (Stanford: Stanford University Press, 1960), 182. It continues, "without anything to avenge, or indeed necessarily anything to do in this world, in whom a vague yet lofty ambition, perpetually foiled by overthought, takes the place of that definite mission which the Prince of Denmark can never decide upon." The similarity between Hamlet and Deronda has also been noted by Linda Bamber in *Comic Women, Tragic Men,* who writes, "Hamlet may be said to occupy the position of the cultural feminine," and calls Deronda "a more or less sexless male into whom Eliot projected many of her own attitudes" but notes that "the difference between Deronda and Hamlet is that Hamlet has a powerful sense of free floating aggression that he uses to heat up the play until it comes to a boil" (89).

7. Eliot, *Mill on the Floss,* 353.

8. Eliot, *Middlemarch,* 765.

9. David Leverenz, "The Woman in Hamlet: An Interpersonal View," in *Representing Shakespeare,* ed. Murray Schwartz and Coppélia Kahn (Baltimore: Johns Hopkins University Press, 1980), 110–28; the quoted words appear on p. 111. Leverenz's allusion may be to Goethe's comparison of Hamlet to an oak tree in a vase. Lawrence Danson's article, "Gazing at Hamlet; or, The Danish Cabaret," makes further study of feminized descriptions of Hamlet in Hazlitt and Victorian writers, as well as of a 1920 film in which a woman, Asta Nielsen, played Hamlet.

10. Bernard Grebanier, *Then Came Each Actor* (New York: David McKay, 1975), 253–54. Grebanier suggests that the common belief in Hamlet's sensitivity encouraged actresses to think of him "as a sister under the skin" (253).

11. See, for example, *Readings on the Character of Hamlet,* ed. Claude C. H. Williamson (London: Allen & Unwin, 1950).

12. George Eliot, *Poems,* in *Works,* 10 vols. (New York: Bigelow, Brown & Co., 1908), 8:416.

13. *Poems,* 420. The biblical image of the lost oracle of Urim and Thummim suggests the Hebraic interest of Deronda, while the "golden emphasis of Will" recalls the many plays on that Shakespearean word in *Middlemarch,* including its association with golden-haired Will Ladislaw.

14. Redinger, *George Eliot,* 366.

15. George Eliot, *Daniel Deronda,* ed. Graham Handley (Oxford: Clarendon Press, 1984), 335. Further page references to this novel will be parenthetically noted in the text.

16. Knoepflmacher, "*Daniel Deronda,*" 28.

17. Charles Shattuck, *Mr. Macready Produces "As You Like It"* (Urbana: Beta Phi Mu, 1962), 55n.
18. Helena Faucit, Lady Martin, *Shakespeare's Female Characters,* 277.
19. Jameson, *Characteristics of Women,* 90–91.
20. Bonnie Zimmerman, "Gwendolen Harleth and 'The Girl of the Period,'" in *George Eliot: Centenary Essays and an Unpublished Fragment,* ed. Anne Smith (Totowa, N.J.: Barnes & Noble, 1980), 196–217.
21. Knoepflmacher, *"Daniel Deronda,"* 28.
22. Ian Adam, *"The Winter's Tale* and Its Displacements: The Hermione Episode in *Daniel Deronda,"* *Newsletter of the Victorian Studies Association of Western Canada* 9 (Spring 1983):10.
23. Thomas Campbell, *Life of Mrs. Siddons* (New York: Harper, 1834), 124, quotes Siddons's description, which also imagines that Lady Macbeth "had probably from childhood commanded all around her with a high hand" (129), like Gwendolen. Gwendolen's pose as Hermione, "her arm resting on a pillar," is borrowed from the stance used by Siddons and other eighteenth-century actresses in this part, in which she was famous, according to Hugh Witemeyer, *George Eliot and the Visual Arts* (New Haven: Yale University Press, 1979), 93–94.
24. See Jacqueline Rose, *Sexuality in the Field of Vision* (London: Verso, 1986), 105–22, on the construction of Gwendolen as spectacle.
25. See Showalter, "Representing Ophelia," in Parker and Hartman, *Shakespeare and Theory,* 77–94, and Auerbach, *Romantic Imprisonment,* 282–91.
26. As the previous chapter mentioned, Eliot wrote out most of Sonnet 29 in the dedication of the copy of *Daniel Deronda* she gave to Lewes. Mordecai's words suggest particularly Sonnet 116's image of "the marriage of true minds." Eliot had appropriated this sonnet in her essay "Woman in France" to write that women's admission to "the whole field of reality" will bring about "marriage of minds" (*Essays,* 81). In *Deronda* she, like Shakespeare, uses the image for love between men. This sonnet's first line appears on her list of fine sonnets discussed in chapter 5, although she refers to it as 115.
27. See Alexander Welsh's view that, in Deronda, Eliot "questions her own steady faith in sympathetic understanding," in *George Eliot and Blackmail* (Cambridge, Mass.: Harvard University Press, 1985), 302.
28. Note the contrast with Felix Holt's more conservative use of Caliban to represent the defects of the working classes. Although there may be other reasons for this contrast, apparently it is easier for George Eliot's heroes to sound relatively progressive in dealing with race than in dealing with class. Deirdre David has argued, *Fictions of Resolution,* 153, that the Jews of *Daniel Deronda* are a displacement of Eliot's ideal of English working-class conduct.
29. Cross, 1:385.

30. Compare Sonnet 120: "If you were by my unkindness shaken / As I by yours, y'have passed a hell of time. . . . / O, that our night of woe might have rememb'red / My deepest sense, how hard true sorrow hits." Barber and Wheeler, *The Whole Journey,* 188, interested in many of the same aspects of the sonnets that George Eliot observes in her notebooks discussed in the previous chapter, calls this "the transformation of passion into compassion."

31. Catherine Gallagher notes, drawing on Eliot's *Theophrastus Such* essay "The Modern Hep! Hep! Hep," which argues against "cosmopolitanism": "By embracing Jewish nationalism, . . . Daniel saves the Jews and himself from abstract universalism." See "George Eliot and *Daniel Deronda:* The Prostitute and the Jewish Question," in *Sex, Politics, and Science in the Nineteenth-Century Novel,* ed. Ruth B. Yeazell (Baltimore: Johns Hopkins University Press, 1986), 57.

32. Two recent critics have opposite views on this openness. Christina Crosby writes, "Eliot is willing to sacrifice Gwendolen to guarantee the salvation of Deronda, of Mordecai, of the Jews as historical man," in *The Ends of History: Victorians and the Woman Question* (New York: Routledge, 1991), 35; Morgan, *Sisters in Time,* writes, "We cannot view Gwendolen as outside history and Daniel as making it because the only history the novel offers is hers" (158). Both writers agree that there is a strong fantasy element in the presentation of Daniel's work for Judaism.

33. Zimmerman, "'The Mother's History,'" 92. It should be noted that these are Mordecai's images. Donald Stone makes the related point that "in Judaism Eliot observed the triumph of the Romantic principle: in the survival of a nation through the power of shared memories and feelings, Eliot saw a Darwinian justification for the survival of the idealism of the authors dear to her." See *Romantic Impulse,* 243. In *The Figure of Theater,* 219, David Marshall construes Daniel's "decision to identify himself with his Jewish heritage . . . as a far-reaching act of sympathy." On the relation to *The Merchant of Venice,* see Michael Ragusis, "Representation, Conversion, and Literary Form: *Harrington* and the Novel of Jewish Identity," *Critical Inquiry* 16 (1989):113–43.

34. Cross, 3:32.

35. See, for example, letters to Emily Cross in January 1875 (6:116) and to Harriet Beecher Stowe in May 1876 (6:247). But note the distinction made in August 1869, about the time of Thornie's death, discussed in the previous chapter: "in proportion as I profoundly rejoice that I never brought a child into the world, I am conscious of having an unused stock of motherly tenderness" (5:52). And compare "We women are always in danger of living too exclusively in the affections. . . . we ought also to have our share of the more independent life" (5:107). She congratulates Mrs. Nassau John Senior, the first woman inspector of workhouses and

pauper schools, by writing, "The influence of one woman's life on the lot of other women is getting greater and greater with the quickening spread of all influences" (5:373).

36. See Beer, *George Eliot*, 180. Beer also notes the active feminism of many of Eliot's close friends: Clementia Doughty, Bessie Rayner Parkes, Barbara Bodichon, and Edith Simcox (181). She recalls that Eliot signed Bodichon's petition in support of the Married Women's Property Bill and distributed sheets for it (169).

37. Compare Gillian Beer's assertion that this novel asks "whether there can be new plots for stories about women," *Darwin's Plots*, 195.

38. Carolyn Heilbrun, *Reinventing Womanhood* (New York: Norton, 1979).

39. *Essays*, 53.

40. Crosby, *The Ends of History*, 12–43, argues that Eliot misconstrues Judaism by universalizing it, yet in the nineteenth century, as William Baker shows in *George Eliot and Judaism* (Salzburg: Institut für Englische Sprache und Literatur, 1975), Jews praised the book, and critical disapproval often gave signs of anti-Semitism. Whatever the weaknesses of Eliot's position on Judaism, which Crosby attacks from a poststructuralist viewpoint, it seems to have been one of the more progressive articulated by a non-Jew in Victorian England.

41. Lewes, *Literary Criticism*, 119.

42. Edgar Rosenberg calls Lapidoth a "tenuous link" with the "Shylock tradition": see *From Shylock to Svengali*, 169. Deirdre David, however, has noted that, in spite of many positive aspects of the Cohen family, they often talk about money, and this "propagates one of the more popular myths about Jewish culture," (*Fictions of Resolution*, 162), and links them with Shylock. The combination of this view with Crosby's view that the novel idealizes Judaism shows the complexity of *Deronda* as well as the difficulty of writing against deep-seated cultural prejudices.

43. They were frequenting the salon of Rahel Varnhagen's widower Karl, a strong supporter of German Jews. Eliot wrote that he gave "appreciatory groans always in the right place when G. was reading 'Shylock'" (Cross, 1:356). See Baker, *George Eliot and Judaism*, 34–37.

44. See Marshall, *The Figure of Theater*, 29.

45. R. A. Foakes, ed., *Coleridge's Criticism*, 24, 181.

46. Moers, *Literary Women*, 59, 71–80; Beer, *George Eliot*, 41–51, adds to the intertextuality with the writers Moers discusses as well.

47. For the contrasting emphasis on the terms of exclusion, see Kathleen McLuskie, "The Patriarchal Bard," in *Political Shakespeare*, ed. Jonathan Dollimore and Alan Sinfield (New York: Methuen, 1985).

48. Cooper, *Voice from the South*, 115. Cooper is discussed further in the introduction to Novy, *Cross-Cultural Performances*. She would not have called herself either feminist or womanist (Alice Walker's term), and her stand-

point is quite different from that of the late twentieth-century critics I discuss here, but she was concerned about injustices against women.

49. The original Eliot passage—"sympathy—the one poor word which includes all our best insight and our best love"—can be found in *Adam Bede* (Boston: Houghton Mifflin, 1968), 407.

50. Juliet Dusinberre, *Shakespeare and the Nature of Women* (New York: Barnes & Noble, 1975), 72; Novy, *Love's Argument*, 3. Another critic who emphasizes such assertiveness is Irene Dash, *Wooing, Wedding, and Power* (New York: Columbia University Press, 1981).

51. See, for example, Clara Claiborne Park, "As We Like It: How a Girl Can Be Smart and Still Popular," in *The Woman's Part: Feminist Criticism of Shakespeare*, ed. Carolyn Ruth Swift Lenz et al. (Urbana: University of Illinois Press, 1980), 100–16; Peter Erickson, "Sexual Politics and Social Structure in *As You Like It*," in Erickson, *Patriarchal Structures*; Catherine Belsey, "Disrupting Sexual Difference," 178–90; and Jean Howard, "Crossdressing, the Theatre, and Gender Struggle in Early Modern England, *Shakespeare Quarterly* 39 (1988):418–40, in addition to chapters in Dusinberre, *Shakespeare and Women*, and Novy, *Love's Argument*.

52. McKewin's article is in *The Woman's Part*, 117–32; Carol Thomas Neely, *Broken Nuptials in Shakespeare's Plays* (New Haven: Yale University Press, 1985).

53. See, for example, Rebecca Smith, "A Heart Cleft in Twain: The Dilemma of Shakespeare's Gertrude," in Lenz et al., *The Woman's Part*, 194–210; Carolyn Heilbrun, "The Character of Hamlet's Mother," *Shakespeare Quarterly* 8 (1957):201–6; Showalter, "Representing Ophelia," in Parker and Hartman, *Shakespeare and Theory*, 77–94. Leverenz, "The Woman in Hamlet," and the chapter on the tragedies in Erickson, *Patriarchal Structures,* contain recent treatments of Hamlet by male feminists; see also Jacqueline Rose, "Sexuality in the Reading of Shakespeare: *Hamlet* and *Measure for Measure*," in Drakakis, *Alternative Shakespeares*, 95–118. *Hamlet* is also considered in Bamber, *Comic Women, Tragic Men*. The most positive recent treatment of Hamlet by a woman may be in Patterson's *Shakespeare and the Popular Voice*, 93–106. More concerned with class than with gender, Patterson is interested in Hamlet's use of popular language; Eliot had made a similar observation about Shakespeare's use of common language even in *Hamlet* in a letter to her prospective French translator. On Coriolanus, see Janet Adelman, "'Anger's My Meat': Feeding, Dependency, and Aggression in *Coriolanus*," in Schwartz and Kahn, *Representing Shakespeare*, 129–49; and, in contrast, Patterson's chapter on this play, which deals with its political context and reception through Brontë and Eliot but does not stress gender.

54. One feminist article that, like Eliot, is interested in the crossing of expected gender positions in the sonnets is Judith Kegan Gardiner, "The

Marriage of Male Minds." See also Carol Thomas Neely, "Detachment and Engagement in Shakespeare's Sonnets: 94, 116, 129," *PMLA* 92 (1977):83–95. In the previous chapter I have shown many links between Eliot's interests in the sonnets and those of Barber and Wheeler, *The Whole Journey*, a work close to feminist criticism.

55. Bamber has also written "Self-Defeating Politics," and, in her article "The Woman Reader in *King Lear*," in *The New Signet Shakespeare*, contrasts our loss of touch with Cordelia's consciousness with the development of Dorothea in *Middlemarch*.

56. The volume of Knight's edition of Shakespeare owned by Lewes and shared by Eliot, now at the Folger, has a marginal notation in the *Othello* volume about Coleridge's claim that "all the sarcasms" on women "in Shakespeare are put in the mouths of villains," with the comment "This is not quite true. Hamlet, for instance."

57. Novy, *Love's Argument*, 202.

58. Germaine Greer, *Shakespeare* (Oxford: Oxford University Press, 1986), 125, 84–87, 17.

59. See, for example, Ania Loomba, *Gender, Race, Renaissance Drama*, and my anthology *Cross-Cultural Performances*.

60. Hélène Cixous, "Sorties," in Hélène Cixous and Catherine Clement, *The Newly Born Woman* (Minneapolis: University of Minnesota Press, 1986), 98. She reads *Antony and Cleopatra* on pp. 122–30, and *Lear* in *Inside* (New York: Schocken, 1985), 126, 136, appropriating his "Come, let's away to prison" speech to Cordelia. In chapter 8 I touch on her use of Shakespeare for the Théâtre du Soleil. For the French association of Shakespeare with liberty, see, for example, Stendhal's *Racine et Shakespeare* (1823) and Hugo's "Préface de *Cromwell*" (1827) as well as works by de Staël and Sand. Selections may be found in *The Romantics on Shakespeare*, ed. Jonathan Bate (New York: Penguin, 1992).

61. Maya Angelou, "Journey to the Heartland." See notes for chapter 5 for further contextualization of this speech.

Chapter 7. Uses of Shakespeare by Twentieth-Century Women Novelists

I would like to dedicate this chapter to the memory of Harriet Gilliam, 1944–1993.

1. Other novelistic Shakespearean rewritings by women of which I am aware are Valerie Miner's *Blood Sisters* and *A Walking Fire*; A. S. Byatt's *The Virgin in the Garden*; Fay Weldon's *Down Among the Women*; Marina Warner's *Indigo*; Michelle Cliff's *No Telephone to Heaven*; Rachel Ingalls's *Mrs. Caliban*; and Elizabeth Jolley's *The Sugar Mother*; in addition to those

discussed in my edited volumes *Women's Re-Visions of Shakespeare* and *Cross-Cultural Performances,* both of which also include discussions of rewritings in poetry and drama as well.

2. See Alice Fox, *Virginia Woolf and the Literature of the English Renaissance* (Oxford: Clarendon Press, 1990), and a forthcoming book by Beth Schwartz. Iris Murdoch's involvement with Shakespeare has also been the subject matter for a book: Richard Todd, *Iris Murdoch: The Shakespearian Interest* (London: Vision, 1979).

3. See, for example, *The Modern Tradition,* ed. Richard Ellmann and Charles Feidelson, Jr. (New York: Oxford University Press, 1965), which includes Keats's definition of "negative capability" as well as passages by such writers as Flaubert, T. S. Eliot, Joyce, Rilke, and Valéry emphasizing the theme of the impersonality of the work of art. See also Hugh Grady, *The Modernist Shakespeare* (Oxford: Clarendon Press, 1991), and Taylor, *Reinventing Shakespeare,* 231–97.

4. *Nebraska State Journal,* May 31, 1896, reprinted in Willa Cather, *The Kingdom of Art,* ed. Bernice Slote (Lincoln: University of Nebraska Press, 1966), 376.

5. Hermione Lee, in *Willa Cather* (London: Virago, 1989), makes the landscape comparison on p. 92 and the Rosamond comparison on p. 227 and analyzes Jim Burden as androgynous, comparing him to "Shakespearean . . . boys dressed as girls dressed as boys," on p. 153.

6. Iris Murdoch, "The Sublime and the Beautiful Revisited," *Yale Review* 49 (1959):262.

7. Virginia Woolf, "George Eliot" (1919), reprinted in *Women and Writing,* ed. Michèle Barrett (London: Women's Press, 1979), 155, 160.

8. Booth, *Greatness Engendered,* 13.

9. See, for example, the many references to Cather's reading Shakespeare in James Woodress, *Willa Cather* (Lincoln: University of Nebraska Press, 1987), as well as in Lee, *Willa Cather.*

10. Willa Cather, "Between the Acts," *Nebraska State Journal,* April 29, 1894, reprinted in "Willa Cather on Shakespeare," *Prairie Schooner* 38 (1964), 68. Contrast the racial/ethnic usage of Shakespeare here to that of Anna Julia Cooper in 1892, discussed in chapter 6.

11. "Willa Cather on Shakespeare," 67. Perhaps this view was a development of Emerson's in *Representative Men:* "he wrote the text of Modern Life; the text of manners: he drew the man of England and Europe; the father of the man in America" (Philadelphia: Henry Altemus, n.d.[c. 1850], 214). Emerson's attitude to Shakespeare shares Cather's populism, but he is much more negative about Shakespeare's connection to the stage. For more on appropriations of Shakespeare for America, see Bristol, *Shakespeare's America.*

12. See Kwame Anthony Appiah, "Race," in *Critical Terms for Literary Study,*

ed. Frank Lentricchia and Thomas McLaughlin (Chicago: University of Chicago Press, 1990), 274–87, for "Anglo-Saxon racialism," the midnineteenth-century construction of the Anglo-Saxons as a race, and its relation to racism and to nationalism.

13. Willa Cather, "As You Like It," *Nebraska State Journal,* April 21, 1895, reprinted in Cather, *The Kingdom of Art,* 431. When she was young she often called herself William, which *might* include Shakespearean associations among the familial ones. For Sylvia Townsend Warner, see her "Women as Writers," reprinted in *The Gender of Modernism,* ed. Bonnie Kime Scott (Bloomington: Indiana University Press, 1990), 544.

14. Willa Cather, "Shakespeare and Hamlet," reprinted in Cather, *The Kingdom of Art,* 434, 426.

15. Sharon O'Brien, *Willa Cather: The Emerging Voice* (New York: Oxford University Press, 1987), 158; see Cather, *The Kingdom of Art,* 349.

16. Cather, "Shakespeare and Hamlet," reprinted in Cather, *The Kingdom of Art,* 434.

17. O'Brien, *Willa Cather,* 158.

18. Cather, *The Kingdom of Art,* 431. The essay also deals with Hamlet's relationship with Gertrude. It twice uses his last line, "The rest is silence," a variation of which ends her 1893 story, "The Elopement of Allen Poole," reprinted in *The Kingdom of Art,* 441. Sharon O'Brien has argued that the essay's description of Hamlet as a frustrated artist, and the interest in his relationship with his mother, illuminate "Allen Poole" and other Cather stories of this time as well. See O'Brien, *Willa Cather,* 206–7.

19. Willa Cather, *My Mortal Enemy* (New York: Knopf, 1926), 87, 89.

20. Cf. David Stouck, *Willa Cather's Imagination* (Lincoln: University of Nebraska Press, 1975), 127.

21. Woolf, *A Writer's Diary,* 274. This passage is quoted in Maria DiBattista, *Virginia Woolf's Major Novels* (New Haven: Yale University Press, 1980), 14.

22. DiBattista, *Woolf's Novels,* 14–15.

23. Woolf, *Room,* 58.

24. Woolf, *A Writer's Diary,* 6.

25. Virginia Woolf, "Professions for Women," based on a 1931 speech, reprinted in Woolf, *Women and Writing,* 59.

26. Phyllis Rose, *Woman of Letters: A Life of Virginia Woolf* (New York: Oxford University Press, 1978), 156.

27. Alison Booth's book thoroughly compares their approaches to this issue in relation to "a certain feminist tradition that affirms a supposed feminine selflessness as it rejects the masculine self-assertion that has conventionally fueled notions of greatness" (3).

28. Woolf, *Room*, 44–45.

29. Woolf, "Men and Women" (1920), reprinted in *Books and Portraits,* ed.
Mary Lyon (London: Hogarth Press, 1977), 28–29; quoted and discussed
in Fox, *Virginia Woolf and the Renaissance,* 101–2.

30. Woolf, *Room*, 86–87.

31. Virginia Woolf, *Night and Day* (London: Granada, 1978), 178. Her
mother's comparison is on p. 277.

32. Woolf, *Night and Day,* 449. See also Carol Thomas Neely, "Epilogue:
Remembering Shakespeare, Revising Ourselves," in Novy, *Women's
Re-Visions,* 246.

33. Adrienne Rich, "Compulsory Heterosexuality and Lesbian Existence,"
in *Blood, Bread, and Poetry* (New York: Norton, 1986), 23–75; see also
Shirley Nelson Garner, " 'Women Together' in Virginia Woolf's *Night
and Day,* " in *The (M)Other Tongue,* ed. Shirley Nelson Garner et al.
(Ithaca: Cornell University Press, 1985), 318–33.

34. Virginia Woolf, *Orlando* (London: Triad Grafton, 1978), 138.

35. Woolf, *Orlando,* 165. For more discussion of Woolf's responses to Shakespeare, see Fox, *Woolf and the Renaissance,* and Christine Froula, "Virginia
Woolf as Shakespeare's Sister: Chapters in a Woman Writer's Autobiography," in Novy, *Women's Re-Visions,* 123–42.

36. Iris Murdoch, "The Sublime and the Good," *Chicago Review* 13 (Autumn
1959):42.

37. Iris Murdoch, "Beautiful Revisited," 261.

38. Murdoch, "Beautiful Revisited," 270.

39. Murdoch, "Good," 42.

40. Murdoch, "Beautiful Revisited," 270.

41. Iris Murdoch, *The Sovereignty of Good* (London: Routledge, 1970), 53;
quoted in Deborah Johnson, *Iris Murdoch* (Brighton: Harvester, 1987), 16.

42. Iris Murdoch, "Against Dryness" (1961), quoted in Todd, *Iris Murdoch,* 27.

43. Iris Murdoch, *The Black Prince* (New York: Viking, 1973), 116.

44. The lecture about Hamlet in this novel is especially interesting to compare with Stephen Dedalus's also somewhat autobiographical specu-
lations about Hamlet and Shakespeare in Joyce's *Ulysses* (New York:
Modern Library, 1934; new ed., 1961), 184–218, which will be discussed
later in this chapter. Stephen focuses more on Shakespeare's father-son
and brother-brother relations than either Cather or Murdoch's Bradley,
and unlike either of the others, Stephen imagines Shakespeare as taking
vengeance through his art.

45. See Brooks-Davies, *Fielding, Dickens, Gosse,* 160–61.

46. Mary Jacobus, "The Question of Language: Men of Maxims and *The Mill
on the Floss,* " in *Writing and Sexual Difference,* ed. Elizabeth Abel (Brighton:

Harvester, 1982), 40, quoted by Deborah Johnson, *Iris Murdoch*, 35. In this essay Jacobus discusses Eliot's critique of the misogynist language of Tom's teacher Stelling, his Latin grammar, and other patriarchal texts. *The Black Prince,* apart from its epilogues and perhaps its prologue, would be the analogue of a whole novel in the voice of a more intelligent but still misogynous Stelling.

47. Johnson, *Iris Murdoch*, 46. Portia, for example, imagines that in her disguise she will "tell quaint lies, / How honorable ladies sought my love, / Which I denying, they fell sick and died" (3.4.69–71). Yet of course these lines were written by a man imitating a woman imitating a man.

48. Iris Murdoch, *Nuns and Soldiers* (London: Penguin, 1981), 284.

49. Cf. Johnson, *Iris Murdoch*, 72–73; on rewriting Shakespeare's Gertrude, see also Elizabeth Dipple, *Iris Murdoch: Work for the Spirit* (Chicago: University of Chicago Press, 1982), 332.

50. Gayle Greene, *Changing the Story: Feminist Fiction and the Tradition* (Bloomington: Indiana University Press, 1991), 7. In her introduction, Greene discusses the literary education of Atwood and Drabble, and their interest in the nineteenth-century novel (4–5), as well as giving many examples of the similar concerns of feminist critics and the protagonists of feminist fiction (8). Greene began as a Shakespeare critic, and her concerns are similar to mine in this chapter, though she deals with recent women novelists' responses to other authors in the English literary tradition as well as to Shakespeare. See also Erickson, *Rewriting Shakespeare,* esp. his discussion of Adrienne Rich on pp. 103–7 and 146–66.

51. Margaret Drabble, *The Waterfall* (London: Penguin, 1971), 87; John Hannay, *The Intertextuality of Fate* (Columbia: University of Missouri Press, 1986), 19–47. On pp. 138–39, Greene, *Changing the Story,* notes allusions to Shakespeare's Sonnet 138 and to Mariana of *Measure for Measure,* but she concentrates on rewritings of nineteenth-century novels and analogies to French feminist theories of women's writing in her excellent chapter on *The Waterfall,* 130–47.

52. After remembering the lines, Mrs. Dalloway "felt it, she was convinced, as strongly as Shakespeare meant Othello to feel it." Virginia Woolf, *Mrs. Dalloway* (1925; reprint, New York: Harcourt Brace Jovanovich, 1985), 51.

53. Drabble, *The Waterfall,* 189.

54. Margaret Drabble, *The Realms of Gold* (New York: Popular Library, 1977), 48–49.

55. Margaret Drabble, *Women Writers Talking,* ed. Janet Todd (New York: Holmes & Meier, 1983), 167.

56. "I Would Like to Have Written," *New York Times Book Review,* December 6, 1981, p. 68.

57. Greene, *Changing the Story,* 220–21, discusses some allusions in *The Radi-*

ant Way—to *The Tempest, Cymbeline,* and *King Lear*—and argues that they show the irrelevance of Shakespeare.

58. Margaret Drabble, *A Natural Curiosity* (New York: Viking, 1989), 208.
59. Marcia's "heterogeneous" life (292), which has made a kind of family out of visitors to her adopted parents' theatrical boardinghouse and now involves a black lover who also "comes from a large and complicated family" with "many legitimate and illegitimate siblings and half-siblings," anticipates some themes in Angela Carter's *Wise Children,* discussed in chapter 8. Cultural hybridity is emerging as one of Drabble's concerns here.
60. Nancy S. Hardin, "An Interview with Margaret Drabble," *Contemporary Literature* 14 (Summer 1973):279.
61. Iris Rozencwajg, "Interview with Margaret Drabble," *Women's Studies* 6 (1979):336; Diana Cooper-Clark, "Margaret Drabble: Cautious Feminist," *Atlantic Monthly,* November 1980, p. 71.
62. Margaret Drabble, "Stratford Revisited: A Legacy of the Sixties," in Novy, *Cross-Cultural Performances.*
63. Dee Preussner, "Talking with Margaret Drabble," *Modern Fiction Studies* 25 (1979–80):570.
64. Margaret Atwood, *Survival* (Toronto: Anansi, 1972).
65. Margaret Atwood, *Life Before Man* (New York: Fawcett Popular Library, 1979), 179.
66. Margaret Atwood, *Cat's Eye* (New York: Doubleday, 1989), 211.
67. An analogous rewriting of a Shakespearean woman—though one seldom as romanticized as Cordelia—occurs in Atwood's "Gertrude Talks Back," in *Good Bones* (Toronto: Coach House Press, 1992), 15–18. In this version, Gertrude tells her son, quite unrepentantly, that she killed Old Hamlet herself. I thank Margaret Atwood for sending me a copy.
68. Atwood's rewriting can also be linked with Janet Adelman's insight, in *Suffocating Mothers* (New York: Routledge, 1992), 126, that "the fantasies enacted in Cordelia's loss and return . . . derive from the very beginnings of nascent selfhood, before consciousness of the gender divide. . . . daughters as well as sons require . . . sacrifice from those we make our mothers."
69. Greene notes that Elaine does not make these connections (212), yet she tells the story in a way that a reader can. In defense of Greene's position, it might be said that the novel will not lead anyone to a feminist analysis who is not ready to make it for other reasons.
70. In the same scene, Cordelia fantasizes about playing the first witch in *Macbeth* the following year. This fantasy of female power—one of the many *Macbeth* allusions rightly noted by Greene—is placed as a fantasy by her difficulty with even her small parts.
71. Margaret Laurence, *The Diviners* (Toronto: Bantam, 1974), 330.

72. For further discussion of Laurence, see Greene, *Changing the Story,* 148–65, as well as Diana Brydon's essay "Sister Letters: Miranda's *Tempest* in Canada," in Novy, *Cross-Cultural Performances,* which discusses revisionary uses of Miranda by other Canadian women writers as well.

73. Margaret Atwood, *Second Words* (Toronto: Anansi, 1982), 344–45.

74. Atwood, "Writing the Male Character" (1982), in *Second Words,* 422. In conversation after a lecture, she has referred to *Life Before Man* as her tribute to *Middlemarch.* There are some parallels between Elizabeth and Rosamond, Lydgate and Nate, Lesje and Dorothea.

75. Atwood, "Writing the Male Character," in *Second Words,* 430.

76. Atwood, "An End to Audience?" (1980), in *Second Words,* 344, 347–48.

77. Atwood, "The Curse of Eve" (1978), in *Second Words,* 226.

78. Joyce, *Ulysses,* 566–67.

79. Jorge Luis Borges, *Labyrinths: Selected Stories and Other Writings,* ed. Donald A. Yates and James E. Irby (New York: New Directions, 1964), 248. This essay has been recently discussed by Barber and Wheeler, *The Whole Journey,* xviii–xix; William Kerrigan, "The Personal Shakespeare: Three Clues," in *Shakespeare's Personality,* ed. Norman Holland, Sidney Homan, and Bernard Paris (Berkeley: University of California Press, 1989), 176–77; and David Willburn, "What Is Shakespeare?" in *Shakespeare's Personality,* 228, an essay that also discusses Henry James's images of Shakespeare.

80. Susan Stanford Friedman, "Remembering Shakespeare Differently: H.D.'s *By Avon River,*" in Novy, *Women's Re-Visions of Shakespeare,* 143–64. Contrast the negative view of Shakespeare, however, in Dorothy Richardson's 1910 experimental novel *Pilgrimage;* her character Miriam Henderson thinks, "there was no reality in any of Shakespeare's women. They please men because they show women as men see them" (London: J. M. Dent, 1967), 2:188.

81. Sylvia Townsend Warner, "Women as Writers," 544.

82. Karen Chase, *Landmarks of World Literature: Middlemarch* (Cambridge: Cambridge University Press, 1991), 91.

83. On the interest of twentieth-century women writers in empathy, a concept whose definitions and relation to sympathy I discuss in chapter 1, see Gardiner, *Rhys, Stead, Lessing.* This interest, however, is not found only in women writers or in feminist critics. See Wayne Booth, *The Company We Keep* (Berkeley: University of California Press, 1988), esp. 451, 456, on sympathy in an author (D. H. Lawrence) and, on sympathy in the reader, Marshall Alcorn and Mark Bracher, "Literature, Psychoanalysis, and the Re-Formation of the Self: A New Direction for Reader-Response Theory," *PMLA* 100 (May 1985):342–54. Yet note how different the tone is in the call for sympathy at the end of Russell Banks's novel, *Continental Drift* (New York: Ballantine Books, 1985), 421: "Good

cheer and mournfulness over lives other than our own, even wholly invented lives—no, especially wholly invented lives—deprive the world as
it is of some of the greed it needs to continue to be itself. Sabotage and
subversion, then, are this book's objectives."

84. Indeed, she has discussed *Life Before Man* as much more in the realist
tradition than her other novels. Her relationship with the feminist movement has often been rather ambivalent as well. Drabble's novels can also
be seen as postmodern, as Greene has shown, and her most recent, *The
Gates of Ivory,* justifiably calls itself so.

85. Elaine Showalter, "The Greening of Sister George," *Nineteenth Century
Fiction* 35 (1980):292–311.

86. Cynthia Ozick, "Puttermesser Paired," *New Yorker,* October 8, 1990, 40–
75; the quote appears on p. 43. See also Ozick in "Who Is the Living
Writer You Most Admire?" *New York Times Book Review,* December 4,
1977, p. 66, on "Mary Ann Evans" as a living writer.

Chapter 8. Shakespeare in the Cultural Hybridity of Contemporary Women Novelists

1. The Anglophile Saladin, consciously hyperbolic, calls *Othello* "worth
the total output of any other dramatist in any other language." Salman
Rushdie, *The Satanic Verses* (New York: Viking, 1989), 398. Saladin uses
his heteroglossic skill (Shakespearean? postmodern?) to inflict jealousy on Gibreel; though Saladin repents, and the men are temporarily
reconciled, at the end both Saladin and his wife, Alleluia, commit suicide.

2. See Diana Brydon, "Sister Letters," in Novy, *Cross-Cultural Performances.*

3. Angela Carter, "Notes from the Front Line," in *On Gender and Writing,*
ed. Michelene Wandor (London: Pandora, 1983), 75. Unlike Drabble and
Atwood, Carter cites Eliot as a model not because of sympathy in her
writing, but because she was both a professional writer and sexually
active, a combination that Carter sees as hardly ever possible for women
before early twentieth-century contraception. (More recent scholars have
discovered evidence of contraception before the twentieth century and
have seen hints of it in Eliot's correspondence.)

4. Angela Carter, "Notes for a Theory of Sixties Style," reprinted in *Nothing
Sacred* (London: Virago, 1982), 87.

5. Angela Carter, *The Passion of New Eve* (New York: Harcourt Brace, 1977),
132. I am indebted to Marjorie Garber for knowledge of this novel. She
discusses it in *Vested Interests: Cross-Dressing and Cultural Anxiety* (New
York: HarperCollins, 1993), 75–76. In the 1987 Virago reprint, which
she quotes there, the end of the passage reads "Rosalind in Elizabethan Arden."

6. Angela Carter, *Nights at the Circus* (New York: Penguin, 1986), 280–81.

7. Angela Carter, *Wise Children* (New York: Farrar, Straus & Giroux, 1992).

8. In another kind of hybridity, this plot element also works as a tribute to South American fiction—*Wise Children* has an affinity to some of its fantastic family sagas.

9. Angela Carter, "Conference Presentation," in *Critical Fictions,* ed. Philomena Mariani (Seattle: Bay Press, 1991), 143. A number of essays in this collection deal with the theme of cultural hybridity, especially in section 2, "'Caliban Speaks to Prospero': Cultural Identity and the Crisis of Representation.'"

10. For her biography, see Kay Bonetti, Interview with Gloria Naylor, American Audio Prose Library, 1988.

11. See especially Cooper, *View from the South;* Maya Angelou, *I Know Why the Caged Bird Sings* (1969; New York: Bantam, 1970); W. E. B. Du Bois, *The Souls of Black Folk* (1903; reprint, New York: Bantam, 1989); Errol Hill, *Shakespeare in Sable* (Amherst: University of Massachusetts Press, 1984); Peter Erickson, *Rewriting Shakespeare*; and my introduction to *Cross-Cultural Performances.*

12. Gloria Naylor, *The Women of Brewster Place* (New York: Penguin, 1983), 147.

13. Erickson, *Rewriting Shakespeare,* 127–28. Erickson's detailed and perceptive study shows how "Naylor plays off two meanings of dream—genuine hope and futile fantasy" (127).

14. Gloria Naylor, *Linden Hills* (New York: Penguin, 1986), 282–83.

15. Elaine Showalter, *Sister's Choice* (Oxford: Clarendon Press, 1991), 41. She quotes Gates, "The Master's Pieces: On Canon-Formation and the Afro-American Tradition" (Paper presented at Princeton University, Spring 1989), 32. Erickson, *Rewriting Shakespeare,* makes a similar point with reference to Willie's image: "Shakespeare comes to symbolize a quest for black recognition that is unattainable within the narrow terms of imitation suggested by the uncomfortable echo effect that ties Willie's name to Will Shakespeare's" (132). Gordimer's Will is named after Shakespeare, but perhaps this device works better because the naming results from his father's love of Shakespeare, which the novel asks us to think about.

16. The novel was published in the same year that Maya Angelou claimed, "I *know* that Shakespeare was a black woman." See my discussion of this appropriation in chapter 5. Erickson, *Rewriting Shakespeare,* contextualizes Angelou's claim, 111–23, and critiques the use of Dante in *Linden Hills,* 212 n. 18.

17. Adrienne Rich, "Dreamwood," in *Time's Power* (New York: Norton, 1989), 35.

18. Gloria Naylor, *Mama Day* (New York: Vintage, 1989), 106.

19. I have discussed such imagery in *Lear* in *Love's Argument*, 195.
20. Erickson, *Rewriting Shakespeare*, 140.
21. My view of this novel has been most influenced by Valerie Traub's "Rainbows of Darkness: Deconstructing Shakespeare in the Fiction of Gloria Naylor and Zora Neale Hurston," in *Cross-Cultural Performances*, but there are also valuable treatments of the novel in Erickson's *Rewriting Shakespeare* and Showalter's *Sister's Choice*. I have condensed my treatment of the aspects of the novel on which I agree with these critics, and concentrated on the treatment of the characters' readings of Shakespeare, a topic on which we disagree somewhat.
22. Nadine Gordimer, *My Son's Story* (New York: Penguin, 1991), 6.
23. See Ania Loomba, *Gender, Race,* and, on Cordelia, Janet Adelman, *Suffocating Mothers* (New York: Routledge, 1992), 124–25.
24. Will has moved from seeing his father as like Claudius or Gertrude into a quite different attitude. The title's characterization of him as "my son" also identifies him in another way with a man always called Sonny; it suggests that somehow Sonny helped Will get the novel published, in spite of the fact that its last line is "this is my first book—that I can never publish." Gordimer has also described her own son, however, as "really torn . . . being a filmmaker, there is also the feeling that you'd like to put into film some of the things you know," in *Conversations with Nadine Gordimer*, ed. Nancy Topping Bazin and Marilyn Dallman Seymour (Jackson: University Press of Mississippi, 1990), 279, so perhaps the allusion is also to him.
25. Bazin and Seymour, *Conversations*, 214.
26. Nadine Gordimer, *The Essential Gesture* (New York: Knopf, 1988).
27. See, for example, Bazin and Seymour, *Conversations*, 37. *Middlemarch* is one of about twenty-seven works and authors listed on this page, but the writers mentioned above are all discussed by Gordimer more frequently and at greater length than either Shakespeare or Eliot.
28. Gordimer, *Essential Gesture*, 66. The other reference praises the 1950s South African black writer Can Themba, who "knew his Shakespeare well and his Dostoevsky"; Bazin and Seymour, *Conversations*, 251.
29. Cornel West, "Diverse New World," *Democratic Left* 19 (1991):7. See also Showalter, *Sister's Choice*, 7. She quotes Homi Bhabha as saying "all forms of culture are continually in a process of hybridity."
30. George Eliot, *Daniel Deronda*, ed. Graham Handley (Oxford: Clarendon Press, 1984), 303–4.
31. Carol Thomas Neely, "Epilogue: Remembering Shakespeare, Revising Ourselves," in Novy, *Women's Re-Visions of Shakespeare*, 245.
32. As I noted in chapter 7, however, Margaret Laurence, in *The Diviners*

(1974), could still give a continuous interest in Shakespeare to a central female character, Morag. See Greene's discussion of Laurence in *Changing the Story*, 148–65. Morag, like Caroline, Daniel, George, and Cocoa, is a Shakespeare reader who has lost a father.

33. Jane Smiley, *A Thousand Acres* (New York: Knopf, 1991). The closest verbal echo of Shakespeare is from *The Merchant of Venice*, when Rose refers to her amputated, cancerous breast as "my pound of flesh" (303). This phrase may be in our "cultural literacy" for people who have never read or seen the play, but on the other hand it, unlike *Lear*, was widely read in high school during the time Rose would have been of high school age.

34. Ginny's attitude here is somewhat like one of Nadine Gordimer's descriptions of her attitude to her characters: "Isn't there a bit of a murderer, isn't there a bit of a prostitute, isn't there a bit of a thief, in all of us? So maybe writers create characters unlike themselves out of suppressed instincts of these kinds," in Bazin and Seymour, *Conversations*, 241. Of course, Gordimer's description doesn't assume the novelist really has attempted murder as Ginny has. Nevertheless the novel's valorization of both psychological understanding and political analysis has affinities with Gordimer's.

35. Showalter, *Sister's Choice*, 169. *A Thousand Acres* won the 1992 Pulitzer Prize for literature.

36. Margaret Drabble, *The Gates of Ivory* (1991; rpt. New York: Viking, 1992).

37. George Eliot, *Daniel Deronda*, 173.

38. See Adrian Kernander, "The Théâtre du Soleil," *New Theatre Quarterly* 2, 7 (August 1986):195–216.

39. See, for example, the interviews with directors in *The Shakespeare Myth*, ed. Graham Holderness (Manchester: Manchester University Press, 1988).

40. Quoted by Dennis Kennedy in "Shakespearean Orientalism," in *Foreign Shakespeare*, ed. Kennedy (Cambridge: Cambridge University Press, 1993). Here Kennedy connects both Mnouchkine's work and postmodernism in general with global travel, refugee movement, and electronic communication, all of which are among Drabble's concerns in *The Gates of Horn*.

41. "The body repeats the landscape. They are the source of each other and create each other. We were marked by the seasonal body of earth, by the terrible migrations of people, by the swift turn of a century, verging on change never before experienced on this greening planet." "The Ancient People and the Newly Come," in *Ripening*, ed. Elaine Hedges (Old Westbury, N.Y.: Feminist Press, 1982), 39.

42. Edith Milton, "Essayists of the Eighties," *Women's Review of Books* 8, 10–11 (July 1991):21, reviewing Janet Sternburg, ed., *The Writer on Her*

Work, vol. 2 (New York: Norton, 1991), notes the repeated theme among many diverse essayists "of a passionate commitment to putting themselves in the service of others, and letting their writing voice the needs of lives and of times beyond their own." (Milton is bothered by what she calls an "unassuming search for usefulness" and "wonders if twenty men would have answered the same exercise so dutifully.") I have consulted the essays in Sternburg, and none of them mentions Shakespeare, although this ideal seems close to the aesthetic that Brontë, Eliot, Woolf, Cather, and Murdoch associated with Shakespeare.

43. Bazin and Seymour, *Conversations,* 155, 169.

44. The essay in which Drabble critiques the subordination of women in *Taming of the Shrew* and *Cymbeline* calls Shakespeare a postmodernist because of his reflexive self-consciousness. At the same time, Drabble was planning her own self-consciously postmodernist novel, *Gates of Ivory.* See "Stratford Revisited," 131–33. This essay was originally published in 1988.

45. In Gates's published version of this talk, in *Loose Canons: Notes on the Culture Wars* (New York: Oxford University Press, 1992), no sentence close to this one appears, and instead he writes, "To reverse Audre Lorde, only the master's tools will ever dismantle the master's house," 37. It would seem that rewritings of Caliban and Miranda now have more revolutionary potential for Gates than for Showalter.

46. But see Susan Baker's discussion of works by both male and female authors in "Rewriting Shakespeare in the Classic Detective Story," an essay presented to Jonathan Crewe's seminar, "Rewriting Shakespeare," at the annual meeting of the Shakespeare Association of America, Kansas City, Missouri, April 18, 1992. One can also see minority perspectives in earlier uses of Shakespeare by males such as Wilde.

47. Alison Lyssa, *Pinball,* in *Plays by Women,* vol. 4, ed. Michelene Wandor (New York: Methuen, 1985). I discuss this play in the introduction to *Women's Re-Visions.*

48. See Elaine Showalter, "Representing Ophelia," in Parker and Hartman, *Shakespeare and Theory,* 80–94, and Lizbeth Goodman, "Women's Alternative Shakespeares and Women's Alternatives to Shakespeare in Contemporary British Theatre," in Novy, *Cross-Cultural Performances.*

49. See Madelon Sprengnether's moving paper, "Mourning Shakespeare: My Own Private Hamlet," delivered at the annual meeting of the Shakespeare Association of America, Kansas City, Mo., April 18, 1992, and also Greene, *Changing the Story,* 220, on *The Radiant Way.*

50. George Eliot, "Notes on Form in Art" (1868), in *Essays,* 433.

51. Patterson, *Shakespeare and the Popular Voice.*

52. For a discussion of a similar search, from a feminist postcolonial per-

spective, for how contradictions between different interlocking power structures "may catalyse the possibility of change," see Ania Loomba, "Hamlet in Mizoram," in Novy, *Cross-Cultural Performances*. For a manifesto on giving up the image of pure identity and celebrating hybridity while being consciously political, see Donna Haraway, "A Cyborg Manifesto: Science, Technology, and Socialist-Feminism in the Late Twentieth Century," in *Simians, Cyborgs, and Women* (New York: Routledge, 1991), 149–81.

53. Virginia Woolf, "The Leaning Tower," in *Collected Essays*, 4 vols. (London: Hogarth Press, 1966), 2:181. I thank B. J. Zamora for this reference. For more on the issue of a common culture in relation to feminist and multicultural re-vision of Shakespeare, see Peter Erickson, *Rewriting Shakespeare*, esp. 171–76.

Bibliography

Abel, Elizabeth, et al. *The Voyage In*. Hanover, N. H.: New England Universities Press, 1983.

Adam, Ian. "*The Winter's Tale* and Its Displacements: The Hermione Episode in *Daniel Deronda*." *Newsletter of the Victorian Studies Association of Western Canada* 9 (Spring 1983): 8–13.

———, ed. *This Particular Web*. Toronto: University of Toronto Press, 1975.

[Adams, William Bridges] Junius Redivivus, pseud. "Coriolanus No Aristocrat." *Monthly Repository* 8 (1834): 41–54, 129–39, 190–202, 292–99.

Adelman, Janet. "'Anger's My Meat': Feeding, Dependency, and Aggression in *Coriolanus*." In *Representing Shakespeare*, edited by Murray Schwartz and Coppélia Kahn. Baltimore: Johns Hopkins University Press, 1980.

———. *Suffocating Mothers*. New York: Routledge, 1992.

Alcorn, Marshall, and Mark Bracher. "Literature, Psychoanalysis, and the Re-Formation of the Self: A New Direction for Reader-Response Theory." *PMLA* 100 (May 1985): 342–54.

Alexander, Christine. *The Early Writings of Charlotte Brontë*. Buffalo: Prometheus Books, 1983.

Allott, Miriam, ed. *The Brontës: The Critical Heritage*. Boston: Routledge, 1974.

Altick, Richard D. *The English Common Reader*. 1957. Reprint. Chicago: University of Chicago Press, 1983.

Angelou, Maya. "Journey to the Heartland." Transcription of an address delivered at the National Association of Local Arts Agencies convention, Cedar Rapids, Iowa, June 12, 1985.

Armstrong, Isobel. "Thatcher's Shakespeare?" *Textual Practice* 3, 1 (Spring 1989): 1–14.

———. *Victorian Scrutinies: Reviews of Poetry, 1830–1870*. London: Athlone Press, 1972.

Armstrong, Nancy. *Desire and Domestic Fiction*. New York: Oxford University Press, 1987.

———. "The Rise of Feminine Authority in the Novel." *Novel* 15 (1981–82):127–45.

Arnold, Margaret. "Coriolanus Transformed: Charlotte Brontë's Use of

Shakespeare in *Shirley.*" In *Women's Re-Visions of Shakespeare,* edited by Marianne Novy. Urbana: University of Illinois Press, 1990.

Ashton, Geoffrey. *Shakespeare's Heroines in the Nineteenth Century.* Buxton: Derbyshire Museum Service, 1980.

Atwood, Margaret. *Cat's Eye.* New York: Doubleday, 1989.

——. *Good Bones.* Toronto: Coach House Press, 1992.

——. *Life Before Man.* New York: Fawcett Popular Library, 1979.

——. *Second Words.* Toronto: Anansi, 1982.

——. *Survival.* Toronto: Anansi, 1972.

Auerbach, Nina. *Romantic Imprisonment.* New York: Columbia University Press, 1985.

——. *Woman and the Demon: The Life of a Victorian Myth.* Cambridge, Mass.: Harvard University Press, 1982.

Austen, Jane. *Emma.* Edited by Lionel Trilling. Boston: Houghton Mifflin, 1957.

——. *Mansfield Park.* Edited by Reuben Brower. Boston: Houghton Mifflin, 1965.

——. *Minor Works.* Edited by R. W. Chapman. Oxford: Oxford University Press, 1986.

——. *Northanger Abbey.* Edited by Anne Ehrenpreis. New York: Penguin, 1972.

——. *Persuasion.* New York: Penguin, 1965.

——. *Pride and Prejudice.* Edited by Tony Tanner. New York: Penguin, 1972.

Awkward, Michael. *Inspiriting Influences: Tradition, Revision, and Afro-American Women's Novels.* New York: Columbia University Press, 1989.

Babcock, Robert. *The Genesis of Shakespeare Idolatry, 1766–1799.* 1931. Reprint. New York: Russell & Russell, 1964.

Baker, Susan. "Rewriting Shakespeare in the Classic Detective Story." Paper presented to the seminar "Rewriting Shakespeare," at the annual meeting of the Shakespeare Association of America, Kansas City, Mo., April 18, 1992.

Baker, William. *George Eliot and Judaism.* Salzburg: Institut für Englische Sprache und Literatur, 1975.

Bakhtin, M. M. *The Dialogic Imagination.* Austin: University of Texas Press, 1981.

Bamber, Linda. *Comic Women: Tragic Men: A Study of Gender and Genre in Shakespeare.* Stanford: Stanford University Press, 1982.

——. "Self-Defeating Politics in George Eliot's *Felix Holt.*" *Victorian Studies* 18 (1975): 419–35.

——."The Woman Reader in *King Lear.*" In *King Lear,* edited by Russell

Fraser and Sylvan Barnet. *The New Signet Shakespeare*. New York: NAL, 1987.

Barber, C. L. *Shakespeare's Festive Comedies*. Cleveland: World Publishing, 1963.

Barber, C. L., and Richard Wheeler. *The Whole Journey: Shakespeare's Power of Development*. Berkeley: University of California Press, 1985.

Barish, Jonas. *The Antitheatrical Prejudice*. Berkeley: University of California Press, 1981.

Barrell, John. *Poetry, Language, and Politics*. Manchester: Manchester University Press, 1988.

Barrett, Dorothea. *Vocation and Desire*. London: Routledge, 1991.

Bate, Jonathan. *Shakespeare and the English Romantic Imagination*. Oxford: Clarendon Press, 1986.

———. *Shakespearean Constitutions*. Oxford: Clarendon Press, 1989.

Battersby, Christine. *Gender and Genius*. Bloomington: Indiana University Press, 1989.

Bazin, Nancy Topping, and Marilyn Dallman Seymour, eds. *Conversations with Nadine Gordimer*. Jackson: University Press of Mississippi, 1990.

Beaty, Jerome. *Middlemarch from Notebook to Novel*. Illinois Studies in Language and Literature, vol. 47. Urbana: University of Illinois Press, 1960.

Beer, Gillian. *Darwin's Plots: Evolutionary Narrative in Darwin, George Eliot, and Nineteenth-Century Fiction*. London: Routledge, 1983.

———. *George Eliot*. Bloomington: Indiana University Press, 1986.

Behn, Aphra. "Preface to *The Dutch Lover*." In *Works*, edited by Montague Summers. 6 vols. 1919. Reprint. New York: Phaeton, 1967.

Belsey, Catherine. "Disrupting Sexual Difference: Meaning and Gender in the Comedies." In *Alternative Shakespeares*, edited by John Drakakis. London: Methuen, 1985.

Bennett, Paula. "Gender as Performance: Shakespearean Ambiguity and the Lesbian Reader." In *Sexual Practice, Textual Theory: Lesbian Cultural Criticism*, edited by Julia Penelope and Susan J. Wolfe. Boston: Blackwell, 1993.

Blake, Kathleen, ed. *Approaches to Teaching Eliot's "Middlemarch."* New York: Modern Language Association, 1990.

Bonetti, Kay. Interview with Gloria Naylor. Columbia, Mo.: American Audio Prose Library, 1988.

Booth, Alison. *Greatness Engendered: George Eliot and Virginia Woolf*. Ithaca: Cornell University Press, 1992.

Booth, Wayne. *The Company We Keep*. Berkeley: University of California Press, 1988.

Borges, Jorge Luis. *Labyrinths*. Edited by Donald A. Yates and James E. Irby. New York: New Directions, 1964.

Bradbrook, Frank. *Jane Austen and Her Predecessors.* Cambridge: Cambridge
University Press, 1967.

Bristol, Michael. *Shakespeare's America, America's Shakespeare.* New York:
Routledge, 1989.

Bromwich, David. *Hazlitt.* New York: Oxford University Press, 1983.

Brontë, Charlotte. *Jane Eyre.* Edited by Margaret Smith. Oxford: Oxford
University Press, 1981.

————. *Shirley.* Edited by Andrew and Judith Hook. New York: Penguin, 1979.

Brooks-Davies, Douglas. *Fielding, Dickens, Gosse, Iris Murdoch, and Oedipal
Hamlet.* New York: St. Martin's Press, 1989.

Brown, John Russell. "On the Acting of Shakespeare's Plays." In *The Seventeenth Century Stage,* edited by Gerard Eades Bentley. Chicago: University
of Chicago Press, 1968.

Browning, Elizabeth Barrett. *Aurora Leigh.* Introduction by Cora Kaplan.
London: Women's Press, 1978.

Brydon, Diana. "Sister Letters: Miranda's *Tempest* in Canada." In *Cross-
Cultural Performances,* edited by Marianne Novy. Urbana: University of
Illinois Press, 1993.

Burke, Edmund. *Philosophical Enquiry.* Edited by J. B. Boulton. Notre Dame:
University of Notre Dame Press, 1968.

Burney, Frances. *Camilla.* New York: Oxford University Press, 1972.

Butler, Judith. *Gender Trouble.* New York: Routledge, 1990.

Campbell, Thomas. *Life of Mrs. Siddons.* New York: Harper, 1834.

Carlisle, Janice. *The Sense of an Audience.* Athens: University of Georgia
Press, 1981.

Carter, Angela. *Nights at the Circus.* New York: Penguin, 1986.

————. "Notes from the Front Line." In *On Gender and Writing,* edited by
Michelene Wandor. London: Pandora, 1983.

————. *Nothing Sacred.* London: Virago, 1982.

————. *The Passion of New Eve.* New York: Harcourt, Brace, 1977.

————. *Wise Children.* New York: Farrar, Straus & Giroux, 1991.

Cather, Willa. "Between the Acts." *Nebraska State Journal,* April 29, 1894. Rpt.
in "Willa Cather on Shakespeare." *Prairie Schooner* 38 (1964): 67–68.

————. *The Kingdom of Art.* Edited by Bernice Slote. Lincoln: University of
Nebraska Press, 1966.

————. *My Mortal Enemy.* New York: Knopf, 1926.

Cavendish, Margaret. *CCXI Sociable Letters.* 1664. Reprint. Menston: Scolar
Press, 1969.

————. "General Prologue." In *Playes.* London: A. Warren, for John Martyn
et al., 1662.

Chase, Karen. *George Eliot, Middlemarch.* Landmarks of World Literature. Cambridge: Cambridge University Press, 1991.

Cheney, Lynne. *Humanities in America.* Washington, D.C.: National Endowment for the Humanities, 1988.

Chodorow, Nancy. *The Reproduction of Mothering: Psychoanalysis and the Sociology of Gender.* Berkeley: University of California Press, 1978.

Cixous, Hélène. *Inside.* New York: Schocken, 1985.

Cixous, Hélène, and Catherine Clément. *The Newly Born Woman.* Minneapolis: University of Minnesota Press, 1986.

Claridge, Laura, and Elizabeth Langland, eds. *Out of Bounds.* Amherst: University of Massachusetts Press, 1990.

Clark, Constance. *Three Augustan Women Playwrights.* New York: Peter Lang, 1986.

Clayton, Jay. "The Alphabet of Suffering: Effie Deans, Tess Durbeyfield, Martha Ray, and Hetty Sorrel." In *Influence and Intertextuality in Literary History,* edited by Jay Clayton and Eric Rothstein. Madison: University of Wisconsin Press, 1991.

Clayton, Jay, and Eric Rothstein, eds. *Influence and Intertextuality in Literary History.* Madison: University of Wisconsin Press, 1991.

Cohn, Ruby. *Modern Shakespeare Offshoots.* Princeton: Princeton University Press, 1976.

Coleridge, Samuel Taylor. *Biographia Literaria.* 2 vols. Edited by James Engell and W. Jackson Bate. Princeton: Princeton University Press, 1983.

Cooper, Anna Julia. *A Voice from the South.* 1892. Reprint. Oxford: Oxford University Press, 1988.

Cooper-Clark, Diana. "Margaret Drabble: Cautious Feminist." *Atlantic Monthly,* November 1980, pp. 69–75.

Cottom, Daniel. *Social Figures: George Eliot, Social History, and Literary Representation.* Minneapolis: University of Minnesota Press, 1987.

Coveney, Peter. "Introduction." In George Eliot, *Felix Holt,* edited by Peter Coveney. New York: Penguin, 1972.

Crosby, Christina. *The Ends of History: Victorians and the Woman Question.* New York: Routledge, 1991.

Cross, J. W., ed. *George Eliot's Life as Related in her Letters and Journals.* 3 vols. Boston: Dana Estes, n.d. [c. 1885]. Reprint. Grosse Pointe, Mich.: Scholarly Press, 1968.

Crump, Jeremy. "Shakespeare in Nineteenth-Century Leicester." In *Shakespeare and the Victorian Stage,* edited by Richard Foulkes. Cambridge: Cambridge University Press, 1986.

Danson, Lawrence. "Gazing at Hamlet; or, The Danish Cabaret." *Shakespeare Survey* 45 (1993): 37–51.

Dash, Irene. *Wooing, Wedding, and Power.* New York: Columbia University Press, 1981.

David, Deirdre. *Fictions of Resolution in Three Victorian Novels: "North and South," "Our Mutual Friend," "Daniel Deronda."* New York: Columbia University Press, 1981.

————. *Intellectual Women and Victorian Patriarchy.* Ithaca: Cornell University Press, 1987.

Davis, Natalie Zemon. *Society and Culture in Early Modern France.* Stanford: Stanford University Press, 1975.

Dentith, Simon. *George Eliot.* Harvester New Readings. Atlantic Highlands, N.J.: Humanities Press International, 1986.

Desmet, Christy. "'Intercepting the Dew-Drop': Female Readers and Readings in Anna Jameson's Shakespearean Criticism." In *Women's Re-Visions of Shakespeare,* edited by Marianne Novy. Urbana: University of Illinois Press, 1990.

DiBattista, Maria. *Virginia Woolf's Major Novels.* New Haven: Yale University Press, 1980.

Dipple, Elizabeth. *Iris Murdoch: Work for the Spirit.* Chicago: University of Chicago Press, 1982.

Dodd, Valerie. *George Eliot: An Intellectual Life.* New York: St. Martin's Press, 1990.

Donohue, Joseph. *Theatre in the Age of Kean.* Totowa, N.J.: Rowman & Littlefield, 1975.

Doody, Margaret. *Frances Burney.* New Brunswick, N.J.: Rutgers University Press, 1988.

————. "George Eliot and the Eighteenth Century Novel." *Nineteenth Century Fiction* 35, 3 (1980): 260–91.

Drabble, Margaret. *The Gates of Ivory.* New York: Viking, 1992.

————. "I Would Like to Have Written." *New York Times Book Review,* Dec. 6, 1981, p. 68.

————. *A Natural Curiosity.* New York: Viking, 1989.

————. *The Radiant Way.* 1987. Reprint. London: Penguin, 1988.

————. *The Realms of Gold.* 1975. Reprint. New York: Popular Library, 1977.

————. "Stratford Revisited: A Legacy of the Sixties." In *Cross-Cultural Performances,* edited by Marianne Novy. Urbana: University of Illinois Press, 1993.

————. *The Waterfall.* 1969. Reprint. London: Penguin, 1971.

Dryden, John. "An Essay of Dramatic Poesy." In *Literary Criticism: Plato to Dryden,* edited by Allan Gilbert. Detroit: Wayne State University Press, 1982.

Duckworth, Alistair. "Jane Austen and the Conflict of Interpretations." In

Jane Austen: New Perspectives, edited by Janet Todd. Women and Literature, n.s., vol. 3. New York: Holmes & Meier, 1983.

Dusinberre, Juliet. *Shakespeare and the Nature of Women.* New York: Barnes & Noble, 1975.

Eigner, Edwin M., and George J. Worth, eds. *Victorian Criticism of the Novel.* Cambridge: Cambridge University Press, 1985.

Eliot, George. *Adam Bede.* Edited by John Paterson. Boston: Houghton Mifflin, 1968.

———. *Daniel Deronda.* Edited by Graham Handley. Oxford: Clarendon Press, 1984.

———. *Essays.* Edited by Thomas Pinney. New York: Columbia University Press, 1963.

———. *Felix Holt, the Radical.* Edited by Fred C. Thomson. Oxford: Clarendon Press, 1980.

———. *The Lifted Veil.* London: Virago, 1985.

———. *Middlemarch.* Edited by David Carroll. Oxford: Clarendon Press, 1986.

———. *Middlemarch Notebooks: A Transcription.* Edited by John Clark Pratt and Victor Neufeldt. Berkeley: University of California Press, 1979.

———. *The Mill on the Floss.* Edited by Gordon S. Haight. Oxford: Clarendon Press, 1980.

———. *Poems.* In vol. 8 of *Works.* 10 vols. New York: Bigelow, Brown, 1908.

———. *Scenes of Clerical Life.* Edited by Thomas A. Noble. Oxford: Clarendon Press, 1985.

———. *A Writer's Notebook, 1854–1879, and Uncollected Writings.* Edited by Joseph Wiesenfarth. Charlottesville: University Press of Virginia, 1981.

Ellmann, Richard, and Charles Feidelson, eds. *The Modern Tradition.* New York: Oxford University Press, 1965.

Erickson, Peter. *Patriarchal Structures in Shakespeare's Drama.* Berkeley: University of California Press, 1985.

———. *Rewriting Shakespeare, Rewriting Ourselves.* Berkeley: University of California Press, 1991.

Erikson, Erik. *Young Man Luther.* New York: Norton, 1958.

Ermarth, Elizabeth D. *George Eliot.* Boston: Twayne, 1985.

———. "George Eliot's Conception of Sympathy." *Nineteenth Century Fiction* 40 (1985): 23–42.

———. "Teaching *Middlemarch* as Narrative." In *Approaches to Teaching Eliot's "Middlemarch",* edited by Kathleen Blake. New York: Modern Language Association of America, 1990.

Evans, G. B., ed. *Shakespeare: Acts of Influence.* Cambridge, Mass.: Harvard University Press, 1976.

Ewbank, Inga-Stina. *Their Proper Sphere.* Cambridge, Mass.: Harvard University Press, 1966.

Faderman, Lillian. *Surpassing the Love of Men.* New York: Morrow, 1981.

Faucit, Helena, Lady Martin. *On Some of Shakespeare's Female Characters.* 5th ed. 1893. Reprint. New York: AMS Press, 1970.

Ferguson, Margaret. "Transmuting Othello: Aphra Behn's *Oronooko.*" In *Cross-Cultural Performances,* edited by Marianne Novy. Urbana: University of Illinois Press, 1993.

Ferguson, Margaret, and Mary Nyquist, eds. *Re-Membering Milton.* New York: Methuen, 1989.

Fetterley, Judith. *The Resisting Reader.* Bloomington: Indiana University Press, 1978.

Fielding, Sarah. *The Adventures of David Simple.* New York: Oxford University Press, 1969.

———. *The History of Ophelia.* New York: Garland, 1974.

———. *The Lives of Cleopatra and Octavia.* Edited by R. Brimley Johnson. London: Scholartis Press, 1928.

Fielding, Sarah, and Jane Collier. *The Cry.* Delmar, N.Y.: Scholars' Facsimiles and Reprints, 1986.

Foakes, R. A., ed. *Coleridge's Criticism of Shakespeare.* Detroit: Wayne State University Press, 1989.

Fox, Alice. *Virginia Woolf and the Literature of the English Renaissance.* Oxford: Clarendon Press, 1990.

Friedman, Susan Stanford. "Creativity and the Childbirth Metaphor." *Feminist Studies* 13, 1 (1987): 49–84.

———. "Remembering Shakespeare Differently: H.D.'s *By Avon River.*" In *Women's Re-Visions of Shakespeare,* edited by Marianne Novy. Urbana: University of Illinois Press, 1990.

———. "Weavings: Intertextuality and the (Re)Birth of the Author." In *Influence and Intertextuality in Literary History,* edited by Jay Clayton and Eric Rothstein. Madison: University of Wisconsin Press, 1991.

Froula, Christine. "Virginia Woolf as Shakespeare's Sister: Chapters in a Woman Writer's Autobiography." In *Women's Re-Visions of Shakespeare,* edited by Marianne Novy. Urbana: University of Illinois Press, 1990.

Gallagher, Catherine. "George Eliot and *Daniel Deronda:* The Prostitute and the Jewish Question." In *Sex, Politics, and Science in the Nineteenth-Century Novel,* edited by Ruth B. Yeazell. Baltimore: Johns Hopkins University Press, 1986.

———. *The Industrial Reformation of English Fiction: Social Discourse and Narrative Form, 1832–1867.* Chicago: University of Chicago Press, 1985.

Garber, Marjorie. *Vested Interests: Cross-Dressing and Cultural Anxiety.* New York: HarperCollins, 1993.

Gardiner, Judith Kegan. "The Marriage of Male Minds in Shakespeare's Sonnets." *JEGP* 84 (1985): 328–47.

——— . "On Female Identity and Writing by Women," *Critical Inquiry* 8 (1981):347–62.

——— . *Rhys, Stead, Lessing, and the Politics of Empathy.* Bloomington: Indiana University Press, 1989.

Garner, Shirley Nelson. " 'Women Together' in Virginia Woolf's *Night and Day.*" In *The (M)Other Tongue,* edited by Shirley Nelson Garner, Madelon Sprengnether, and Claire Kahane. Ithaca: Cornell University Press, 1985.

Gaskell, Elizabeth. *The Life of Charlotte Brontë.* New York: Penguin, 1975.

Gilbert, Sandra, and Susan Gubar. *The Madwoman in the Attic.* New Haven: Yale University Press, 1979.

——— . *No Man's Land.* Vol. 1, *The War of the Words.* New Haven: Yale University Press, 1988.

Gilligan, Carol. *In a Different Voice.* Cambridge, Mass.: Harvard University Press, 1982.

Goodman, Lizbeth. "Women's Alternative Shakespeares and Women's Alternatives to Shakespeare in Contemporary British Theatre." In *Cross-Cultural Performances,* edited by Marianne Novy. Urbana: University of Illinois Press, 1993.

Gordimer, Nadine. *The Essential Gesture.* New York: Knopf, 1988.

——— . *My Son's Story.* New York: Penguin, 1991.

Grady, Hugh. *The Modernist Shakespeare.* Oxford: Clarendon Press, 1991.

Graver, Suzanne. *George Eliot and Community.* Berkeley: University of California Press, 1984.

——— . " 'Incarnate History': The Feminisms of *Middlemarch.*" In *Approaches to Teaching Eliot's "Middlemarch,"* edited by Kathleen Blake. New York: Modern Language Association, 1990.

Grebanier, Bernard. *Then Came Each Actor.* New York: David McKay, 1975.

Greene, Gayle. *Changing the Story.* Bloomington: Indiana University Press, 1991.

Greer, Germaine. *Shakespeare.* Oxford: Oxford University Press, 1986.

Haight, Gordon. *George Eliot: A Biography.* Oxford: Oxford University Press, 1968.

Hall, Stuart. "Encoding/Decoding." In *Culture, Media, Language,* edited by Stuart Hall et al. London: Hutchinson, 1980.

Hannay, John. *The Intertextuality of Fate.* Columbia: University of Missouri Press, 1986.

Hardin, Nancy S. "An Interview with Margaret Drabble." *Contemporary Literature* 14 (Summer 1973):273–95.

Hardy, Barbara. "Middlemarch and the Passions." In *This Particular Web,* edited by Ian Adam. Toronto: University of Toronto Press, 1975.

————. *The Novels of George Eliot.* London: Athlone Press, 1959.

Harris, Jocelyn. "Anne Elliott, the Wife of Bath, and Other Friends." In *Jane Austen: New Perspectives,* edited by Janet Todd. Women and Literature, n.s., vol. 3. New York: Holmes & Meier, 1983.

Hayles, N. Katherine. "Anger in Different Voices: Carol Gilligan and *The Mill on the Floss.*" *Signs* 12, 1 (Autumn 1986): 23–39.

Hazlitt, William. *Complete Works.* Edited by P. P. Howe. 21 vols. 1930. Reprint. New York: AMS Press, 1967.

Heilbrun, Carolyn. "The Character of Hamlet's Mother." *Shakespeare Quarterly* 8 (1957): 201–6.

————. *Reinventing Womanhood.* New York: Norton, 1979.

Helsinger, Elizabeth, Robin Sheets, and William Veeder, eds. *The Woman Question: Society and Literature in Britain and America, 1837–1883.* 3 vols. Chicago: University of Chicago Press, 1989.

Hill, Erroll. *Shakespeare in Sable.* Amherst: University of Massachusetts Press, 1984.

Holderness, Graham. *The Shakespeare Myth.* Manchester: Manchester University Press, 1988.

Holland, Norman, Sidney Homan, and Bernard Paris, eds. *Shakespeare's Personality.* Berkeley: University of California Press, 1989.

Homans, Margaret. *Bearing the Word.* Chicago: University of Chicago Press, 1986.

Howard, Jean E. "Crossdressing, the Theatre, and Gender Struggle in Early Modern England." *Shakespeare Quarterly* 39 (1988):418–40.

————. "Renaissance Antitheatricality and the Politics of Gender and Rank in *Much Ado About Nothing.*" In *Shakespeare Reproduced,* edited by Jean E. Howard and Marion R. O'Connor. New York: Methuen, 1987.

Howard, Jean E., and O'Connor, Marion R., eds. *Shakespeare Reproduced: The Text in History and Ideology.* New York: Methuen, 1987.

Hume, David. *A Treatise of Human Nature.* Oxford: Clarendon Press, 1896.

Hunt, Linda. *A Woman's Portion.* New York: Garland, 1988.

Jackson, Russell. " 'Perfect Types of Womanhood': Rosalind, Beatrice, and Viola in Victorian Criticism and Performance." In *Shakespeare Survey* 32, edited by Kenneth Muir. Cambridge: Cambridge University Press, 1979.

Jacobus, Mary. "The Question of Language: Men of Maxims and *The Mill on the Floss.*" In *Writing and Sexual Difference,* edited by Elizabeth Abel. Brighton: Harvester, 1982.

Jameson, Anna. *Shakspeare's Heroines: Characteristics of Women: Moral, Political, and Historical.* New ed. London: George Bell, 1889.

Jehlen, Myra. "Archimedes and the Paradox of Feminist Criticism." *Signs* 6 (Summer 1981):575–601.

Johnson, Deborah. *Iris Murdoch.* Brighton: Harvester, 1987.

Jones, Ann Rosalind. *The Currency of Eros: Women's Love Lyric in Europe, 1540–1620.* Bloomington: Indiana University Press, 1990.
Joyce, James. *Ulysses.* Rev. ed. New York: Modern Library, 1961.
Keats, John. *Letters.* Edited by Hyder Rollins. 2 vols. Cambridge, Mass.: Harvard University Press, 1958.
Kennedy, Dennis, ed. *Foreign Shakespeare.* Cambridge: Cambridge University Press, 1993.
Kernander, Adrian. "The Theatre du Soleil." *New Theatre Quarterly* 2, 17 (August 1986):195–216.
Kerrigan, William. "The Personal Shakespeare: Three Clues." In *Shakespeare's Personality,* edited by Norman Holland, Sidney Homan, and Bernard Paris. Berkeley: University of California Press, 1989.
King, Jeannette. *Tragedy in the Victorian Novel.* Cambridge: Cambridge University Press, 1970.
Kinnaird, John. *William Hazlitt.* New York: Columbia University Press, 1978.
Kirkham, Margaret. *Jane Austen: Feminism and Fiction.* New York: Barnes & Noble, 1983.
Knoepflmacher, U. C. "*Daniel Deronda* and William Shakespeare." *Victorian Newsletter* 19 (1961):27–28.
———. *George Eliot's Early Novels.* Berkeley: University of California Press, 1968.
Kolodny, Annette. "Dancing Through the Minefield: Some Observations on the Theory, Practice, and Politics of a Feminist Literary Criticism." *Feminist Studies* 6 (1980):1–25.
Kucich, John. *Repression in Victorian Fiction.* Berkeley: University of California Press, 1987.
Landis, Joan Hutton. "'Another Penelope': Margaret Hutton Reading William Shakespeare." In *Women's Re-Visions of Shakespeare,* edited by Marianne Novy. Urbana: University of Illinois Press, 1990.
Lanser, Susan. *Fictions of Authority.* Ithaca: Cornell University Press, 1992.
Laurence, Margaret. *The Diviners.* Toronto: Bantam, 1974.
Lee, Hermione. *Willa Cather.* London: Virago, 1989.
Lenz, Carolyn, Gayle Greene, and Carol Thomas Neely, eds. *The Woman's Part: Feminist Criticism of Shakespeare.* Urbana: University of Illinois Press, 1980.
Leverenz, David. "The Woman in Hamlet: An Interpersonal View." In *Representing Shakespeare,* edited by Murray Schwartz and Coppélia Kahn. Baltimore: Johns Hopkins University Press, 1980.
Levin, Harry. *The Gates of Horn.* New York: Oxford University Press, 1963.
Levine, George. *The Realistic Imagination.* Chicago: University of Chicago Press, 1981.

Lewes, G. H. Autograph Journal for 1857. Beinecke Library, Yale University, New Haven, Conn.

————. *Life of Goethe.* 2d ed. London: Smith, Elder, 1864.

————. *Literary Criticism.* Edited by Alice Kaminsky. Lincoln: University of Nebraska Press, 1964.

————. Marginal notes on *Othello* 2.1, edited by Charles Knight. Folger Shakespeare Library, Washington, D.C.

————. "The Novels of Jane Austen." *Blackwood's Edinburgh Magazine* 86 (July 1859):99–113.

————. *On Actors and the Art of Acting.* 1875. Reprint. New York: Greenwood, 1968.

Longhurst, Derek. " 'Not for all time, but for an Age': An Approach to Shakespeare Studies." In *Re-reading English,* edited by Peter Widdowson. New York: Methuen, 1982.

Loomba, Ania. *Gender, Race, Renaissance Drama.* Manchester: Manchester University Press, 1989.

Lyssa, Alison. *Pinball.* In *Plays by Women,* vol. 4, edited by Michelene Wander. New York: Methuen, 1985.

McKewin, Carole. "Counsels of Gall and Grace." In *The Woman's Part,* edited by Carolyn Lenz, Gayle Greene, and Carol Thomas Neely. Urbana: University of Illinois Press, 1980.

McLuskie, Kathleen. "The Patriarchal Bard." In *Political Shakespeare,* edited by Jonathan Dollimore and Alan Sinfield. New York: Methuen, 1985.

Mariani, Philomena, ed. *Critical Fictions.* Seattle: Bay Press, 1991.

Marsden, Jean, ed. *The Appropriation of Shakespeare: Post-Renaissance Reconstructions of the Works and the Myth.* New York: St. Martin's Press, 1991.

Marshall, David. *The Figure of Theater: Shaftesbury, Defoe, Adam Smith, and George Eliot.* New York: Columbia University Press, 1986.

Martin, Robert. *The Accents of Persuasion: Charlotte Brontë's Novels.* London: Faber & Faber, 1966.

Martin, Theodora Penny. *The Sound of Our Own Voices: Women's Study Clubs, 1860–1910.* Boston: Beacon Press, 1987.

Mineka, Francis. *The Dissidence of Dissent: The Monthly Repository, 1806–1838.* Chapel Hill: University of North Carolina Press, 1944.

Moers, Ellen. *Literary Women.* Garden City: Anchor/Doubleday, 1977.

Moldstad, David. "*The Mill on the Floss* and *Antigone.*" *PMLA* 85 (1970):527–31.

Montagu, Elizabeth. *An Essay on the Writings and Genius of Shakespear.* 1769. Reprint. New York: Augustus M. Kelly, 1970.

————. *Letters of Mrs. Elizabeth Montagu,* 4 vols. 1813. Reprint. New York: AMS Press, 1974.

Morgan, Fidelis. *The Female Wits: Women Playwrights on the London Stage, 1660–1720.* London: Virago, 1981.

Morgan, Susan. *Sisters in Time.* New York: Oxford University Press, 1989.

Muir, Kenneth. *Shakespeare's Sonnets.* London: Allen & Unwin, 1979.

Murdoch, Iris. *The Black Prince.* New York: Viking, 1973.

————. *Nuns and Soldiers.* 1980. Reprint. London: Penguin, 1981.

————. *Sovereignty of Good.* London: Routledge, 1970.

————. "The Sublime and the Beautiful Revisited." *Yale Review* 49 (1959):247–71.

————. "The Sublime and the Good." *Chicago Review* 13 (Autumn, 1959):42–55.

Nadel, Ira Bruce, ed. *Victorian Fiction: A Collection of Essays from the Period.* New York: Garland, 1986.

Naylor, Gloria. *Linden Hills.* New York: Penguin, 1986.

————. *Mama Day.* New York: Vintage, 1989.

————. *The Women of Brewster Place.* 1982. New York: Penguin, 1983.

Neely, Carol Thomas. *Broken Nuptials in Shakespeare's Plays.* New Haven: Yale University Press, 1985.

————. "Detachment and Engagement in Shakespeare's Sonnets: 94, 116, 129." *PMLA* 92 (1977):83–95.

————. "Epilogue: Remembering Shakespeare, Revising Ourselves." In *Women's Re-Visions of Shakespeare,* edited by Marianne Novy. Urbana: University of Illinois Press, 1990.

Newton, Judith Lowder. *Women, Power, and Subversion.* Athens: University of Georgia Press, 1980.

Novy, Marianne. *Love's Argument: Gender Relations in Shakespeare.* Chapel Hill: University of North Carolina Press, 1984.

————, ed. *Cross-Cultural Performances: Differences in Women's Re-Visions of Shakespeare.* Urbana: University of Illinois Press, 1993.

————, ed. *Women's Re-Visions of Shakespeare: On Responses of Dickinson, Woolf, Rich, H.D., George Eliot, and Others.* Urbana: University of Illinois Press, 1990.

O'Brien, Sharon. *Willa Cather: The Emerging Voice.* New York: Oxford University Press, 1987.

Odell, George. *Shakespeare from Betterton to Irving.* 2 vols. 1920. Reprint. New York: Dover, 1966.

Ohmann, Carol. "Charlotte Brontë: The Limits of Her Feminism." *Female Studies* 6 (1972):160–64.

Orel, Harold, ed. *Victorian Literary Critics.* New York: St. Martin's Press, 1984.

Ozick, Cynthia. "Puttermesser Paired." *New Yorker,* October 8, 1990, pp. 40–75.

Paris, Bernard, *Experiments in Life*. Detroit: Wayne State University Press, 1965.

Park, Clara Claiborne. "As We Like It: How a Girl Can Be Smart and Still Popular." In *The Woman's Part*, edited by Carolyn Lenz, Gayle Greene, and Carol Thomas Neely. Urbana: University of Illinois Press, 1980.

Parker, G. F. *Johnson's Shakespeare*. Oxford: Clarendon Press, 1989.

Patterson, Annabel. *Shakespeare and the Popular Voice*. Cambridge: Blackwell, 1989.

Paxton, Nancy. *George Eliot and Herbert Spencer*. Princeton: Princeton University Press, 1991.

Poovey, Mary. *The Proper Lady and the Woman Writer: Ideology as Style in the Works of Mary Wollstonecraft, Mary Shelley, and Jane Austen*. Chicago: University of Chicago Press, 1984.

Postlethwaite, Diana. "When George Eliot Reads Milton: The Muse in a Different Voice." *ELH* 57 (1990):197–22.

Preussner, Dee. "Talking with Margaret Drabble." *Modern Fiction Studies* 25 (1979–80):563–77.

Rackin, Phyllis. *Stages of History*. Ithaca: Cornell University Press, 1990.

Ragusis, Michael. "Representation, Conversion, and Literary Form: *Harrington* and the Novel of Jewish Identity." *Critical Inquiry* 16 (1989):113–43.

Redinger, Ruby. *George Eliot: The Emergent Self*. New York: Knopf, 1975.

Rich, Adrienne. *Blood, Bread, and Poetry*. New York: Norton, 1986.

Rose, Jacqueline. *Sexuality in the Field of Vision*. London: Verso, 1986.

———. "Sexuality in the Reading of Shakespeare: *Hamlet* and *Measure for Measure*." In *Alternative Shakespeares*, edited by John Drakakis. New York: Methuen, 1985.

Rose, Phyllis. *Parallel Lives: Five Victorian Marriages*. New York: Vintage, 1984.

———. *Woman of Letters: A Life of Virginia Woolf*. New York: Oxford University Press, 1978.

Rosenberg, Edgar. *From Shylock to Svengali*. Stanford: Stanford University Press, 1960.

Ross, Deborah. *The Excellence of Falsehood: Romance, Realism, and Women's Contributions to the Novel*. Lexington: University Press of Kentucky, 1991.

Rowe, Karen. " 'Fairy-born and human-bred': Jane Eyre's Education in Romance." In *The Voyage In*, edited by Elizabeth Abel et al. Hanover, N.H.: New England Universities Press, 1983.

Rozencwajg, Iris. "Interview with Margaret Drabble." *Women's Studies* 6 (1979):335–47.

Rushdie, Salman. *The Satanic Verses*. New York: Viking, 1989.

Russell, Anne. "Rosalind, Viola, and Early Nineteenth Century Gender Ideologies." Dissertation, York University, Toronto, Ontario, 1987.

Schwartz, Murray, and Coppélia Kahn, eds. *Representing Shakespeare.* Baltimore: Johns Hopkins University Press, 1980.

Schweickart, Patrocinio. "Reading Ourselves: Toward a Feminist Theory of Reading." In *Gender and Reading,* edited by Elizabeth A. Flynn and Patrocinio Schweickart. Baltimore: Johns Hopkins University Press, 1986.

Shattuck, Charles. *Mr. Macready Produces As You Like It.* Urbana: Beta Phi Mu, 1962.

Showalter, Elaine. "Feminist Criticism in the Wilderness." Rpt. in *The New Feminist Criticism,* edited by Elaine Showalter. New York: Pantheon, 1985.

———. "The Greening of Sister George." *Nineteenth Century Fiction* 35 (1980): 292–311.

———. *A Literature of Their Own: British Women Novelists from Bronte to Lessing.* Princeton: Princeton University Press, 1977.

———. "Representing Ophelia: Women, Madness, and the Responsibilities of Feminist Criticism." In *Shakespeare and the Question of Theory,* edited by Patricia Parker and Geoffrey Hartman. New York: Methuen, 1985.

———. *Sister's Choice.* Oxford: Clarendon Press, 1991.

Shuttleworth, Sally. *George Eliot and Nineteenth-Century Science: The Make-Believe of a Beginning.* Cambridge: Cambridge University Press, 1984.

Sircy, Otice C. " 'The Fashion of Sentiment': Allusive Technique and the Sonnets of *Middlemarch.*" *Studies in Philology* 84 (1987):219–43.

Skura, Meredith. *The Literary Use of the Psychoanalytic Process.* New Haven: Yale University Press, 1981.

———. *Shakespeare the Actor.* Chicago: University of Chicago Press, 1993.

Smiley, Jane. *A Thousand Acres.* New York: Alfred A. Knopf, 1991.

Smith, Adam. *The Theory of Moral Sentiments.* New Rochelle, N.Y.: Arlington House, 1969.

Smith, Bruce. *Homosexual Desire in Shakespeare's England.* Chicago: University of Chicago Press, 1990.

Smith, Rebecca. "A Heart Cleft in Twain: The Dilemma of Shakespeare's Gertrude." In *The Woman's Part,* edited by Carolyn Lenz, Gayle Greene, and Carol Thomas Neely. Urbana: University of Illinois Press, 1980.

Southam, B. C., ed. *Jane Austen: The Critical Heritage.* Rev. ed. London: Routledge, 1986.

Spivak, Gayatri. "Three Women's Texts and a Critique of Imperialism." *Critical Inquiry* 12, 1 (1985):243–61.

Sprengnether, Madelon. "Mourning Shakespeare: My Own Private Hamlet." Paper presented at the annual meeting of the Shakespeare Association of America, Kansas City, Mo., April 18, 1992.

Staël, Madame de [Anne-Louise-Germaine Necker]. *Corinne; or, Italy.* Translated by Isabel Hill. New York: W. I. Pooley, 1870.

Stavisky, Aron Y. *Shakespeare and the Victorians: Roots of Modern Criticism.* Norman: University of Oklahoma Press, 1969.

Stock, R. D. *Samuel Johnson and Neoclassical Dramatic Theory.* London: University of Nebraska Press, 1983.

Stone, Donald. *The Romantic Impulse in Victorian Fiction.* Cambridge, Mass.: Harvard University Press, 1980.

Stouck, David. *Willa Cather's Imagination.* Lincoln: University of Nebraska Press, 1975.

Tave, Stuart. *The Amiable Humorist.* Chicago: University of Chicago Press, 1960.

Taylor, Gary. *Reinventing Shakespeare.* New York: Weidenfeld and Nicholson, 1989.

Thomas, Clara. *Love and Work Enough.* London: Macdonald, 1967.

Thompson, Dorothy. "Women and Nineteenth Century Radical Politics: A Lost Dimension." In *The Rights and Wrongs of Women,* edited by Juliet Mitchell and Ann Oakley. New York: Penguin, 1976.

Thompson, E. P. *The Making of the English Working Classes.* New York: Penguin, 1980.

Tintner, Adeline. *"As You Like It* as George Sand Liked It." *Revue de Littérature Comparée* 3 (1986):337–44.

Todd, Janet, ed. *Jane Austen: New Perspectives.* Women and Literature, n.s., vol. 3. New York: Holmes & Meier, 1983.

——— . *The Sign of Angellica: Women, Writing, and Fiction, 1660–1800.* London: Virago, 1989.

——— , ed. *Women Writers Talking.* New York: Holmes & Meier, 1983.

Todd, Richard. *Iris Murdoch: The Shakespearian Interest.* London: Vision, 1979.

Tompkins, J. M. S. *The Popular Novel in England, 1770–1800.* London: Constable, 1932.

Traub, Valerie. "Rainbows of Darkness: Deconstructing Shakespeare in the Work of Zora Neale Hurston and Gloria Naylor." In *Cross-Cultural Performances,* edited by Marianne Novy. Urbana: University of Illinois Press, 1993.

Uglow, Jennifer. *George Eliot.* New York: Pantheon, 1987.

van den Broek, A. G. "Additional Notes to Shakespearean Entries in the Pforzheimer Holographs." *George Eliot/George Henry Lewes Newsletter* 12–13 (1988):6–11.

——— . "Reading George Eliot Reading Shakespeare." Ph.D. diss. Dalhousie University, 1990.

Vickers, Brian, ed. *Shakespeare: The Critical Heritage, 1623–1801.* 6 vols. London: Routledge, 1974–81.

Warhol, Robyn. *Gendered Interventions.* New Brunswick: Rutgers University Press, 1989.

Warner, Sylvia Townsend. "Women as Writers." In *The Gender of Modernism,* edited by Bonnie Kime Scott. Bloomington: Indiana University Press, 1990.

Wasserman, Earl. "The Sympathetic Imagination in Eighteenth-Century English Theories of Acting." *JEGP* 46 (1947):264–72.

Watson, Nicola J. "Kemble, Scott, and the Mantle of the Bard." In *The Appropriation of Shakespeare,* edited by Jean Marsden. New York: St. Martin's Press, 1991.

Wayne, Valerie, ed. *The Matter of Difference.* Ithaca: Cornell University Press, 1991.

Weissman, Philip. *Creativity in the Theater.* New York: Basic Books, 1965.

Welsh, Alexander. *From Copyright to Copperfield: The Identity of Dickens.* Cambridge, Mass.: Harvard University Press, 1987.

———. *George Eliot and Blackmail.* Cambridge, Mass.: Harvard University Press, 1985.

West, Cornel. "Diverse New World." *Democratic Left* 19 (1991):7.

Wheeler, Michael. *The Art of Allusion.* New York: Barnes & Noble, 1979.

Willbern, David. "What Is Shakespeare?" In *Shakespeare's Personality,* edited by Norman Holland, Sidney Homan, and Bernard Paris. Berkeley: University of California Press, 1989.

Williams, Ioan, ed. *Novel and Romance, 1700–1800.* New York: Barnes & Noble, 1970.

Williams, Raymond. *The Country and the City.* New York: Oxford University Press, 1973.

Williamson, Claude C. H., ed. *Readings on the Character of Hamlet.* London: Allen & Unwin, 1950.

Wilson, William A. "The Magic Circle of Genius: Dickens' Translations of Shakespearian Drama in *Great Expectations.*" *Nineteenth-Century Fiction* 49 (1985):154–74.

Wimsatt, W. K., ed. *Samuel Johnson on Shakespeare.* New York: Hill & Wang, 1960.

Wise, T. J., and J. A. Symington, ed. *The Brontes, Their Lives, Friendships, and Correspondence.* 4 vols. Oxford: Blackwell, 1932.

Witemeyer, Hugh. *George Eliot and the Visual Arts.* New Haven: Yale University Press, 1979.

Wittreich, Joseph. *Feminist Milton.* Ithaca: Cornell University Press, 1987.

———. " 'John, John, I blush for thee!': Mapping Gender Discourses in *Paradise Lost.*" In *Out of Bounds,* edited by Laura Claridge and Elizabeth Langland. Amherst: University of Massachusetts Press, 1990.

Wolfson, Susan. "Explaining to Her Sisters: Mary Lamb's *Tales from Shakespear.*" In *Women's Re-Visions of Shakespeare.* Urbana: University of Illinois Press, 1990.

Wollstonecraft, Mary. *The Female Reader,* ed. Moira Ferguson. 1789. Facs.
Delmar, N.Y.: Scholars' Facsimiles and Reprints, 1980.

——. *A Vindication of the Rights of Woman.* Edited by Carol H. Poston. Rev.
ed. New York: Norton, 1988.

——. *A Vindication of the Rights of Woman.* 3d ed. London: J. Johnson, St.
Paul's Churchyard, 1796.

Woodress, James. *Willa Cather.* Lincoln: University of Nebraska Press, 1987.

Woolf, Virginia. *Books and Portraits.* Edited by Mary Lyon. London: Hogarth
Press, 1977.

——. *Collected Essays.* Vol. 2. London: Hogarth, 1966.

——. *Mrs. Dalloway.* 1925. Reprint. New York: Harcourt Brace Jovanovich, 1985.

——. *Night and Day.* 1919. Reprint. London: Granada, 1978.

——. *Orlando.* Reprint. 1928. London: Triad Grafton, 1978.

——. *A Room of One's Own.* New York: Harcourt Brace Jovanovich, 1929.

——. *Women and Writing.* Edited by Michèle Barrett. London: Women's
Press, 1979.

——. *A Writer's Diary.* New York: Harcourt, Brace, 1954.

Yaeger, Patricia. *Honey-Mad Women.* New York: Columbia University
Press, 1988.

Zimmerman, Bonnie. " 'The Dark Eye Beaming': Female Friendship in
George Eliot's Fictions." In *Lesbian Texts and Contexts: Radical Revisions,*
edited by Karla Jay and Joanne Glasgow. New York: New York University
Press, 1990.

——. *"Felix Holt* and the True Power of Womanhood." *ELH* 46
(1979):432–51.

——. "Gwendolen Harleth and 'The Girl of the Period.' " In *George Eliot:
Centenary Essays and an Unpublished Fragment,* edited by Anne Smith.
Totowa, N.J.: Barnes & Noble, 1980.

——. " 'The Mother's History' in George Eliot's Life, Literature, and
Political Ideology." In *The Lost Tradition: Mothers and Daughters in Litera-
ture,* edited by Cathy N. Davidson and E. M. Broner. New York: Fredric
Ungar, 1980.

Index